PRAISE FOR *RESULTS THAT LAST*

"Change is hard for many people. That's what makes this book so valuable. Quint Studer lays out a formula that tackles one of the daunting tasks a leader must face—changing human behavior in order to improve organizational performance—and makes it feel doable. Reading this book before the next big change initiative at your company will make your job much easier... and infinitely more rewarding."

—Richard Lepsinger, President, OnPoint Consulting, LLC, and coauthor of *Flexible Leadership: Creating Value by Balancing Multiple Challenges and Choices*

"Anyone can be great once—even blind squirrels find a few nuts to store away. Quint Studer shows you how to consistently amaze your customers, connect with your employees, and outperform your competitors. And if that doesn't interest you, perhaps you are browsing in the wrong section of the bookstore."

—Randy Pennington, author of *Results Rule! Build a Culture That Blows the Competition Away*

"As companies everywhere break through borders and expand across the globe, achieving strong organizational performance takes on a new urgency. Without an unshakable foundation—one based on proven business principles—you won't survive growth and change. Quint Studer can help. He explains how standardizing your leadership practices sets you up for the kind of consistent, day-to-day, employee-to-employee, customer-to-customer excellence that ensures global success. Don't miss this book."

—Tom Travis, author of *Doing Business Anywhere: The Essential Guide to Going Global*

"Here's what I like about Quint Studer: He gets that the *employee* experience and the *customer* experience are intertwined and inseparable. Make the former happy and the latter will follow organically. And as Studer rightly points out, it all starts with great leadership. His book overflows with practical, why-didn't-I-think-of-that tactics for building a culture around service. You'll want to try these tactics the minute you read them—and I suspect they'll fit like a tailor-made suit."

> —Scott Deming, international speaker and business consultant, author of *The Brand Who Cried "Wolf"*: *Deliver on Your Company's Promise and Create Customers for Life*

"Not only are the most powerful leaders goal-oriented, disciplined, and passionate, they're connectors. They've mastered the art of human relationships. Quint Studer intuitively knows how to connect with others and persuade them to buy into a vision. If you're charged with leading others, don't just read *Results That Last*; live it. It will change the way you interact with your people, which in turn will change the course of your business for the better."

> —Dennis F. Haley, founder and CEO, Academy Leadership, and coauthor of *The Leader's Compass, 2nd Edition: A Personal Leadership Philosophy Is Your Key to Success*

"Quint Studer's new book, *Results That Last*, is a must-read for anyone who is serious about leadership and the steps that can be taken to help improve morale and productivity in the workplace. He takes the principles he has refined as a distinguished leader in the healthcare industry and applies those to other corporate cultures. Studer bases his commonsense thesis on what he calls evidence-based leadership practices, which he breaks down into three key elements: Aligned Goals, Aligned Behavior, and Aligned Processes. He then weaves all three into a leadership formula that is both practical and attainable and will inspire and motivate anyone wishing to improve their leadership skills. It's what success is all about."

> —Charles S. Lauer, retired publisher, *Modern Healthcare* Magazine

"Quint Studer, the foremost healthcare service consultant, has already taught us how to hardwire excellence. His latest book, *Results That Last*, is sure to be a classic in the annals of business management."

> —Floyd D. Loop, M.D., former CEO (1989–2004), Cleveland Clinic

RESULTS THAT LAST

Hardwiring Behaviors That Will Take Your Company to the Top

QUINT STUDER

John Wiley & Sons, Inc.

Published by John Wiley & Sons, Inc., Hoboken, New Jersey.
Published simultaneously in Canada.

Wiley Bicentennial Logo: Richard J. Pacifico

For general information on our other products and services or for technical support, please contact our Customer Care Department within the United States at (800) 762-2974, outside the United States at (317) 572-3993 or fax (317) 572-4002.

Wiley also publishes its books in a variety of electronic formats. Some content that appears in print may not be available in electronic books. For more information about Wiley products, visit our web site at www.wiley.com.

Library of Congress Cataloging-in-Publication Data:

Studer, Quint.
  Results that last : hardwiring behaviors that will take your company to the top / Quint Studer.
     p. cm.
  Includes bibliographical references.
  ISBN-13: 978-0-471-75729-0 (cloth)
    1. Leadership. 2. Organizational behavior. 3. Corporate culture. I. Title.
HD57.7.S787 2007
658.4′092—dc22

                                                              2007014619

Printed in the United States of America.

10 9 8 7 6 5 4 3 2 1

CONTENTS

Introduction   Evidence-Based Leadership   xi

KEY TACTICS

CHAPTER 1 Up or Out   Deal with Low Performers
               and Move Your Organization to the
               Next Level   3
               Defining High, Middle, and Low Performers
               Dealing with High, Middle, and Low Performers

CHAPTER 2 Round for Outcomes   25
               Five Critical Elements Employees Want
                  from Managers
               Nine Steps for Starting Rounding

CHAPTER 3 Manage Up to Improve Performance   35
               We/They Phenomenon
               Art of Managing Up
               Handling Handoffs
               Create a Cultural Shift (Feedback Systems)

THE CORE

CHAPTER 4 Build the Foundation (Passion and Purpose)   55
Flywheel
Five Pillars
Connect the Dots

CHAPTER 5 Reduce Leadership Variance   75
Why Leaders Don't Standardize Behaviors
Why Organizations Don't Achieve Lasting Results
Five Ways to Reduce Leadership Variance

CHAPTER 6 Measurement 101   89
What Gets Measured Gets Improved
Focus on Moving 4s to 5s
Transparency—Helping People Understand
   the Metrics
Demonstrating Return on Investment

CHAPTER 7 Align Behaviors with Goals and Values   105
Holding Leaders Accountable
Leader Evaluation Tool
How to Roll Out the Leader Evaluation Tool

CHAPTER 8 Create and Develop Leaders   123
Principles for Developing Leaders
Phases of Change
Leadership Development Institutes

EMPLOYEE TACTICS

CHAPTER 9 Satisfied Employees Mean a Healthy
   Bottom Line   143
Three Building Blocks of Employee Satisfaction

CHAPTER 10 Know Your Employees' *What*   161
Pursuing the *Whats*

CHAPTER 11 Improve Employee Selection and Retention   171
Peer Interviewing
Thirty- and Ninety-Day New-Employee Meetings

Contents

CHAPTER 12 Build Individual Accountability   187
Renters versus Owners
Strategies to Transform Renters into Owners

CHAPTER 13 Harvest Intellectual Capital   199
Hardwiring Harvesting

CHAPTER 14 Recognize and Reward Success   211
Small Prizes Have a Big Impact
Reward and Recognition Change as You Mature
Power of Reward and Recognition
Hardwiring Thank-You Notes
How to Implement Reward and Recognition

CHAPTER 15 Find and Recognize Difference Makers   225
Power of Hero Recognition
How to Find Heroes

CUSTOMER TACTICS

CHAPTER 16 Build a Culture around Service   235
Standards of Behavior
Impact of Key Words

CHAPTER 17 Implement Pre- and Post-Customer-
Visit Calls   251
Impact on Customer Likelihood to Recommend
Ability to Exceed High Customer Expectations
Impact on Bottom Line
Opportunity to Retain a Customer Even When
Things Go Wrong

CHAPTER 18 Round on Your Customers: Determine
Your Customers' *What* and Give It
to Them!   267
Importance of Asking Customers Their *Whats*
Rounding on Customers
Three Faces of Rounding
Random Rounding

CONTENTS

Relationship Rounding
Deep-Impact Rounding

CHAPTER 19 Key Words at Key Times   281
What Are Key Words?
How to Develop Key Words
AIDET
When to Use Key Words for Greatest Impact
Service Recovery

About Studer Group   295

Other Leadership Books By Quint Studer and Studer
  Group   297

Index   299

What truly creates results that last?

It's not the products and services an organization offers. These can change and, besides, the minute they hit the global marketplace competitors can and do copy them. It's not particular employees. People leave organizations every day. It's not even individual leaders. They, like the employees who serve under them, come and go over time.

What creates results that last is *leadership*—leadership that's consistently excellent from leader to leader, department to department, division to division. Standardize the right leadership practices and you will find that organizational performance improves across the board . . . and *stays* improved.

The strategies and tactics in this book have been "road tested" by Studer Group, an outcomes-based firm devoted to teaching its client organizations how to create and sustain service and operational excellence. We know they work, and work well. Our partner organizations attest to their validity.

Evidence-based leadership (EBL) enables us to create results that last. What *is* EBL? It's a strategy centered on using the current "best practices" in leadership—practices that are proven to result in the best possible outcomes. The "evidence," in this context, is the reams of data collected from study after study that aim to determine what people really want and need from their leaders. When leaders apply these tried-and-true tactics to every corner of our organizations, we achieve consistent excellence. Our organization's success is no longer dependent on individuals. It's hardwired. No matter who leaves, the excellence remains.

It seems important to mention that evidence-based leadership is a spinoff of *evidence-based medicine*—a philosophy based on using current "best evidence" to make decisions about the care of individual patients. What works for doctors and nurses will also work for CEOs and managers. It just requires a different way of thinking about how we lead.

Ironically, many organizations balk at standardizing their leadership practices. They standardize all sorts of other (less critical) items, from how they display their logos to what time employees arrive at work to how the phone must be answered. And yet the most important aspect of any organization—leadership—is allowed to be inconsistent.

We have all heard employees say things like: *I will work for this boss but not that one*, or *The north-side store is so much better than the other ones*. And we've all heard them ask questions like: *Why do that leader's employees get to interview potential co-workers and we don't?. . .* or *How come employees can get away with behavior with some bosses but not others?. . .* or *Why does this leader get a better evaluation than a higher-performing person who works for another boss or in another division?*

The tools and techniques in this book will stop those comments and questions. They will help virtually any organization get its leadership practices aligned.

At the beginning of each chapter you will see this graphic:

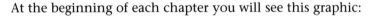

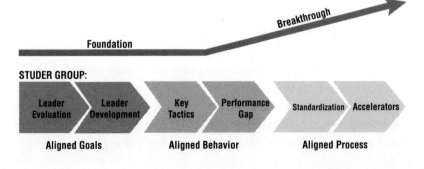

It illustrates how the components of evidence-based leadership work together to create results that last. A circled area on the graphic will show you where the tactic addressed in that chapter fits into the process.

As you can see, there are three major components to evidence-based leadership: *Aligned Goals, Aligned Behavior,* and *Aligned Processes.* The book goes into detail about how to implement the tactics under each component, but here's a brief overview:

- *Aligned Goals.* Organizations must implement an objective evaluation system that tells leaders not only what they're supposed to be doing, but also what their priorities are. In addition, leaders must be thoroughly trained in order to be successful.

- *Aligned Behavior.* There are certain behaviors that an organization must agree to implement at the leadership level to ensure that every employee gets a consistent experience—whether it's the presence of daily rounding or a certain way of showing appreciation. (These aligned behaviors cascade down to employees to create a consistent experience for customers.) Standardizing leader behavior ensures predictable responses from our employees. And aligning behaviors forces us to deal with performance gaps. We must move low performers up or out or eventually our improvement efforts will not be sustained.

- *Aligned Processes.* We must identify certain processes that are consistent throughout the company—how people are hired, for instance. Consistency in process allows people to move more effectively and opens the door to acceleration—the phase in which results start getting better and better.

Let me take a moment to explain how I've categorized the tactics in this book.

Chapters 1 through 3 cover the three most powerful **Key Tactics** a company can adopt: *high, middle, and low conversations, rounding for outcomes,* and *managing up.* Even if a leader takes none of the other suggestions in this book, he or she usually finds that implementing these three tactics leads to big dividends.

You might think of Chapters 4 through 8 as **The Core.** This section covers the philosophy behind the tactics and explains the intricacies of reducing leadership variance, measuring the important things, aligning behaviors with goals and values, and training leaders. It creates the foundation of an organization so all employees are working toward the same goals and all employees are held accountable.

Chapters 9 through 15 focus on **Employee Tactics.** We'll learn how to determine what employees really want from us—which is the heart of evidence-based leadership—and how to give it to them. We'll also learn how to build individual accountability in people and how to benefit from the wealth of knowledge our employees possess.

Finally, Chapters 16 through 19 reveal critical **Customer Tactics.** We'll discuss various tools and techniques leaders can use to build a culture around service. When an organization understands what "great service" really looks like to its customers, it has a much greater likelihood of consistently providing it. The result is that customers keep coming back and refer us to their friends, family members, and colleagues.

Please understand: You do *not* have to adopt every single tactic in this book to enjoy significant results. Decide which ones make the most sense for your organization and get started on those. However, the foundation described in the Core chapters is necessary if you are to achieve breakthrough.

Likewise, you don't have to follow a particular sequence. You may want to begin with one of the three very powerful tactics we explain right up front—high, middle, and low conversations, rounding for outcomes, and managing up—because we've found they have a tremendous impact on organizational performance.

Figure out what you want to accomplish and dive right in with the tactic that best fits your goals. The sudden improvement you see will boost morale and motivate everyone to strive for even better results. Remember to align these behaviors with all leaders so the results last.

By the way, don't worry that you're creating a company of lookalike leaders; each person will always bring his or her own personality into the workplace. What you *are* doing is creating consistency based on the foundation of best practices. You're also creating a culture of excellence. A great culture outperforms strategy every time. A great culture, combined with a great strategy, is unbeatable.

And here's the bottom line: Not only will your customers have consistently excellent experiences with your company, your employees will as well. Happy, loyal customers and happy, loyal employees are two sides of the same coin—and that coin is the currency that buys you results that last.

KEY TACTICS

CHAPTER 1

UP OR OUT
Deal with Low Performers and Move Your Organization to the Next Level

Why This Chapter Is Important

MOST ORGANIZATIONS DON'T HAVE TROUBLE *GETTING* BETTER RESULTS AT first. The problem lies in *keeping* them.

Much like marathon runners, companies hit a performance wall. After their initial achievements, they find themselves running with an anchor dragging behind them. And the name of that anchor is often "the low performer." Until low performers are moved up or out, an organization or department will never move beyond short-term gains. The wall will stop progress every time.

And that fact is why I put this chapter up front.

I've heard many leaders say that step one is to get everyone on board. I disagree. *You'll never get everyone on board.* At Studer Group, we have found that 34 percent of people will improve their performance and stay at their new higher level, 58 percent will do so *if* their behavior is properly reinforced, and 8 percent will flat-out refuse to budge.

3

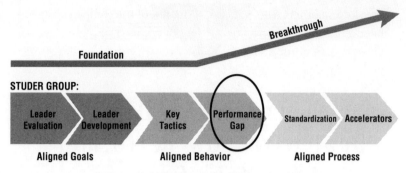

Figure 1.1 Evidence-based Leadership

This chapter is about spending 92 percent of your time retaining the 92 percent of your employees who want to be on board, and 8 percent of your time dealing with the 8 percent who don't. The outcome is results that last.

● ● ●

Whom do we take home with us every night? Who dominates our conversations about work? Who causes the vast majority of the problems we face? It's low performers. They are the men and women who block our efforts to build lasting results. They drain the energy, initiative, and creativity right out of us and our organizations.

Have you ever walked into your department and had the distinct feeling that one co-worker was holding you and the others hostage? Is there an employee in your company who keeps you guessing—someone who follows path A for several weeks, then suddenly, with a sense of glee, zigzags onto path B? Have you found yourself worrying more about how one particular employee might react to a new process than about anyone else in the entire organization?

If you recognize any of these scenarios, you've experienced firsthand the devastating impact of the low performer. Consider this classic example:

> Karen handles the corporate web site. She is intelligent and has moments of brilliance. However, she talks negatively about all others involved in the programming of the web site. As she "manages down"

the site and others who work on it, the rest of the company loses confidence and faith in the site. At the same time, tasks that have been given to Karen just aren't getting done. Every three weeks or so she puts forth a flash of effort, but the rest of the time nothing seems to happen and negativity continues to breed in the office.

When you meet with Karen, she always has an array of excuses as to why her items aren't getting completed. She may then follow up this litany of blame and finger-pointing by offering an ambitious new Internet proposal. Frankly, Karen's hot-and-cold work ethic and her negativity are wearing you out. Her co-workers just try to work around her to the best of their abilities.

Here's the unpalatable truth: Most organization leaders spend 80 percent of their supervisory time on the "Karens" in their companies. Although we wish these low performers would leave, they bring new meaning to the word *tenacious*. The Karens of this world know from experience that they can outlast the latest "change initiative" if they just hang on a little longer. They have outlasted more than one supervisor. Their workplace prayer is "This, too, shall pass."

LOW PERFORMERS COME IN MANY SHAPES AND SIZES

Your low performer may not look like time-wasting, deliberately inconsistent Karen. She may look more like rude, surly, disruptive Mary, who actively undermines every management policy and nearly dares you to fire her. Or maybe your low performer resembles arrogant salesman Eric, who specializes in pitting one co-worker against another—in between the roster of cell phone calls, text messages, and games of computer solitaire that seem to take up his workday. (Needless to say, after three weeks of no sales—just when you're on the verge of letting him go—Eric brings in a big contract.)

Leaders can be low performers, too. Think of a leader who says all the right things in meetings but seems to go back and manage her employees in a completely different manner.

As you can see, low performers don't fit a single neat stereotype. Generally, though, they can be recognized by their penchant to coast along with their inconsistent work output, collecting their paychecks and infecting everyone else with their negative attitudes. When we try to initiate change in our organization, it's the low performers who dig in their heels and resist—sometimes to our face, most often behind our back.

Once after coaching a manager on how to address a low-performer situation, I checked back to see how the conversation had gone with this difficult person. She told me, "He convinced me that *I* was the problem." Amazing, isn't it? Low performers are masters of blame and diversion. These tactics are their special survival skills. When confronted, they will do one of three things:

1. Blame others for their low performance.

2. Point the finger at you, claiming that you haven't given the proper training or tools.

3. Unload some personal problem with the aim of playing on your sympathies and diverting attention away from their low performance.

We, leaders tell ourselves that a warm body is better than a void in the company. We'd rather have a familiar personnel problem (the devil we know) than hire a whole new set of problems (the devil we don't). Or we may play the "blame game" and say Human Resources is the culprit and won't let us fire the low performer. Or we may even blame that ever-popular scapegoat, the union, for protecting him or her.

As you read this, you've probably already started thinking about the low performers in your organization. We all know who they are. They are the people we usually work around when we really want to get something done, the leaders from whom employees are constantly seeking to transfer away. We're willing to admit that our low performers don't contribute often—and in some ways we've made our peace with that fact—but we may not realize how much real damage they do to our organization.

HOW DO THEY DAMAGE? LET US COUNT THE WAYS . . .

First of all, in a company where low performance is allowed to exist, customers get neglected. Low performers may ignore them—or at least fail to fully engage in helping them—and everyone else is too busy picking up the slack to serve them properly. In this way, low performers squelch profitability and service goals.

Yet, customer neglect is only the tip of the iceberg. Here's why. As they grow, change, and move toward peak performance, all organizations hit a psychological wall. High and middle performers come to perceive the performance gap between themselves and the low performers as unfair, thus they begin to pace themselves and results tail off. The organization may even slip back to lower performance levels than before. Meanwhile, our Karens, Marys, and Erics spread distrust and misinformation as they pull others, particularly the middle performers, down to their level. They "knew the new systems would not work," and don't hesitate to tell their co-workers. (See Figure 1.2.)

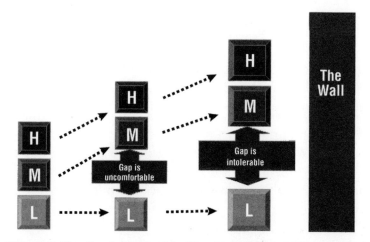

Figure 1.2 The Gap Is Intolerable (H = high, M = middle, L = low)

Once this occurs, employees lose faith in their organization's ability to create and sustain long-term gains. Many leaders don't see their own failure to address low performers as the problem. Instead they embark on a search for a new "program of the month." Because low performers aren't being properly handled, their organization's performance is inconsistent. They go up, then they go down, and then (maybe) they go up again. The problem is that the subsequent "ups" aren't quite as high as they were before because leaders can't get their people as excited as they did early on.

This slow spiral into mediocrity is only part of the picture. Another reason performance suffers is that the top staff members leave. High performers simply won't stay in an environment where low performers are tolerated. Eventually, what's left is an organization of medium and low performers trudging along.

REVERSING THE SPIRAL: HIGH, MIDDLE, AND LOW CONVERSATIONS

So how can you reverse the spiral into mediocrity and produce long-term high organizational performance? *You must do something about the low-performer problem.* You must instigate conversations specifically designed to re-recruit high performers, develop middle performers, and hold low performers accountable. Here's why this solution works: It creates an uncomfortable gap as low performers become more isolated from their higher-performing co-workers. Ultimately, low performers improve or leave, which unlocks the full potential of the organization as it scales the wall separating it from peak performance. (See Figure 1.3.)

WHO'S WHO IN TERMS OF PERFORMANCE

Figuring out who's who in your organization is the first step. In our work at Studer Group, we have found the best approach is to place your staff into high-, middle-, and low-performance groups. A useful tool is the Differentiating Staff Worksheet, which ranks each employee across five performance areas: *professionalism, teamwork,*

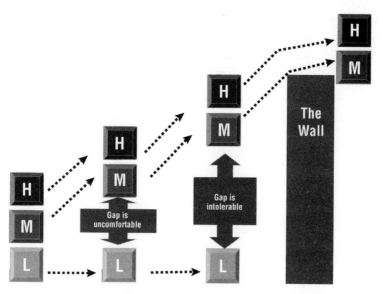

Figure 1.3 Over the Wall

knowledge and competence, communication, and *workplace (or safety) awareness.* (See Figure 1.4.)

As you evaluate each staff member in these areas, you examine how well he or she adheres to policies, demonstrates commitment to the organization, strives for continued professional development, and comes to work with a positive attitude.

You'll find that your high performers create solutions when problems arise. Middle performers can identify a problem, but may lack the experience or self-confidence to bring solutions to the table. Low performers blame others for problems, demonstrating a real lack of ownership.

During this evaluation process, you will most likely run across at least one employee who is technically competent but difficult to work with in some way. If he is very talented, you are often tempted to rate him a high or middle performer. You shouldn't. High and middle performers must be excellent both technically *and* as team members.

In fact, we have recommended to our clients that they terminate employees—even leaders—who get results but don't role model

Below is a differentiating staff worksheet that SG has developed based on the findings from its national learning lab. Use this to help complete an assessment of your staff. In terms of the actual assessment, the most difficult issue for leaders tends to be for an employee who has four out of five good qualities but the last quality holds them back and actually hurts the performance of the department. A good question to ask yourself is "Knowing what I know, would I hire them again?"

We encourage you to customize the specific characteristics based on your own organization's standards of behaviors and expectations.

	High	Middle	Low
Definition	Comes to work on time. Good attitude. Problem solver. You relax when you know they are scheduled. Good influence. Use for peer interviews. Five Pillar ownership. Brings solutions.	Good attendance. Loyal most of the time. Influenced by high and low performers. Wants to do a good job. Could just need more experience. Helps manager be aware of problems.	Points out problems in a negative way. Positions leadership poorly. Master of We/They. Passive aggressive. Thinks they will outlast the leader. Says manager is the problem.
Professionalism	Adheres to unit policies concerning breaks, personal phone calls, leaving the work area, and other absences from work.	Usually adheres to unit policies concerning breaks, personal phone calls, leaving the work area, and other absences from work.	Does not communicate effectively about absences from work areas. Handles personal phone calls in a manner that interferes with work. Breaks last longer than allowed.
Teamwork	Demonstrates high commitment to making things better for the work unit and organization as a whole.	Committed to improving performance of the work unit and organization. May require coaching to fully execute.	Demonstrates little commitment to the work unit and the organization.
Knowledge and Competence	Eager to change for the good of the organization. Strives for continuous professional development.	Invested in own professional development. May require some coaching to fully execute.	Shows little interest in improving own performance or the performance of the organization. Develops professional skills only when asked.
Communication	Comes to work with a positive attitude.	Usually comes to work with a positive attitude. Occasionally gets caught up in the negative attitude of others.	Comes to work with a negative attitude. Has a negative influence on the work environment.
Safety Awareness	Demonstrates the behaviors of safety awareness in all aspects of work.	Demonstrates the behaviors of safety awareness in all aspects of work.	Performs work with little regard to the behavior of safety awareness.

Figure 1.4 High-, Middle-, and Low-Performers Conversation

their organization's standards of behavior. Such employees are very damaging to overall employee morale. The harm they do in this area outweighs the good they do in others.

SCHEDULE THE CONVERSATIONS

Next, use an employee tracking log to monitor each interview. The log should include name, rating, initial meeting date, and follow-up date and comments.

Introduce the interview process at an employee meeting. Tell your people that the corporation is committed to feedback and professional development. Add that over the next so-many weeks, each leader is going to meet one-on-one with each employee and provide each of them with performance feedback. This way everybody will know the interviews are coming.

It is crucial to meet with the high performers first, middle performers next, and low performers last. This sequence accomplishes two things:

1. High performers can dispel fear about the meetings when other employees ask why the boss wanted to meet with them.

2. Leaders become energized and are better fortified for the difficult low-performer conservations after having met with the employees they value the most.

The objectives and outcomes are distinct for each type of conversation.

High-Performer Conversations: Recruit to Retain

High performers share your company's values, display proactive attitudes, and suggest changes for process improvement. They are open to new ideas from anywhere within the organization and have the ability to get the job done. Characterized by their positive attitudes, high performers are good role models and mentors to new employees. They also naturally transfer what they learn. (See Figure 1.5.)

During high-performer conversations you want to:

- *Tell them where the organization is going.* High performers want to work for an organization that is going in the right direction.

- *Thank them for their work.* High performers want to know that the organization feels their work is worthwhile.

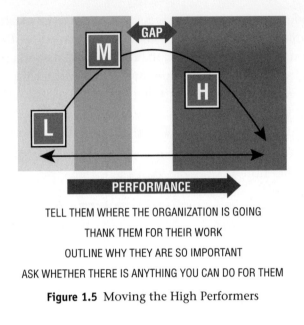

TELL THEM WHERE THE ORGANIZATION IS GOING

THANK THEM FOR THEIR WORK

OUTLINE WHY THEY ARE SO IMPORTANT

ASK WHETHER THERE IS ANYTHING YOU CAN DO FOR THEM

Figure 1.5 Moving the High Performers

- *Outline why they are so important.* Be specific. High performers get turned off by general statements. Share specific examples of how their work aligns with the goals and direction of the organization.

- *Ask whether there is anything you can do for them.* High performers will often ask for more training, more responsibility, or more opportunity.

Below is an example of a high performer conversation:

"John, O'Sullivan Creel wants to be the dominant, most technically advanced CPA and consulting firm in Northwest Florida. We are opening branch offices in several cities and investing $700,000 in new equipment and training each year.

"I wanted to thank you for being a part of O'Sullivan Creel. You are integral to this firm accomplishing its goals. Your work in the corporate tax group has been excellent. The partners and I appreciate the extra time you put into the Baskerville/Donavan Engineering Firm Account. It wouldn't have gone off smoothly without your efforts.

"John, your leadership and willingness to help your co-workers is appreciated also. Thank you specifically for helping Mike meet our client's important deadline. I am very comfortable giving you any project. I know it will get done and the client will be satisfied.

"We hope you stay here for a long time. Is there anything we can do for you? Is there anything I can do differently to better support you?"

Now here is a surprising fact. Studer Group has helped organizations hold more than 300,000 of these conversations. *Not once* has a high performer asked for money. High performers know the salary structure. They're mature enough to understand the realities of compensation and comparisons.

High performers—if they're not overwhelmed by just having this conversation—tend to ask for one of three things:

1. More training, because they want to be the best.

2. More responsibility, because high performers always want to impact the organization in a positive manner.

3. More opportunity, because high performers are always looking for more ways to help.

One of our clients brought a high performer in for his performance conversation. When they were finished, the high performer said, "I'd really like to be more involved in training new employees." The boss almost fainted. He never imagined the employee would want to take on *more* duties. In fact, his fear had been that the employee would think he was already being asked to do too much. Yet, the high performer realized training new employees was so important that he volunteered!

Don't be surprised when your high performers ask for more work, because achievement is what turns high performers on. High performers take extra batting practice. High performers get involved in the community. Quite simply, high performers live up to their name!

Remember, the central point of these conversations is to re-recruit high performers to retain them. Make sure your meeting clearly conveys the sentiment: "I value you. What can I do to help you and your departments achieve our goals?"

Middle-Performer Conversations: Support—Coach—Support

Middle performers are good, solid employees. They make or break an organization. They usually support the leaders in your company and will let leadership know if there is a problem. Your goal here is to help middle performers become even better. (See Figure 1.6.)

When meeting with middle performers, inform them early on that you want to retain them as employees. This immediately reduces their anxiety and they will be able to focus on the conversation. We recommend a three-step process for each conversation:

1. *Support.* Tell the employee why she is important to the organization. Be specific.

   "Joanne, your detailed work in the recent automation of our customer files and the key words you developed to use when we talk to our customers about their information are excellent. Because of your efforts, we can locate customer data quickly, schedule appointments well, and service customer requests much better than we could before. Our customer

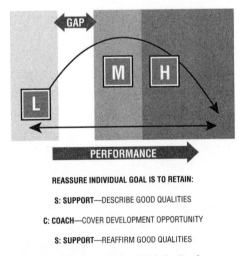

REASSURE INDIVIDUAL GOAL IS TO RETAIN:

S: SUPPORT—DESCRIBE GOOD QUALITIES

C: COACH—COVER DEVELOPMENT OPPORTUNITY

S: SUPPORT—REAFFIRM GOOD QUALITIES

Figure 1.6 Moving the Middle Performers

satisfaction score has improved by 20 percent this quarter, and our ability to service our customers efficiently has contributed to this improvement. Thank you...."

2. *Coach.* Share one area for development and improvement with the middle performer. Let her know that you have a concern, but share only one area. This keeps the conversation positive and the item seems doable.

"Joanne, now that the conversion is complete, I would like you to focus on using the system and key words we have developed in a more consistent manner. I have observed a lack of consistency depending on workload or time of day, and I need you to focus on standardizing these elements into every customer conversation. I want you to role-model the key words to use in every customer interaction...."

3. *Support.* (Yes, again.) End the meeting with a statement of support. Let her know you are committed to her success. Ask if there is anything you can do to help her in the area you just identified.

"Joanne, thank you again for all your hard work to set up our new system and develop key words to use in our customer interactions. Our company is now more efficient and our customer is better served because of your efforts. Is there anything we can do to support you more?"

What has been accomplished? You have now moved the middle performers' performance up, thus creating a wider gap between them and the low performers. Remember, your goal is to *isolate* the low performers, and you're well on your way to accomplishing that.

Keep in mind that low performers are the smallest percentage of your staff. The only way they keep their power is by influencing middle performers. These conversations are helping you build a healthy emotional bank account with your middle performers, so they're much less likely to be pulled down by low performers.

Document, Document, Document! (A Cautionary Tale)

Let me tell you a story from earlier in my career. Like most leaders, I had taken on a supervisory role without first having any formal leadership training. Early on at a meeting an employee said something in a way that I felt was less than professional. Today, I would have talked with him about the matter. Back then, I did not know how to handle it. I decided that to get the employee more positive I would spend more time with him so as to win him over. Now I see that I just reinforced the negative behavior. At the time, however, things seemed to get better.

Some months later, a similar situation arose. Instead of handling it on the spot, I rationalized that his evaluation was coming up and that would be a good time to discuss the issue. Plus, if I said something now, he may ask me why now and why not earlier when he exhibited the same behavior. In this way, I rationalized not taking action. (Truth to tell, I was avoiding confrontation because it felt uncomfortable to me.) His behavior got better a few months before the end of the year, and at evaluation time I rationalized he was trending in the right direction, so why put a damper on it? I checked "meets expectations" on his yearly evaluation.

A few months later the third negative situation took place. I was motivated now! I told some other supervisors who knew about my previous problems with the employee that I was going to Human Resources. I sat down with a person in HR and let him know of the three negative instances. The person said, "Hold on, Quint, let me get his personnel file." Of course, I knew what was in his file: no documentation of issues, just the evaluation I completed that said he was meeting expectations. I quickly changed strategy, from an exit for the employee to an exit for *me* out of the Human Resources office. I quickly thanked him for his help, told him I knew how to handle the situation, and left, hoping he would not tell anyone I had not documented anything. As I walked back to my work area, another manager asked me what happened. I answered, "Human Resources won't let you fire anyone around here!"

Now here's the question I hope you'll ask regarding this little story: Was the problem really Human Resources—or was it *me*? The answer is *me*. Too often, HR departments get blamed for a leader's lack of skill set, and failing to document the transgressions of low performers is a prime example.

Low-Performer Conversations: The *DESK* Approach

Here's an interesting item that we've discovered about low performers: Many have not been written up as problem employees.

Recently, I had the department leaders of an organization write down the names of the employees who were not meeting expectations, employees the leaders would not rehire. Nearly 10 percent of the company's employees—about 200 people—were listed as low performers. We then turned the names over to Human Resources and asked them to pull all their files. *Less than one-third* of the employees identified as low performers had issues that had been documented on their evaluations! We have found since then that this situation is the rule with most organizations, not the exception.

The point is that we may have to admit that we haven't done a great job in dealing with low performers. That doesn't mean we can't move forward. In fact, we *must*. Our high and middle performers deserve to be in a better work environment. They shouldn't have to work with low performers, and as I mentioned before, many of them *won't*.

Once you've identified your low performers, tell your boss who they are. Doing so sets up a situation in which you expect the boss to ask about them in the future. This expectation creates an extra layer of accountability. It helps ensure that you don't lose your initial motivation to deal with these employees.

Make no mistake: Your low performer is more experienced with difficult conversations than you are. That's why it's important to practice and role play with your boss.

If you don't go in prepared, the low performer will eat you for lunch. He probably had difficult conversations in the second grade, in the sixth grade, in high school, in the last job he had, and in every relationship he's been involved in. Low performers usually "survive" because they've evolved survival skills that most leaders haven't even considered.

Some low performers will quickly blame others. Some will point the finger at their boss. Some will lay a huge personal problem in front of you: *My mother's sick. . . . My wife's leaving me.* These employees will do everything they can to keep the conversation away from them and their performance.

Before your upcoming low-performer conversation, go to Human Resources. Don't assume HR won't let you take action with this person. Just lay out everything you have on him or her. You might find that—even though your records are not as organized as you'd like—Human Resources might allow you to go farther than you expect.

By the way, if you have to start fresh because you haven't been documenting infractions as you should have, it's okay to say to the individual, "I've made a mistake as a leader. I should've addressed these issues with you. I can't go backward, but we're starting from today."

When you have your conversation with the low performer, be very specific in telling the person what he or she is doing wrong and what you expect to be done differently in the future. All employees deserve specific feedback.

We recommend what we call the *DESK* approach (Figure 1.7):

D. *Describe* what has been observed: "Karen, you are missing deadlines on the projects assigned to you. Our last brochure mailed three weeks late. This has impacted sales. Other employees have stepped in to make sure key communications get done on time. This is unfair and is causing morale problems among your co-workers."

E. *Evaluate* how you feel: "Your continued missed deadlines are not up to the standards we've set for this department. We have discussed this problem, most recently two weeks ago,

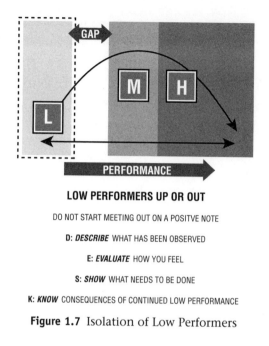

LOW PERFORMERS UP OR OUT

DO NOT START MEETING OUT ON A POSITVE NOTE

D: *DESCRIBE* WHAT HAS BEEN OBSERVED

E: *EVALUATE* HOW YOU FEEL

S: *SHOW* WHAT NEEDS TO BE DONE

K: *KNOW* CONSEQUENCES OF CONTINUED LOW PERFORMANCE

Figure 1.7 Isolation of Low Performers

regarding the new product brochure missed deadline. I'm disappointed because you assured me you would take steps to work more efficiently. You signed the organizational standards of behavior commitment. I'm concerned that you aren't following them."

S. *Show* what needs to be done: "Karen, you need to meet all upcoming deadlines. Over the next two weeks, I am going to work directly with you and show you how to budget your time and create a system to ensure deadlines are met. Tomorrow morning at 8:30, I want you to present your revised work schedule that notes all upcoming deadlines and plans in place to meet the deadlines. Every morning we will meet at 8:30 to review your progress and mark off the tasks as they're accomplished."

What you've done in this step is provide training so that the low performer can't complain you haven't. If you skip this step—and maybe even if you don't—she will surely say, "I'm running down to Human Resources now," or "I'm going to run to my union steward because nobody's given me the training I need." It's important to be as proactive as possible.

K. *Know* consequences of continued low performance: "Karen, I'm now giving you a verbal warning. If this happens again, it'll be followed by a written warning. If it continues to happen, you will have to leave the company." Then have Karen summarize this conversation in an email.

Because low performers are so skilled at excuses, guilt, and righteous indignation, managers often find these conversations difficult. Hey, leaders are only human! But you can't let your dread and discomfort—or your low performer's manipulation tactics— dissuade you. You must stay calm, objective, and clear about consequences if performance doesn't improve by a date you specify. Set short evaluation periods.

Then, be relentless in your *follow-up.* If you see it, say it—both good and bad. If you see a marked improvement in the low performer's behavior, acknowledge it. A sincere effort deserves a sincere compliment. However, the next time your "Karen" (or Mary or Eric) rolls into the parking lot at 8:45, takes a two-hour lunch, or comes up short at deadline time, you must be quick to submit the promised written warning. And if it happens again, it is time for her to leave the organization. I believe strongly in the adage, "Select slow, deselect fast."

SUBTRACTION REALLY IS ADDITION

Our work at Studer Group shows that in most organizations:

- Thirty-four percent are high performers.

- Fifty-eight percent fall in the middle category.

- Eight percent are labeled low performers.

We have found that in the low-performer category, one-third will improve their performance to the middle level. Another third won't change behavior and will deselect themselves when they realize management is serious. The remaining third will stubbornly hold on until we terminate them. We also have learned that no low performers will improve or deselect themselves until at least one low performer is terminated.

It's never easy to fire someone. If it were, low performers wouldn't be an issue and you wouldn't be reading this chapter. When you decide to do it, just do it. Have your documentation in hand and be decisive and straightforward. You can simply say, "I followed our policies, and at this time your employment is being terminated."

When you apply the advice in this chapter to your own low performer, you may balk. That's understandable. Not only is firing someone unpleasant—particularly when that person has been with the company for a long time—it creates a vacuum in the organization. And isn't even a low performer better than nothing?

A client once said, "But isn't 25 percent better than zero?" In other words, isn't a very-low-performing employee preferable than no employee at all? Our answer is *absolutely not*. By hanging on to a low performer, not only are you impacting all your other employees in a negative way, you're also holding a spot that, potentially, a high performer could fill.

Look at it this way: Subtraction is really addition. Employees who had to deal with this person felt that they had a foot pressing down on their chests. When you fire him or her, the foot is pulled away. Chances are, your other employees will be thrilled and you'll find that you *can* attract a better person. And from there, great things will start to happen. So, yes, you have to make that leap of faith—but it's a leap that almost always takes you closer to becoming a high-performance organization. (Figure 1.3.)

WHAT YOU'VE ACCOMPLISHED

Most clients tell us they have come to realize that they can't become great leaders or great departments if they don't deal with their low performers.

The higher up in the organization the low performer is, the more damage is done. Just pick up the *Wall Street Journal* and you'll see that when a high-profile person is a low performer, it can actually ruin an entire organization and cost hundreds of thousands of people their jobs and their pensions.

But here's an even better reason to deal with low performers: You simultaneously deal with high performers. When you follow the steps in this chapter, you're doing more than addressing the 8 percent of your employees who need to move up or out. You're also spending 92 percent of your time dealing with people you want to keep.

How powerful is this time spent with medium and high performers? An anecdote from my work with one client may best illustrate the answer. The manager had just met with one high performer when the employee said, "I need to tell you something. You're a good boss. People like working for you. You're not afraid to get down into the trenches." The manager was so touched she started crying.

You see, the reason leaders don't always feel great about being leaders is that we tend to surround ourselves with the people who perpetually tell us what's wrong, instead of the 92 percent of our employees who actually *want* to work with us. That makes sense, right?

To recap: What have you accomplished when you follow the advice in this chapter? Well, you've talked to all of your employees one-on-one. Every single employee, including leaders and followers, knows exactly where he or she stands.

- *For the high performers:* You've let them know how much you appreciate them. You've told them specifically why they're valued, and talked about what you can do to keep them— which is usually more training, more opportunity, or more responsibility.

- *For the middle performers:* You've told them that you want to retain them. You've also discussed professional development and shared your commitment to it. Your middle performers have walked out of these meetings feeling great. They know they're wanted; and not only that, they have an organization committed to their development.

- *For the low performers:* You've put them on notice. They won't be surprised, although they may pretend otherwise. (Those in Human Resources verify how rare it is for an employee to come to them shocked over a bad performance review that they had no idea was coming.) You've outlined exactly what they were doing that needs improvement. You've told them how you feel, you've gone over step by step what they need to do to meet expectations, and you've told them the consequences of not doing so.

In the end, you have shown value-driven leadership for every single employee in the organization. That's what this thing called *leadership* is all about: working within the organization to maximize the human potential inside it.

KEY POINTS FOR HARDWIRING RESULTS

- Low performers can cause serious damage to your organization. Because of them your customers may get neglected, your middle performers may get pulled down, and your high performers may become disenchanted and leave. You risk ending up with an organization filled with medium and low performers trudging along.

- Schedule conversations about performance with all employees, using Studer Group's *Employee Tracking Log* tool (download a sample on studergroup.com). Have all leaders meet one-on-one with each of their employees to provide performance feedback, meeting with high performers first, middle performers next, and low performers last.

- Your conversations with high performers should focus on *recruit to retain.* Your middle-performer conversations should focus on *support—coach—support*, while your low-performer conversations should take the *DESK* approach:

*D*escribe what has been observed.

*E*valuate how you feel.

*S*how what needs to be done.

*K*now the consequences of continued low performance.

- As a result of implementing these tactics, you'll spend 92 percent of your time with the high and middle performers. They'll feel reengaged, you'll move the entire organization's performance curve, and everyone will enjoy great results— results that last.

CHAPTER 2

ROUND FOR OUTCOMES

Why This Chapter Is Important

AT STUDER GROUP, WE HAVE FOUND THAT THE TOP DRIVER OF STAFF performance is the skill of the leader. There are proven leadership behaviors that create better organizational performance—and rounding for outcomes is one of them.

Rounding for outcomes is a skill set that engages staff and customers. It achieves multiple results. It increases staff retention, improves operational efficiency, and gets quicker action on performance issues. It enables a leader to play *offense,* not *defense.*

Leaders who are skilled at rounding find their jobs much easier. Organizations see a quick return on investment as employee turnover decreases and efficiency increases from the get-go.

Rounding itself is not new; leaders have done it for years in their conversations with employees. But rounding for outcomes—approached in the way described in this chapter—takes the best practices to increase performance and packages them to be more effective and efficient for leaders and employees alike.

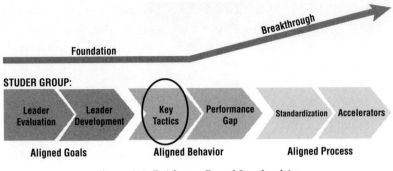

Figure 2.1 Evidence-Based Leadership

• • •

As leaders, we want employees to be happy, productive, and loyal. Indeed, it's our job to create conditions that facilitate these qualities. The reason we're not always as successful as we'd like to be boils down to two factors: *information* and *time*. It's hard to know what problems our team is facing, solve them, show our people we care, *and* handle all the other tasks on our plate.

Here's the good news: There *is* a way we can stay on top of what our employees really want and need. It's a concept from the healthcare arena called *rounding*—and it can also be a powerful management tool for leaders in all sectors of the business world. When we study high-performing leaders, they list the ability to engage staff as the number-one item that drives areas to high performance.

Rounding is the method doctors in hospitals traditionally use to check on patients. The image of the white-coat-wearing, stethoscope-wielding doctor paying bedside visits to patient after patient is one that has practically become a national archetype. But doctor/patient rounding is only the tip of the rounding iceberg.

In our work with hospitals, we urge CEOs to also make daily rounds, but not necessarily to check on patients. In the case of hospital CEOs, they make rounds to check on their managers, to see what's going right (and *wrong*) in their respective worlds. Those same managers are also trained to round on the people who work under them. And the rounding continues on down the hierarchy chain.

We call this *rounding for outcomes* because the goal is not to provide friendly banter or put in less-than-sincere face time. No; the rounding we recommend is highly focused and *outcome*-driven.

The same idea can be used in other businesses, as with a CEO, VP, or department manager making the rounds to check on the status of his or her employees. Rounding allows you to gather information in a structured way. It is proactive, not reactive. It is a way to get a handle on problems before they occur, and also to reinforce positive and profitable behaviors. Best of all, it is an efficient system that yields maximum return on investment.

Making rounds in a business setting requires leaders to take time each day to touch base with their employees to make personal connections, find out what projects or techniques are successful, and determine what improvements can be made. Quite simply, it's a way to consistently gather the information we leaders need to do our job and do it well—in a timely and efficient manner.

WHAT EMPLOYEES WANT: FIVE GOOD REASONS TO ROUND

When done properly, rounding is much more than superficial "face time" or wandering around. It is meaningful. And it is the heart and soul of what we call *evidence-based leadership*—a term inspired by another health care concept, evidence-based medicine. The *evidence,* in this context, is the reams of data collected from study after study that aim to determine what people really want and need from their leaders.

There are five critical elements employees look for from their managers. Rounding helps us accomplish each and every one of them:

1. *Employees want a manager who cares about and values them.* The number-one reason people leave their jobs is because they feel they are not valued. What's more, people don't leave their *team*—they leave their direct supervisor. And we can't assume our employees *know* that we value them. Some may, but others may not. When we round properly, we

automatically build strong relationships with *all* of our employees. It just happens naturally.

> There are moments of reality for each employee when an action by a leader will either cement his loyalty or begin his exit journey. The story of Vinnie exemplifies this truth. Vinnie worked for a small company. About a year ago, the company was purchased. In effect, he went from being a big fish in a small pond to being a medium-sized fish in a big pond.
>
> During the transition, Vinnie did a lot of soul-searching about his new role in the company. In December, he shared with me that he was seriously thinking of looking at other options. That very week he received a handwritten letter from the president of the company. In it, the president thanked Vinnie and shared his excitement about the future. Vinnie not only stayed, he made a big commitment to the new organization and moved his family from Florida to California to be closer to company headquarters . . . and all because a leader showed that he cared.

2. *Employees want systems that work and the tools and equipment to do the job.* Obviously, a major part of job satisfaction centers on being able to actually *do* our job. From time to time, most companies experience equipment breakdowns that stymie and frustrate employees. In some cases, people have complained among themselves for years about inefficient systems and processes. (As we all know, employees are far more likely to vent to each other than to a leader who might be able to do something about the complaint.) Rounding solves these problems and gives productivity a boost.

> Mike shared this story with me. As he was walking through an area of his organization, he asked some employees if they had the tools and equipment they needed to do the job that day. One lady said no. She told him they needed more of a certain type of equipment. Mike made sure they got it that day.

A few weeks later, as Mike was visiting the area again, the lady came up to him and said, "The other day was going to be my last day, but when you asked about equipment I decided to give you a chance. When you delivered on your promise I decided to stay." Such moments of reality, however unplanned, are often make-or-break moments for us, our staffs, and our organizations.

3. *Employees want opportunities for professional development.* Rounding is a natural avenue for discovering whose skill sets need improvement and for initiating professional development discussions. Daily rounds present the ideal scenario for suggesting training to someone who clearly needs it, or to ask one employee to mentor another. Rounding also gives us many opportunities to help high performers move to an even higher level. A leader wishing to instigate such a conversation might say something like, "We want to keep you in our organization and are committed to helping you excel professionally. Is there any training that you feel might be helpful to you?"

4. *Employees want to be recognized and rewarded for doing a good job.* A big part of the rounding process involves asking people who among their peers is demonstrating exceptional performance—and then passing the compliments on. It's an excellent way to build morale, as praise from one's peers is probably the most meaningful kind.

5. *Employees don't want to work with low performers.* Nothing makes employees as discouraged and resentful as having to coexist with people who don't pull their own weight. In fact, low performers usually drive high performers right out the door. Rounding naturally solves this problem. Of course, once we find out who the low performers are, we have to move them up or out—as we discussed in the first chapter. It's not easy, but it's absolutely necessary.

As powerful as rounding is, it cannot succeed in a vacuum. We must standardize rounding skills, teach the process to all managers, and hardwire it into our organizations. And please, don't assume that rounding is easy. It isn't. It requires some serious training and self-discipline—but over time we'll see that the results are worth the effort.

ROUNDING 101: NINE SIMPLE STEPS FOR GETTING STARTED

1. *Give your employees a heads-up.* Before you incorporate rounding into your organization, explain to your employees what you plan to do. Any time a leader modifies his or her behavior, employees tend to get anxious. Be honest. Explain to them up front: "I want to be a better leader and I need your help. I am here to recognize and reward people and to find out what's working well in this company—and what's not working so well."

2. *Prepare a scouting report.* When preparing a scouting report, start out with a basic knowledge of what the current problems are. For instance, if you know a department is short-staffed, put it on the report. Or if you know there's a chronic problem with equipment breaking down, write it down. When you start rounding, you'll be able to talk intelligently about the issues. (Sample report on page 47.)

3. *Make a personal connection.* Rounding shouldn't be all business. It is important on occasion to express interest in an individual's life outside of work. Ask her how her sick mother is doing or ask him how his child did on college entrance exams. This is relationship building. Be genuine.

4. *Mention an issue he or she raised during your last rounding visit.* Illustrate to the employee that you have solved the problem or that you are working on it. "Steve, I know you told me Monday that the spreadsheet software needs to be updated. I've asked Melanie to take care of it and she'll be following up with you about it soon."

5. *Ask these questions,* keeping your tone and words as positive as possible:
   - What is working well today?
   - Are there any individuals I should be recognizing?
   - Do you have the tools and equipment you need to do your job?
   - What systems could work better?

6. *When someone brings up an issue or concern, assure him or her that you will do the best you can to resolve it.* If you can't, explain why not without blaming your boss or company. Obviously, there will be circumstances you can't control. But people appreciate knowing that you will try. Sincere effort goes a long way. Be careful, though, not to foster a *we/they* division by subtly pinning the blame on your superiors. Remember, there is only one team and it is *we.*

7. *Record issues that arise in a rounding log.* Remember the scouting report I mentioned in step 2? The rounding log is a continuation of that report. Taking notes on what you learn during the rounding process will help you keep what needs to be done "top of mind." It will also help you hardwire the process into your company. Writing things down makes it more likely that they'll get done, and it makes things seem more official. (See Figure 2.2.)

8. *Recognize/reward those who are identified by peers as high performers.* This might mean conveying a sincere word of thanks—being sure to cite who complimented him or her—or sending a written thank-you note. It might even be a small bonus.

9. *Repeat the process.* Round daily, if possible. At least do it several times a week. Don't risk losing momentum or you'll give it up before you start seeing results.

Does this process sound contrived or unnatural to you? It felt pretty awkward the first several times I did it. It's like starting a jogging regimen after being sedentary for years. You may feel

Hardwiring: Sample Rounding Log

Complete and return once a week to supervisor:	
Name:	
Key Words or Questions:	
Look Out For: (e.g., environmental safety)	

Rounding for:	Comments:
System Issues Identified:	
Supply or Equipment Needs Identified:	
Staff Action or Recognition:	
Physician Action or Recognition:	
Tough Questions:	
Other:	
Area or Number of Staff Rounded In:	

Note: For a full size copy, log on to www.studergroup.com and type in "rounding log"

Figure 2.2 Rounding for Outcomes

self-conscious huffing and puffing through your neighborhood the first day out, but after you've done it for a few weeks the neighbors will stop staring and pointing. And once you start looking fit and feeling better you're glad you put on those running shoes.

Rounding is like exercise in another way, too. If you don't round every day, religiously, it will take much longer to accomplish your goals and it will be far more painful. You must make it part of your routine. Proactive leadership is far more effective than reactive leadership. It allows you to consciously and deliberately build the kind of culture in which people feel a sense of purpose, a sense that their work is worthwhile, and a sense that they're truly making a difference.

KEY POINTS FOR HARDWIRING RESULTS

- Rounding for outcomes—based on the concept of physician rounds performed in hospitals—is a highly focused, outcome-driven technique for gathering valuable information in a structured way. It helps leaders get a handle on problems before they occur and reinforce positive, profitable behaviors.

- *Evidence-based leadership* confirms that the majority of employees look for five critical elements from their managers and leaders. Employees want (1) a manager who cares about them, (2) working systems with the tools and equipment to do the job, (3) opportunities for professional development, and (4) recognition for doing good work. Number (5) is the one thing they *don't* want . . . low performers as co-workers.

- Here are a few tips for successful rounding:
  - Start the process by explaining to all of your employees what you intend to do and why.
  - Prepare a scouting report to serve as a baseline for your discussions.
  - Ask the following questions: *What is working well today? Are there any individuals I should be recognizing? Do you have the tools and equipment you need to do your job? What else would you like me to know?*
  - Following each discussion, record issues discussed in your rounding log.
  - If someone identifies a high performer, take the opportunity to send the high performer a quick thank-you note.

CHAPTER

3

MANAGE UP TO IMPROVE PERFORMANCE

Why This Chapter Is Important

IN OUR TRAINING SESSIONS WITH THOUSANDS OF LEADERS, WE ASK THE following question after the first few days of training: "Based on what you know right now, what are your top three takeaways?"

Here is what we almost always hear: "I will deal with low performers, round for outcomes, and manage up to stop the 'we/they' communication that's dividing my company." (Now you see why those three topics are first in this book!)

A critical task in getting organizations aligned is teaching leaders how to quit playing the "blame game" and start positioning others—individuals, departments, and so forth—in a positive light. That's managing up. We all need to learn to manage up ourselves as well as managing up our employees, our leaders, and our organizations.

Managing up eliminates the *we/they phenomenon,* which is the primary reason employees and customers lose confidence in the organization. It's an easy trap to fall into. I know I have played

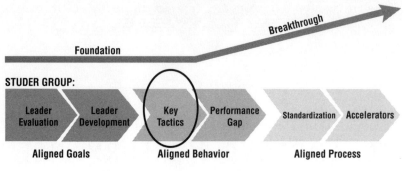

Figure 3.1 Evidence-Based Leadership

the we/they game—and perpetuated the lack of confidence in top leaders and thus the organization—at one time or another in my career.

Often, we/they has been going on inside a company for so long that its leaders don't even recognize it. In this chapter, we show you how to remove this destructive practice from your organization so you can go on to achieve high-performance results that last.

• • •

Few of us were educated to be leaders. Rather, we have leadership thrust upon us. Instead of choosing our first management position, many of us literally fall into it or have it fall on us. Go to a construction site and ask somebody why he's laying brick. Chances are he *won't* say, "Well, I'm just doing brickwork so someday I can be a foreman."

Common sense tells us that most of us start out looking for jobs that involve tasks that we enjoy. (A teacher usually wants to teach. Typically, she *doesn't* go into the field with a burning desire to be a principal.) Then somewhere along the line, we end up in a leadership position. More times than not, it's because our boss quit. The organization needs to fill the position quickly, so we get the call.

This lack of training means many leaders don't know how to explain and carry messages to employees. It's a shortcoming that can be disastrous. Why? Because the way messages are communicated within an organization is critical to that organization's culture.

There are two types of corporate cultures: those divided by blame and finger-pointing, and those united by teamwork and shared responsibility.

THE *WE/THEY* PHENOMENON

Playing the we/they card hurts an organization and its leadership. What is the *we/they card,* you ask? Basically, it's making oneself look better at the expense of others. I will give you a hypothetical example:

> Let's say I am an untrained (or inadequately trained) leader. The pay raises in my company have been in the 3 percent range because that's what was approved for this year. Oh, I may have had some 3.1 percent and 2.8 percent increases, but most were right at 3 percent.
>
> A member of my staff, Rick, comes up to me and says, "You know, Quint, I'm really upset. I've worked harder this year than ever before, but I got the same pay raise as everyone else. I thought I deserved more."
>
> My response is something like this: "Rick, I can understand how you feel." (After all, I want to show empathy, right?) "If it were up to me it wouldn't have been like that," I continue. "But you know pay raises are really out of my hands. That's something that Human Resources dictates." (Or, same tune different lyrics: "That's something that comes from corporate headquarters.")

See what I've done? I've just made the employee feel better. He may even see me as his friend. Unfortunately, I've done it at the expense of either another department or my boss.

Okay, let's give Hypothetical Untrained Me the benefit of the doubt. I didn't respond this way to Rick because I wanted to put down HR or corporate. I did this because I didn't know how *not* to do it.

I firmly believe leaders want to do a good job. However, most of us don't get the training we need to make it happen. In our two-day coaching and educational seminars, we explain how to stop the we/they phenomenon in an organization. In the years that we've held these sessions with thousands of people, one of the top three things leaders tell me that they're going to accomplish when they get back to their organization is this: "I'm going to stop creating and enabling the we/they phenomenon."

It's quite possible to play the we/they card subconsciously. We don't *intend* to subtly shift the blame, but we do so anyway, and for the most human of reasons: to make other people like us. Let me give you an example:

> Most leaders are likely to say "yes" to an employee immediately if the answer is yes. So when Tricia says, "My son's graduating from eighth grade on Friday. We're having a big party. Would it be okay if I leave just a little early that day?" If the answer is yes, I'm quick to say, "Absolutely, Tricia. I'd be disappointed if you didn't."
>
> Now, if the answer might be *no*, I'll probably say, "Hmmm, you know it's okay with me, but let me run it by Bob (the boss's boss)." Even though the answer might be *yes*, the employee's going to thank me for going to bat for her. If the answer's *no*, she will still thank me for trying and she will understand the boss is "the heavy."

So what stops an organization's flywheel—that self-perpetuating energy-and-enthusiasm cycle that keeps employees striving for excellence—from turning? It's we/they.

Examples of employees shifting the blame are encountered almost every day. Did your meal arrive cold or undercooked? It's not the server's fault; the kitchen is understaffed (or overwhelmed)! Does your new computer refuse to operate properly? It's not a hardware problem; the software's at fault! Are the company's newest employees struggling to do their work properly? Either the training department didn't do its job or the recruiting/employment department hired weak candidates (depending on whom you ask).

Has an unexpected turn in the economy lowered the company's sales? Top management should have seen it coming. Or has a sudden spurt in the economy caught the company's inventory in a shortfall? Again, top management should have seen it coming.

One way to diagnose the we/they phenomenon in your company is to do an employee attitude survey. Believe me, I've seen how it works. I was hired as president for Baptist Hospital in Pensacola, FL just after an employee attitude survey was completed. The survey ranked the supervisors a little below average. However, the top administration had an off-the-chart negative rating. And as the results were rolled out, the supervisors I could see had a look in their eye that said, "Phew, we're bad, but my God, look what we're dragging around with us here: this senior administration!"

Now, let me ask you: Where do most employees get their perception of corporate leadership? From their supervisor, of course! And here's a related question: Where do most customers get the perception of the corporation or the manager? From the employees. I am not saying top administration can't do better. The key is providing managers with the training required to drive results. It is about values. A value-driven organization trains its leaders.

When dealing with a disgruntled customer the employee can say, "Gosh, it's not up to me. *They're* the ones that do the pricing, not *me*. I don't know why we don't have that in stock, either. I tell them all the time...." (He continues in this vein, building a nice little rapport with the customer based on finger-pointing and mutual eye-rolling over those dimwits in corporate.)

Here's the rest of the story: The customer thinks, "That's a nice employee, but I'm never coming back here again." Likewise, disgruntled employees might think, "I like my boss but I don't like this company." Ultimately, both lead to people leaving. The customer never comes back and the employee eventually follows him.

Do you see how destructive the we/they phenomenon can be?

When we consult with organizations, they often discover that they are subject to we/they divisiveness. It is really a key finding. It just comes naturally to people. If it didn't, our seminar attendees wouldn't consistently label it the "number-one thing for my organization to stop doing." But they always do ... and most people don't realize what a severe problem it is.

Ed, president of an organization in Hoffman Estates, Illinois, took the leaders offsite for training. They were all asked to put their arms around each others' shoulders to form a circle. Ed said, "Okay, everybody move." It was a mess, with people lurching around in different directions. So right away they realized that they needed some leadership. Then he said, "Everybody move to the left." It still took a few missteps before they got it right. Then he asked one person not to move and the whole flywheel stumbled.

I think that story accurately illustrates the effects of teamwork and what happens in its absence. We/they is the *antithesis* of teamwork. It's people working against each other, rather than with each other. Even one person committing this sin can stop your forward progress. We/they is the stumbling block that hurts the culture of an organization and holds it back from moving from good to great.

THE ART OF MANAGING UP

So how *do* we prevent we/they? How do we keep the flywheel spinning? The answer is that we look for ways to manage up. Essentially, *managing up* is positioning something or someone in a positive light. For example:

> When you're talking to your boss, be sure to tell her about an employee who's done a good job. By relaying an employee's positive efforts, the boss can come out and say, "Kathy, I was talking to Mike and I asked him which employees are doing a particularly good job. He specifically mentioned you, Kathy. He mentioned the fact that you had a tight timeline on a project and you turned it around quickly. Kathy, I would just like to thank you for your dedication."

What has happened? Well, by getting Kathy's name from Mike, the boss has reinforced positive behavior—and reinforced and recognized behavior gets repeated. She not only managed up Kathy, but she also managed up Mike in the eyes of Kathy and the rest of the staff. I have done this with thousands of people, in our workshops and when I was in a leadership position, and I guarantee you Kathy will say, "Wow, that was really nice of Mike." And she will thank the boss for passing along the praise.

A big part of managing up is refraining from managing down. Now obviously, few leaders would deliberately manage down a person or an event at their company. Often, we take the "no comment" approach. But human nature being what it is, people often take the liberty of assuming the worst. Leaders need to find ways to position positively, and we need to be proactive about it. Let me give you an example:

> When I was president of a division of an organization, the corporation decided to review our 401(k) choices because they thought they might be able to get a better one. Now that impacted all the managers, but it also impacted all the employees who were involved in the 401(k). The CEO said that he wanted to head that committee.
>
> How could I have managed this situation down? Well, I could just say nothing. (And saying nothing would probably be the equivalent of managing down, as many employees would not know the CEO's role.) Or I could use this as an opportunity to manage up my boss and the corporation.
>
> At the employee meetings, I said, "How many of you have money invested in our 401(k)?" Probably 90 percent of the hands went up. "Let me update you on what's going on. The corporate people felt that our 401(k) *might* be fine the way it is now, but they want to be certain. So they've started an intense look into our 401(k) to ensure the employees are being charged correctly for the service and that we are getting the maximum investment opportunity and return for that money." The employees nodded their heads. "Now, because our CEO, Mr. Vickery, is so dedicated to this workforce, he is chairing that committee personally because he wants to make sure that you get the very best return on your money."

Remember, this story represents only one example of the deliberate managing up I did at this company. It was a conscious, ongoing effort. Over the year, employee satisfaction with corporate administration went from being a "minus 8" standard deviation, to a "plus 6." Corporate didn't change its behavior; they were fine already. The rating changed because how the administration was positioned with the employees was handled entirely differently.

Whether you realize it or not, you see managing up all the time. Take the restaurant industry. When a server waits on you, instead of just pointing to a blackboard with the daily specials, she says, "I tried today's pasta special before my shift and it's fabulous." Or when it is time for dessert, she says, "Gee, I don't know if you know this, but we've got an executive chef who was trained in New Orleans at Commanders Palace. He's creating our desserts today." You walk away from the meal feeling positive about the restaurant, and after giving your server a nice tip. Why? Because the waitress did a good job of managing up and positioning the restaurant, the chef, and the food.

How do you position your product? How do your employees position it? Let me state unequivocally that positioning must be authentic. Ask an employee or a manager to manage up something he doesn't believe in and you will quickly turn him off. You have to say to your employees, "If you don't believe in our product, then please tell us so we can correct it, or so we can educate you." It's this component of managing up that is often overlooked. As leaders, we need to help employees understand and support the product and the corporation.

Certain workplace cultures are themselves roadblocks to managing up. In the health care industry, everyone tends to be critical. Don't get me wrong; being critical certainly has its uses. Health care workers are trained to focus on what's wrong, and for good reason: What's wrong can kill someone. It's not hard to understand why this managing up philosophy has been slow to take hold in health care!

It's always easy to point out what's wrong. Ever notice how often people accentuate the negative? We don't necessarily do it overtly. Usually, we do it by default. How many times have you called your facilities department and told them the temperature in your office is perfect? Or called City Hall to let them know how well timed all the traffic lights are? But if it's 85 degrees in the office in the middle of July, or the traffic lights are changing every five seconds, you can bet that someone's phone will be ringing off the hook!

A good self-audit is to ask yourself this question: "When I go home, does someone in my family remind me that I'm no longer at work?" If the answer is yes, do you think it's because you are being so positive? Probably not! Likewise, has anyone in your family ever said, "We don't work for you"?

According to research, it takes a ratio of three positives to one criticism for one human being in the workplace to feel good about another human being. So we unconsciously operate on a negative cultural foundation, then wonder why we feel bad when we go home. The truth is, managing up—positioning people and products in a positive light—is somewhat countercultural. It may not come naturally, but it is worth the effort. It makes everyone feel better about themselves, their bosses, their co-workers, and the corporation.

Hot Topic is a chain of 650 stores that sell music-related clothing and accessories to teenagers, usually in malls. With annual sales of more than $720 million, this innovative retailer recently made the list of Fortune's "100 Best Companies to Work For" by encouraging its youthful employees to manage up the store's merchandise, as well as the customers who purchase it.

Salespeople are paid to attend local rock concerts and youth events, after which they write up scouting reports about what rock stars and other concertgoers were wearing. Salespeople are also expected to call the company's buyers with tips on fashion trends and to ask questions about incoming merchandise. Practices like these not only result in highly aware, well-trained salespeople, they also encourage the salespeople to "talk up" new fashions and fads with customers, co-workers, and friends. The employees feel empowered and important—circumstances that are highly unusual among retail sales clerks.

WELL-HANDLED HANDOFFS—AND THEIR PAYOFFS

When you look at customer satisfaction, one fact that always comes through loud and clear is this: If the customer is unhappy, it's usually due to lack of coordination, weak teamwork, or poor handoffs.

In health care, many lawsuits can be traced back to a handoff between caregivers or departments characterized by weak communication.

Anytime you hand off a customer, you need to clearly explain what is happening to each party involved. If possible, do the handoff in front of the other person instead of saying, "The guy down there told me this or told me that." Balls tend to be dropped when customers move from person A to person B, and the reason is that person B doesn't fully understand the situation.

> Just as bad handoffs can lead to lawsuits, great handoffs can lead to delighted customers and jingling cash registers. A friend of mine, Randy Hammer, recently shared this story with me. He had moved to Louisville and found a salon that gave him a great haircut. The next time he needed a trim he dropped in at the same place. He discovered that his stylist wasn't there, but he was assured that he could still get a great haircut. When he sat down, the new stylist said, "Now from what I've read, you like your hair cut like this." Then, he proceeded to describe the desired style in amazing detail. My friend was absolutely stunned. The salon owner explained that whatever her stylists do for a customer gets entered in the salon's computer system. Then, when the customer comes back, the stylist is sure to know exactly what he wants.

Now, if my friend's favorite salon can do it, so can every business in the country. It's how well we manage those moments of truth—handoffs—that really show that we have good teamwork, good coordination, and most of all, a good organization.

Handoffs are also perfect occasions to manage up your coworkers. Anytime you pass a customer on to another department or another team member, you should view it as an excellent opportunity for managing up. For example:

> My daughter's battery is running out and the car won't start. I jump the battery and drive the car to Whibbs Automotive. The front-desk person, Bob, listens to my problem and says, "Mr. Studer, we're sending your car to Bay 7. Steve is our mechanic today. He will check out both

your battery and your alternator. I want you to know that Steve is a certified mechanic. In fact, when it comes to fixing the alternator, Steve is one of the very best people we have in this entire garage."

Now, I'm thanking Bob for giving me to Steve, and I'm already genuinely happy that Steve's fixing my car. See the power of managing up? Obviously, you don't want to tell a customer something that's not true. But I find that most of the time we *do* work with talented people who know what they're talking about—we just don't think to relay that to customers.

MANAGING UP TO REDUCE ANXIETY

By managing up co-workers every time you get a chance, you reduce the customer's anxiety. Let me share another one of my experiences with handoffs:

When my wife, Rishy, was in the labor room about to give birth to Mallory, both of us were scared to death. I may have been even more frightened than she was. Childbirth is usually a time when the man looks at the size of the stomach, then looks at the "exit strategy," and says, "I don't think this is possible." You get very dependent on the caregiver, and that's exactly what happened to us. We bonded, Superglue style, with our nurse. She was constantly in and out of the room, reading the heartbeat of the child, taking ultrasounds, tracking the progress of dilation, and so on. We were feeling that we got lucky.

And then all of a sudden the nurse came in and said, "I'll be going home now." We were stunned. It never occurred to us that labor might go over a shift. My wife looked at me like, "Do something! I don't want this lady to leave!" In fact, if Rishy had to choose at that moment who should leave the room—the nurse or me—I would be on the other side of the door.

Now, what if that nurse had said, "Mrs. Studer, I'm going home to my family now, but I want to talk to you about the nurse who's taking my place. I just told her all about you. She'll be down here in a few minutes to meet you. Sue's an excellent nurse. She's been with us a year and I helped train her. We are so lucky that she decided to practice medicine at our hospital. I always hear so many nice compliments from parents whose babies she's delivered. I wanted you to know what good hands you're in." *Bingo!* Anxiety goes down and customer confidence goes up.

So when we talk about managing up, we're really talking about reducing anxiety. When you manage up the company or the boss, you reduce anxiety for the employee, because she wants to believe that she's working for a good place or that her boss is a nice guy. And when you manage up the company, you reduce anxiety for the customer. You help him feel he's in the right place.

CREATING THE CULTURAL SHIFT

At this point you may be feeling a bit discouraged. You may be wondering how you'll ever get your employees and colleagues (and maybe yourself) to reject we/they and embrace managing up. Don't worry. It's definitely doable. You can create a cultural shift in your company that will change everything. Here's how:

1. *Conduct employee attitude surveys.* These management tools give you a good idea of how strong a hold we/they has on your organization. Plus, taking a survey will allow you to set some benchmarks by which you can measure your progress in changing your corporation culture from one of blame to one of shared accountability and teamwork.

2. *Send scouting reports* (Figure 3.2). Employees want to know the boss. It's what we constantly hear from middle managers, "I wish my boss were more visible. The employees would like to meet him." Sending the boss a scouting report makes it more likely that he will visit.

Bosses have several reasons for not visiting branch offices and other departments. First, many are just too swamped. Also, they often figure you're in charge of the area, not them, and they don't want to interfere. Finally, though they might not admit it, bosses

To: Quint Studer
From: Rachel Azare
Date: 9/30/06, 10:43 a.m.

Subject: Scouting Report: Marketing

Quint:

Next time you're in the Marketing Department, please make note of the following:

> • We've reorganized in the department. Bob Mosley is handling all media relations—print, radio, and television. Diana Roberts takes care of all marketing materials—brochures, promotional materials, and newsletters. Joy Beckham manages graphic design and writers. They're proud of how it makes our department more responsive to the rest of the corporation.

> • We recently launched an in-house newsletter that is very popular. Joy and Diana worked together on the basic design. I've attached a copy of the latest one.

> • Also please recognize Gloria Casio, our new administrative assistant. She has reorganized our marketing library and helped get the individual department reports to complete the in-house newsletter. She is coming up on her one-year anniversary with the company.

A good time to come by would be next Thursday around 9:30 a.m. after our regular staff meeting.

Thanks,
Rachel

Figure 3.2 Scouting Report

usually get slammed by the employees and would rather avoid any confrontations.

The scouting report eases the boss's anxiety, makes his visit much more productive, and generally facilitates managing up in your organization. Instead of telling the boss just what's wrong in your area, give him the good news, too. Consider this experience from my own career:

When I was president of a hospital, I got an e-mail that said "Heads up. Bad day in the operating room. Some angry surgeons down here;

you might want to come on down." *I don't think so,* I told myself. Do you blame me? No one wants to answer a summons that inspires dread and foreboding!

I preferred to receive scouting reports from department heads and supervisors. They can be written or verbal. I would have been much happier if the "angry surgeons" e-mail had included the following scouting report: "Hey, when you come to my area to talk to the surgeons, here's some equipment that we've improved that you might want to mention because the employees are excited to get it. Here are some projects that I'd like you to ask about, because the employees are really feeling good about what they've done. Here's the name of a few employees that I'd like you to recognize and here's why."

3. *Send regular notes to the bosses.* Bosses want to know whom to reward and recognize. Don't be afraid to drop your boss a note. Tell her the name of an employee to whom you would like her to send a note and the specific behavior or accomplishment you would like her to write about. And suggest that she send it to the employee's home. You've just managed up the employee to the boss, who, when she writes the note, will say she got the information from you.

4. *Help employees develop key words.* (See Chapter 19, "Key Words at Key Times," to learn more.) You want your frontline employees to tell the customer that your product is the best and that the people behind the scenes are doing a great job. Even if it's uncomfortable at first, you will find that the customer appreciates it.

Meet with your frontline employees and make sure they understand the product and the roles and qualifications of others who help create, service, and deliver it. Teach them how to communicate this to the customer in a way that feels comfortable and natural. For example: "Our luxury bath soaps are the very best. They are milled in Provence, France, using fresh herbs and flowers grown in the French countryside by farm families whose ancestors have done this for centuries. I love our lavender soap; I even keep a bar of it in my dresser drawer."

Let's revisit our restaurant example. Good restaurants huddle with their waitstaff before their shift and make sure they understand all the specials. They let them sample entrees and advise them on what wines may complement each one. The manager will visit the tables, manage up the server and the chef, and ask for feedback to relay to the staff later on.

5. *Continually emphasize honest, open communication between employees.* Here's a scenario that may seem all too familiar: Gerald is upset that his co-worker, Bob, left him out of a meeting in which he would normally be included. He shares his displeasure with Bob with their leader, who discusses it with the Chief Operating Officer, who discusses it with the president. The COO spends time talking to Gerald, his supervisor, and others involved in the meeting. These conversations take time—time that is, frankly, mostly unproductive. The leader simply could say up front to Gerald, "Have you talked to Bob?"

Things like this happen all the time. We carry messages for people we shouldn't. As leaders, we must teach our people to carry such messages themselves. The reality is we've got to be able to have adult conversations in the workplace. If there is a problem or issue, it is best that the two parties discuss it first between themselves. If they can't reach resolution, *then* it's time to bring in the boss. Otherwise, the problem gets caught up in the organizational chart and never handled.

6. *Develop written department feedback systems.* Large corporations have numerous departments. All are interconnected, but few may know each others' goals and objectives. This lack of communication can lead to many we/they situations. For example:

> A weekly newspaper's editorial staff has as its goal to turn in all its stories to production by 3:00 P.M. so that they can begin reviewing the final pages the next morning before the publication is sent to the press. They're upset because the production department doesn't have the page laid out for them when they arrive at 7:30 A.M. What they don't know is production has placed a priority on finishing the ad designs and *their* goal was to complete the editorial pages by noon. They didn't even know the editorial staff was upset. It's the publisher who hears all the complaints.

Written feedback systems help eliminate passive-aggressive behavior between departments. When the two departments have to evaluate each other on a weekly basis, they are forced to talk out the issues and modify their operational goals. As a department head, I have to write my name on the evaluation. My boss sees it and so do you. Now, if I rank you too high then I can't use you as an excuse to my boss anymore. So I'm probably going to rank you accurately. The first time I give you that 3 when you think you're a 5, we'll have a talk. It may not be pleasant, but it's best to get difficult conversations out of the way early on.

Do you see the value of creating feedback systems? They open up dialogue and help move the organization forward. That's always a good thing.

KEY POINTS FOR HARDWIRING RESULTS

- The we/they phenomenon creates negative images and feelings among employees. Leaders who try to make themselves look good at the expense of others—even unconsciously—contribute to an atmosphere of distrust, blame, and finger-pointing.

- Managing up helps organizations overcome we/they. Basically, it means positioning something or someone—top management, other departments, outside suppliers, and so forth—in a positive light. Managing up leads to better customer service, better leadership, and higher employee satisfaction.

- Make it a point to manage up as you coordinate handoffs from one customer service provider to another. Well-designed recordkeeping—through computer databases, file cards, or any other techniques that capture and retain customer data—can help you do this more effectively. When customers realize that each person in your organization understands their problems and needs, their level of satisfaction skyrockets.

- Employees at all levels of an organization should always look for an opportunity to talk up the company with customers, vendors, suppliers, visitors, and others. By managing up our co-workers every time we get a chance, we reduce the customer's anxieties and create an expectation of good service.

- Here are a few tips for creating a cultural shift in your company from blaming to managing up:
  - Conduct employee attitude surveys to set some benchmarks by which you can measure your progress.
  - Send scouting reports to your boss. A scouting report detailing what your people are doing is likely to motivate the boss to visit more often and become more visible.
  - Also, send regular notes to your boss identifying employees who deserve reward and recognition. Doing so helps her send thank-you notes, which are an important component of managing up.
  - Help employees to develop key words for managing up.
  - Emphasize honest, open communication between your employees.
  - Finally, develop written departmental feedback systems so all employees can know each other's departmental goals and objectives. (See sample on studergroup.com, search departmental feedback.)

THE
CORE

CHAPTER

4

BUILD THE FOUNDATION (PASSION AND PURPOSE)

Why This Chapter Is Important

EMPLOYEES WANT TO HAVE PURPOSE AND DO WORTHWHILE WORK THAT makes a difference. This truth is at the heart of our drive to lasting results. That's why the hub of the flywheel is purpose, worthwhile work, and making a difference.

Leaders who help their employees connect the dots between their work and its purpose outperform those who don't.

There are certain building blocks that we've found—through our work and research—are essential to hardwiring excellence in an organization and achieving lasting results. These blocks form a foundation that, when applied properly, works for any organization in any industry.

The foundation gives you a framework for helping others understand the purpose of their work and how it makes a difference. Once you and your employees integrate this framework into your mindset, you will see a dynamic positive change within your organization.

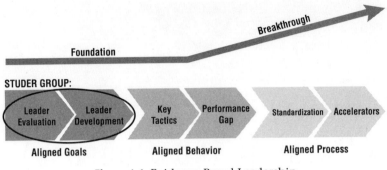

Figure 4.1 Evidence-Based Leadership

Read on and let's get the flywheel turning.

• • •

What sets one person apart from another? What makes one organization succeed where another organization flounders? Very often being "good enough" is the biggest barrier keeping an organization from moving to the next level. How do you create a sense of urgency to take your organization to the next level? How do you sustain gains and continue to take success to yet a higher level?

There's a story of a man (let's call him Michael) who goes for a stroll one day and comes upon three bricklayers working on a construction project. Michael approaches Bricklayer #1 and asks, "What are you doing?" The man replies, "What's the matter with you? Are you blind or something? What's it look like I'm doing? I'm laying bricks!"

Michael then goes up to Bricklayer #2 and asks, "What are you doing?" The second man looks up with a smirk and says, "I'm just doing whatever they tell me to do, as long as they keep paying me twelve dollars per hour!"

Finally he goes up to the third man and asks, "What are you doing?" Bricklayer #3 pauses in his work and takes a moment to look over the construction site before answering. "Why, I'm helping to build a beautiful church," he replies. "Someday, families will come here to worship. They'll bring their babies here to be baptized and their sons and daughters will be married here. For many years to come, people of all walks will celebrate the joys of life and find solace from sorrow in this beautiful church that I am helping to build!"

Pretend for a moment that you are Michael. Which of these three workmen would you believe has a genuine passion for his job? All three perform the exact same type of work, but which of them is driven by a sense of purpose and believes his work to be worthwhile? Which man feels he is making a difference in the lives of others? Which of them cares that he is building something that will last?

Of course, the "Michael" in this story could just as easily be the CEO of an automobile factory or the manager of a flower shop. Regardless of the nature of his job, he (or she) doesn't want employees who merely "install windshields" or "shove rose stems into vases." No; he or she wants employees who "build sleek automobiles that people can drive with exhilaration and pride," or "make beautiful bouquets that help people express their feelings, hopes, and dreams." In short, he wants a whole company full of "Bricklayer #3s."

Employees who succeed (and who help their organizations succeed) do so because their commitment flows from the right reasons: They want to feel that their job and organization has purpose, that they do worthwhile work, and that they make a difference.

THE ORGANIZATIONAL FLYWHEEL

The *organizational flywheel* works in much the same way that the flywheel on a steam engine drives a train. When you listen to the sound of the engine, you can hear the push that starts it purring. Then as the engine moves, the train gains momentum, until the momentum is so great, it's difficult to stop. Some say it takes eight miles for a locomotive to stop.

It is the same with the organizational flywheel. When organizations help employees reconnect to their values and passion for doing worthwhile work, they balance the flywheel and inspire them to commit to some prescriptive *to-do's* that turn it. This creates results that generate increasing momentum for more results

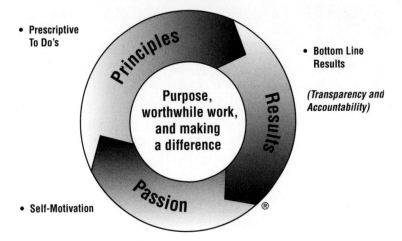

- Prescriptive To Do's

- Bottom Line Results

(Transparency and Accountability)

- Self-Motivation

Figure 4.2 Purpose, Worthwhile Work, and Making a Difference

on the journey to service and operational excellence—until those to-do's are *hardwired*. In other words, an organization can sustain the gains, even if great leaders come and go.

It all starts with a commitment to *purpose, worthwhile work*, and *making a difference* (Figure 4.2). Those three values drive most people to embrace change and seek to become better at what they do. By continually reinforcing how daily choices and actions connect back to these values (i.e., the hub of the flywheel), leaders will reinforce behaviors and effect change more quickly.

SELF-MOTIVATION

The passion that people bring to their work sets the organizational flywheel in motion. Of course, some workers may well seem to be more passionate than others; pilots are notably passionate about passenger safety. But in any line of work it shouldn't be hard to discover the passion that drives individuals to put forth their best effort. Even in a "widget" factory you should find people who eat, breathe, live, and die for widgets. As leaders it is important for us to connect the dots with employees on how what they do impacts the organization and beyond.

Gina is a quality control manager at a company that makes food storage containers. She didn't feel much of a sense of purpose, worthwhile work, and making a difference until management asked her to listen in on some focus groups that the product design team was holding. One mom in the focus group said, "I hate it when the containers leak. One day I got a call from my kindergartner's teacher at school. My daughter Maddie was in tears because her yogurt had spilled and soaked her sandwich, so she refused to eat lunch. The other kids were making fun of her mess at the lunch table. I'd pay extra if you could guarantee me a leak-proof container!" From that day on, Gina's quest for quality control was personal. And so was her team's. They thought of little Maddie each time they inspected lids.

At first glance, this doesn't sound like a job that would inspire passion. But if Gina remembers the impact that that storage container will have on all the "Maddies" out there—not to mention their moms—she'll feel her work is affecting people positively. Gina is no longer just making a food storage container, but a tool that helps others to demonstrate love and thoughtfulness.

Passion, Purpose, Worthwhile Work ... and Insurance

When you think of insurance, do purpose and worthwhile work come to mind? They do at SASid. SASid is an internet-based insurance company that focuses on developing and distributing insurance products that are smart and simple. Below is a letter that was recently sent to the president of SASid.

Dear Mr. Kennedy,

I wanted to share the impact your staff and insurance product had on my life. I was laid off from a company I had worked at for three years. They offered me COBRA insurance but the cost was going to be over $1,300 per month. This was a cost I just could not

(Continued)

Passion, Purpose (*Continued*)

afford—and what was the chance something would happen in the time my family and I would not be covered?

My wife wasn't sure she wanted to take that chance. So, I looked up COBRA insurance on the internet to find more information and ended up calling your company. I spoke with Robin, who graciously explained what COBRA meant and that there were alternatives. We ended up with temporary health insurance for 1/3 of the price my previous employer had quoted me.

Thank God we did. A month after I was laid off my daughter was in a car accident. It was terrifying. My wife and I were with her constantly. Thanks to our policy with your company and the help of Robin, we didn't have to worry about medical bills or our financial future. My daughter is doing great now.

I wanted you to know that I will never think of insurance as a hassle or unwarranted cost again. I am grateful to your company for educating me and providing me with an affordable alternative.

Sincerely,
Glen

P.S. During the time my daughter was hospitalized, I repeatedly called your organization. It didn't matter whom I spoke with; I was treated kindly and felt your staff cared.

The insurance professionals at SASid know that what they do impacts lives. If they ever forget, letters like this one serve as great reminders.

Self-motivation born of passion is what gets the flywheel spinning. Motivated leaders and employees keep it spinning in the face of long days, endless paperwork, and cranky clients.

PRESCRIPTIVE TO-DO'S

Prescriptive to-do's are the actual techniques, tactics, and behaviors that direct the passion of the employees toward the organization's desired results. They're based on aligned behaviors that have been proven to create service and operational excellence. In Studer Group's work, we have developed and regularly use the *Nine Principles* (see sidebar). We share several prescriptive to-do's in this book (rounding for outcomes; high, middle, and low conversations; and so forth) but it is important for each organization to determine what techniques need to be standardized to drive their desired results.

Nine Principles for a Solid Foundation

If our corporate culture does not deeply embed core values and key processes, then we will never be able to sustain excellence in our organizations. How do we create the necessary cultural values, habits, beliefs, and methods among our leaders and employees? We believe that the following Nine Principles are central to any attempt to transform an organization's culture:

1. **Commit to excellence:** Focus on measurable goals of excellence.

2. **Measure the important things:** What gets measured gets focused on.

3. **Build a culture around service:** Use tools and techniques to drive performance.

4. **Create and develop leaders:** They're the flag bearers for any effort to achieve excellence.

5. **Focus on employee satisfaction:** The best barometers of problems are your employees.

6. **Build individual accountability:** Create ownership with employees.

7. **Align behaviors with goals and values:** Leaders must be accountable for culture change.

(Continued)

> **Nine Principles (*Continued*)**
>
> 8. **Communicate at all levels:** Learn how to position others well.
>
> 9. **Recognize and reward success:** Recognized behaviors get repeated.

RESULTS

This is the third element of the flywheel. Without tangible results, the flywheel slows, and leaders become disheartened and lose momentum. When an organization and its employees see results, the flywheel sets in motion a positive, upward spiral of success that engenders more success. The employees become more excited by the results. They become ever more motivated, and they work harder at the prescriptive to-do's. This leads to more positive bottom-line results and the flywheel continues to spin.

Many leaders ask, "How can I keep my staff motivated?" I urge them to focus on two things: (1) Drive the prescriptive to-do's that are included throughout this book because they bring results, and (2) always connect results back to purpose, worthwhile work, and making a difference. These things feed and strengthen self-motivation.

The most successful leaders understand and organize around *passion, prescription, and results* because this combination leads us back to the hub of our deep and universal yearning to have purpose, do worthwhile work, and make a difference. In fact, I urge leaders to explicitly make this connection for their employees. They don't always realize it on their own. They need to hear it from their leaders.

THE FIVE PILLARS OF EXCELLENCE

While the flywheel drives the momentum of the organization, it is the *Five Pillars* and the *organizational goals* we set for each of them that provide the structure. The Five Pillars—Service, Quality, People, Finance, and Growth—is a universal concept that applies equally well to all types of service and industrial organizations: retailers, manufacturers, government, education, technology, and so forth. It provides the foundation for setting organizational goals and direction to achieve service and operational excellence. It also provides a consistency and focus that allows an organization to resist new fads.[1]

When we set goals under the Five Pillars we keep the flywheel spinning in the same direction for the entire organization.

The Five Pillars keep you from getting sidetracked by the latest buzzword or program of the month and keep you focused on an aligned vision. Now, I'm not saying there's anything wrong with programs or buzzwords in and of themselves. But the sheer volume of them makes people—executives, managers, and employees alike—confused. Leaders need to do is create a corporate culture that will last. That means we've got to help our employees understand what makes the organization go.

Remember, employees want jobs that have purpose, that are worthwhile, and that make a difference. It doesn't matter whether the job is with a tire company, a fast-food restaurant, or a Wall Street brokerage firm; if it doesn't have these three criteria, an employee won't engage wholeheartedly. And if the program you're trying to implement doesn't speak to them on this same deep and meaningful level, your employees will never buy into it.

Fortunately, the Five Pillars model is a powerful tool for organizational transformation that is also easy to explain and implement. By realigning your organization into operational pillars, you provide the foundation for setting organizational goals and direction for service and operational excellence that the majority of employees will accept.

---

[1]In his wonderful book, *Creating the New American Hospital: A Time for Greatness* (New York: John Wiley & Sons, 1993), Clay Sherman expressed the concept of four pillars. I adapted his model by adding a fifth pillar (which I define as "Growth," or access) and moving "cost" within a new Finance pillar, which better describes financial goals.

Avoiding the Buzz

In 1992, America's greatest technology company had fallen upon very hard times. IBM, a company that boasted it had never conducted an employee layoff in nearly 100 years of operation, was facing serious financial losses and many, many jobs were in danger of being cut. The technology marketplace had evolved radically and IBM's mainframe computers, which once ruled the business world, were rapidly becoming high-tech dinosaurs.

To stem the prospect of disaster IBM brought in Louis Gerstner, an experienced executive and turnaround specialist. Gerstner could have drummed up a campaign or slogan to bolster IBM's troops, but he knew that IBM's talented employees needed an authentic, down-to-earth approach to rescue the organization. Instead, he traveled throughout the company, listening to employees and gathering information that would help revitalize IBM.

One day during this period a reporter asked Gerstner if he had a vision for the future of IBM. Gerstner replied, "The last thing IBM needs right now is a vision." He was widely mocked and ridiculed for that comment, which seemed to fly in the face of conventional management wisdom. But Gerstner was right. IBM's employees didn't need a buzzword or a slogan; they needed to get a grasp on the company's problems, to focus on what needed to be done, and to work as a team to make things better. Within a few years IBM's fortunes had completely turned around and they reclaimed their position as a worldwide leader in technology.

Together, the Five Pillars also provide the framework for an evaluation process, since all leaders are evaluated against established metrics under each pillar. (This subject will be covered later.) In addition, the Five Pillars help keep the organization balanced in its short- and long-term objectives. The pillars are interrelated and give added purpose and meaning to the work of employees.

The Five Pillars of Excellence				
Service	Quality	People	Finance	Growth
Fewer Complaints	Improved Products or Processes	Reduced Turnover	Controlled Costs	Larger Market Share
Higher Customer Satisfaction	Reduced Defects and Rework	Controlled Costs	Improved Collections	Greater Share Value
Higher Customer Retention	Reduced Waste	Improved Productivity	Higher Profit Margins	
Improved Word of Mouth		Improved Morale		Increased Sales or Customers
				Increased Volume

To hardwire the strategic direction of the organization, we recommend three things:

1. Set all meeting agendas by pillars to provide focus.

2. Establish a leader evaluation tool by pillars to create accountability (Chapter 7).

3. Create department or organization communication boards by pillars to update staff on measurable progress.

The synergy of the pillars gives purpose and meaning to the work of employees. The model helps Jill in Quality Control understand how her actions affect, say, Troy, the cashier in the Duluth store.

Every organization is dependent on these five key components, even if they're not accustomed to thinking of them in precisely this way. Almost every company has some type of *service* channel through which it connects with the customer. It also has a *quality* component, whether it is quality management, parts preventative maintenance, or clinical quality for patients. Every organization that hires and employs human beings also has a *people* component.

Of course, no company survives without understanding financial management, and thus the *financial* component. In finance, we *know* the goal. As soon as the variance gets to a certain point, whether it's five days or seven days, we're already taking corrective action to bring it back in line.

And finally, there is *growth*. You might call it *volume*. Or perhaps you call it *access*: Are enough customers utilizing our services or products?

The goals set under each pillar—Service, Quality, People, Finance, and Growth—are desired targets. What will it take to achieve excellent results under each pillar? It depends. Each organization needs to define *excellence* in its own marketplace. These goals then cascade down. Each leader sets his or her goal for the organization, facility, division, and department based on all of the pillars. The end result is an entire company focused on the same organizational results.

Building a Culture of Excellence, Not Perfection

Too often we confuse "excellence" with "perfection," but they're not the same thing. Perfection is an unrealized ideal. Excellence is an *achievable* goal. While we sometimes use the term "perfect" to describe a result or a state of being, few people realistically believe that perfection can be achieved. When you hold people up to the standard of perfection you are setting them up for failure. To be branded less than perfect is disheartening, discouraging, and ultimately counterproductive in our efforts to achieve excellence.

A culture of excellence doesn't mean that mistakes will not be made or that failures won't occur. They will—that's unavoidable. Creating a culture of excellence means that when there *are* mistakes, when failures *do* occur, that they will be examined, *learned from,* and (hopefully) not repeated. Far from sabotaging a culture of excellence, mistakes can be a powerful engine for achieving higher levels of performance.

In short, a culture of excellence is not a culture of perfection. Instead, it's a culture in which employees at every level are given "permission" to take certain risks, to make mistakes without dire consequences, and competent about making changes that will help move the entire organization in the direction of excellence. Without this type of *supportive atmosphere* change will be much harder, with a great deal of employee and management resistance and a much greater likelihood of failure.

Seven Steps to Creating a Supportive Environment

1. **Reconnect with your passion for your work.** If you have lost the passion you once held for what you do, look for creative ways to rediscover it. Talk to customers about what your products and services mean to them; ask how you can meet their needs even better. If possible, delegate responsibilities that no longer fulfill you, and try to get back in touch with the aspects of your work that drew you to your profession, company, or field. You'll never achieve excellence as a leader without passion.

2. **Never make excuses. Don't tolerate them in your employees.** Announce the "no-excuses" policy and do your best to live by it. Empower leaders to do what they feel is in the best interest of your company and its goal of achieving excellence. When people know they are responsible for coming up with solutions, and that *they have the latitude to do so,* they will be far less likely to fall back on excuses. If you catch an employee making an excuse, call her on it (but remember, be constructive).

3. **Allow yourself to be vulnerable. When you make a mistake, admit it.** For many leaders, vulnerability is scary. People fear they'll be rejected if they show weakness or admit that they failed. Interestingly, the opposite is true.

(Continued)

Building a Culture of Excellence (*Continued*)

Leaders more often gain greater employee loyalty when they show that they are human.

1. **Accept criticism graciously. Try not to take failure personally.** You are setting an example for your employees. Leaders who take it personally when an idea doesn't pan out, or when someone points out a mistake, discourage risk-taking in others. You want to create a culture in which principles matter more than egos.

2. **Build a culture in which it's okay to challenge leaders.** Invite your people to challenge you if they disagree with something you say or do. A company of yes-men and yes-women rarely achieves excellence. People must be free to express their ideas without censure, even if you don't act on their recommendations.

3. **When you issue challenges, do so publicly, not privately.** This creates accountability both for the challenger and the challenged. Goals that are made public have a way of getting accomplished in a way that "secret plans" rarely do. It's okay to risk failure by making your plans public, since that increases your likelihood of success.

4. ***Never* punish someone for an honest mistake.** Remember, mistakes are stepping stones on the journey to excellence. As long as employees learn from their mistakes and don't repeat them, they are valuable partners on that journey.

HELPING EMPLOYEES CONNECT THE DOTS

Even if we don't officially call them the "Five Pillars," it's essential that we create standardized operational goals/components that all employees can understand, and that we communicate the goals organizationwide. Once the leadership agrees on the goals and how they work together for the good of the overall organization, we need to find a way to help each employee understand his or her *big picture* role. Just like those puzzles where children have to draw lines connecting a series of dots in order to see the final picture, we have to help our employees "connect the dots" between themselves and each of the goals.

In one organization where I served, many people viewed the chief financial officer as if he were a greedy, money-pinching miser. The common opinion seemed to be that all this man did was sit in his office, rub his hands together, and mutter "money, money, money" under his breath like a mantra. Anyway, I asked him at a staff meeting why he was so aggressive in collecting money. He replied that the more he was able to collect, the more he could reinvest back into the employees and equipment they need. When he finished speaking, you could tell that everybody in the meeting looked at him differently. He had connected the dots for everyone in that room. (See Figure 4.3.)

Results-oriented companies help employees at all levels and in all departments connect the dots. In plant operations, the work crews must understand that the preventive maintenance they do reduces downtime. Reducing downtime improves the efficiency of their co-workers and, ultimately, improves customer service.

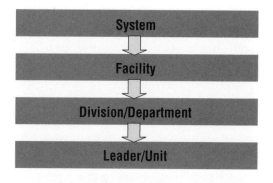

Alignment of goals creates momentum!

Figure 4.3 Cascading Goals

Boosting efficiency and customer service improves the financial bottom line. Thus, the work of plant operations is worthwhile and has purpose.

How do you convey this message to your employees? It depends. Sometimes, connecting the dots is specific and personal. It's a one-on-one conversation a leader has with an employee who doesn't seem to get it. You can also address the subject in a speech you give at your annual holiday party, or via the Q&A portion of a department meeting (you might "plant" a colleague who will ask a prearranged question that gets the ball rolling), or in an article in your company newsletter. The idea is to seize "teachable moments" to connect the dots in a natural, relevant way.

Sometimes, connecting the dots can even save jobs. I wish I could write a book that said you'd never have to lay off staff, but with technology and changes in the market such a promise is unlikely to be kept. Every company at one time or another will face some level of financial challenge. Still, instead of immediately moving to laying off employees, you might look for creative ways to save money. Explain to your staff how these seemingly unrelated (or at least, only distantly related) actions could make the company healthier and, ultimately, save jobs. This brings home the connections between people and departments in a very powerful way.

For example, if the company or department had fewer costly errors, it would obviously be more solvent. In health care, every time a patient falls, it costs as much as $11,000 in out-of-pocket expenses alone. Yes, a financially strapped hospital could reduce staff, but what if it prevented four falls per year instead? That's $44,000 that could probably pay for a staff member. When you explain this principle to employees, it clearly demonstrates the connection between Ralph, the man who keeps the floors clean and dry, and Marjorie, the training specialist who would be the first to go in the event of a layoff. It helps them really understand the Five Pillars of your organization, why they are important, and how they relate to their jobs and the overall success of the organization.

Instant Alignment

There is an activity that Bob Murphy, former hospital CEO and now national speaker with Studer Group, shared with me. It can be done in the new employee orientation that will lead to instant alignment with the organization's goals and objectives. In the handouts provided to each new employee, include a page with five interlocking circles. At the top of the page is the question, "Where would you focus?" Break the employees into groups of five or six people with this instruction: "You have just been promoted to CEO. Where would you focus?"

The employees fill in each of the five circles with the things they would focus on if they were CEO. After a few minutes' discussion, solicit the ideas from the groups. No matter how many times you do this, the new folks always identify the Five Pillars: Service, Quality, People, Finance, and Growth.

It gives you the opening to explain what would be measured under each pillar. For example, if a group reports that they would focus on employee satisfaction, you can link that to the People pillar and discuss key goals such as lowering turnover below a certain percentage. Then explain why lowering turnover is important for quality, physician collaboration, satisfaction of other employees, and lowered costs of replacement. You should be able to connect the dots and explain many of the goals of the organization.

Ultimately, what we as leaders need to do as often as possible is to help employees see how what *they* do impacts the organization and its customers. People work for the paycheck, yes, but they also want to make meaningful contributions to their little corner of the world. It's what makes them feel good about themselves. It's what makes their efforts seem worthwhile.

Remember our bricklaying analogy from the beginning of the chapter? Let's close with a similar story about bricks. Years ago at the University of Wisconsin, researchers studied the impact of pay on the quality of work. The study involved a group of workers whose job was to move bricks from one place to another. Once the bricks were all moved, the laborers moved them back to the original spot. The researchers doubled the workers' pay. Even though the work wasn't physically exhausting and they made more money than ever before, the workers quit after a few weeks. Why? Because they didn't see any progress and they had no vision of a beautiful completed building at the end of their labors. The job did not fulfill the workers' need to feel they were doing something worthwhile.

It's all about a commitment to do the things you've always done *even better*. We're talking about helping people understand the cause and effect of their work. Connecting the dots is all about reinforcing an existing truth about what a company is. It's about reminding employees that what they do every day does have purpose . . . it is worthwhile . . . and it does make a difference. When they *really* understand it on a heart-and-soul level, they're ready to truly start creating results that last.

KEY POINTS FOR HARDWIRING RESULTS

- The hub of the flywheel—*purpose, worthwhile work,* and *making a difference*—drive most people to become better at what they do. No buzzword, or management fad, or best-selling book can supplant the self-motivation that compels individuals—or organizations—to improve.

- Before you can transform an organization's culture, you must build two *foundations*. The first foundation for the organization's leaders, called the *flywheel*, generates those behaviors and practices that lead to improvements, better results, and organizational success. The second foundation, called the *Five Pillars of Excellence*, helps organizations set goals and measure progress toward reaching those goals. It's a framework within which each organization defines excellence, recognizes critical areas of focus, and communicates core values to all stakeholders.

- The flywheel has three elements that drive organizational change: *passion, principles* (expressed as prescriptive to-do's), and *results*. The passion people bring to their work sets the organizational flywheel in motion. Prescriptive to-do's lead the organization to achieve the goals that they set forth under the Five Pillars of Excellence. Achieving the necessary results fuels more passion, drives more prescriptive actions, and leads to better results, setting in motion a positive, upward spiral of success.

- The Five Pillars—Service, Quality, People, Finance, and Growth—are interrelated and give added purpose and meaning to the work of employees. They provide a framework for measuring results, evaluating leaders, and achieving true organizational excellence.

- Leaders have to find ways to help employees connect the dots. When people see the big picture and understand how their job performance fits in, they are more likely to understand and support your organization's Five Pillars of Excellence. Storytelling is an excellent way to communicate the impact of your employees' efforts on a human level.

- *Excellence* is not a synonym for *perfection*. It really is okay for people to make mistakes; that's part of the growth process. Work hard to create a supportive environment inside your organization.

CHAPTER 5

REDUCE
LEADERSHIP VARIANCE

Why This Chapter Is Important

MOST ORGANIZATIONS HAVE STRICT RULES ON HOW TO USE THEIR LOGO
and its tag line. We call it corporate identity. Break the rules, and the
logo police are in your office. Why is this so? Because it's important
to convey a consistent visual message about your company.

We also standardize what we buy, from whom we buy it, and
how we buy it. We measure variances in the financials all the time.
And when one variance falls outside a certain range, we fix it.

But there is one thing most companies struggle to standardize,
and ironically, it's the most important part of our efforts to gain
and sustain results. It is *leadership*. If a company has 500 leaders, it
may have 500 different ways to interview prospective employees,
500 different answers to the same questions, and 500 different ways
to deal with a given situation.

Companies that standardize leadership best practices create a
map showing the way to high performance—a map that all leaders
can share.

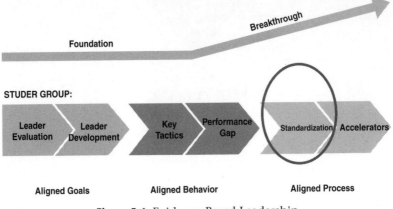

Figure 5.1 Evidence-Based Leadership

This chapter explores the reasons why leadership variance is such a common problem and why, therefore, so many organizations fail to achieve their desired results. It builds a strong case for adopting a system that enables your company to utilize best leader practices consistently so that everyone is working together to create results that last.

• • •

When we fly, we're grateful that the pilot has a checklist that he follows when he lands the plane. We want every landing to be the same—smooth, safe, and uneventful. No one on the plane wants the pilot to experiment with some new technique that just hit him while the passengers were watching the in-flight movie.

The same is true when we dine out. Our favorite franchise food tastes the same whether we order it in Phoenix, Arizona, or Opp, Alabama. We count on our burgers and fries being cooked and seasoned to the same specifications in all cities. If for some odd reason the food isn't identical, our confidence in that franchise is weakened.

With our medical care, we have the same sorts of expectations. Doctors have spent long hours perfecting their treatments and procedures. Many surgeons perform the same operation several times in a week. Although individual cases may require more skill than others, the basic core procedures that are followed are the same. We don't want our cardiovascular surgeon to suddenly use his left hand instead of his right because he was bored and wanted to shake things up.

Pilots, restaurant owners, and doctors seek standardization and wish to reduce variances from one landing, meal, or patient to another. They strive for consistent outcomes. We can learn from this principle as we move our organizations toward achieving lasting results.

TAKE A CUE FROM YOUR FINANCE LEADERS

Finance departments have focused on accounting variations for decades. Financial managers watch each and every expense variation like hawks to contain costs and preserve the quality of care.

At our "Taking You and Your Organization to the Next Level" seminars, we often ask a financial officer in the audience, "If one of your managers has exceeded his or her expense budget for the month, how long will it be before you ask for an action plan to bring expenses back into line?" They inevitably answer, "About five minutes," a joke that's not far off the mark. The bottom line is that variances in managing expenses are not going to be tolerated.

If we don't tolerate variances in expenses, then why do we tolerate variances in other aspects of leadership and management? When we ask leaders about variances in other areas (such as Service, People, Quality, and Growth), their action plans and accountability are often sketchy. They say that correcting those types of variances may take weeks or months—or that it may never actually happen.

This is the case because the nonfinancial areas, at first glance, appear more difficult to measure objectively than sales, overtime, or other such items. But making the effort is definitely worth it.

Setting measurable goals for areas other than finance leads to improved outcomes. When leaders track and trend results, variances can be monitored. For instance, when all leaders set a goal to reduce turnover to 10 percent, the organization can find high-performing areas for others to use as benchmarks. It allows an organization to respond at the beginning of a negative trend and create action plans immediately.

The fact is that most organizations would be better off if leaders ran their operations like financial managers, because they focus a great deal on measurement metrics and reducing variances. Sometimes these financial managers are so focused on reports and metrics that other people in the organization suspect that the Finance Department is more concerned about numbers than about people.

We believe financial managers *are* concerned about people. However, they understand that consistency and standardization in operations come first. If we can't ensure operational excellence, we can't build a great place for employees to work, leaders to lead, and customers to receive excellent service.

It may *involve* numbers, but it isn't *about* numbers. It's about people!

CONSISTENCY EQUALS SUSTAINABLE RESULTS

An example from my work with one hospital may serve to illustrate this point. Leaders at this hospital wanted to reduce the number of people who left the Emergency Department (ED) without being seen. These "lost patients" equal lost revenue. Typically, people who leave are those who have other options for care and are more likely to be able to afford it. Also, people who leave without being seen are a liability to the hospital.

Let's say Susan brings her young daughter into the Emergency Department on a Saturday morning. The child is exhibiting a fever, chills, and vomiting. Susan suspects her daughter has the flu but is seeking assurance that it's nothing more. After waiting two hours without any update from ED staff, Susan gets frustrated and decides to leave. After all, it is most likely the flu, right? But what if it *isn't?*

If it turns out Susan's young daughter actually has meningitis, for instance, the hospital is liable.

To reduce the number of people leaving without being seen, the ED charge nurse or triage nurse was asked to round on patients and families in the waiting area of the Emergency Department. The rounding needed to happen consistently, so the nurse was asked to round every hour on the hour using specific key words (see sidebar). The timing and wording were based on a study by the *Alliance for Health Care Research (AHCR)*. The study showed that using consistent rounding and key words was effective at reducing the likelihood that people would leave the ED without being seen. (Access the full study at www.studergroup.com.)

Key Words for Patients and Families in the Emergency Department Reception Area

SCRIPT: IN RECEPTION/LOBBY

Julie: Good afternoon. I am the ED Charge Nurse (or Triage Nurse) today in the ER. There is about a 45-minute wait to go to the treatment area right now. Please let me or the greeter, Leigh, know if your condition worsens, and I will keep you informed every hour. Dr. Pablo knows you are here. He is the ED doctor today and he is an excellent physician.
Julie: *Documents the round on the rounding log.*

This standardized process resulted in an *additional* 4 percent improvement in preventing patients from leaving without treatment. Now 4 percent may not sound like a lot, but in a busy Emergency Department it adds up to a lot of patients. The improvement netted the hospital *an additional $432,000 per year!*

This is just one example of how reducing the variance in the way a process is administered can result in bottom-line improvements. (See the sidebar for other improvements based on reducing variance by standardizing behaviors.) We should also note that the other improvement here, besides the $432,000 savings, was the increase in the perception among patients that the hospital's staff was genuinely interested in them.

Reducing Variance = Return on Investment

We believe that any organization in any industry—not just health care—can improve the quality of performance and enhance both customer satisfaction and employee performance by eliminating variances. (See Figure 5.2.)

ROI—ED

ISSUE	RETURN ON INVESTMENT	Estimated Value*
Left-Not-Seen Rate	A 4% improvement in left-without-treatment yields an additional 1440 patients x $300.	$432,000/yr
Volume Growth Patient Sat	An additional 1% increase in volume from improved word of mouth yields 360 patients/year x $300.	$108,000/yr
Registration	An improvement of 5% collections from accurate registration information yields revenue from an additional 1800 patients/year × $300.	$540,000/yr
Litigation	A reduction of door-to-doc time from 60 minutes to under 30 minutes decreases potential litigation claims from 4.16 to .9 (0–30 minutes = .9, 30–60 minutes = 2.74, >60 minutes = 4.16)	$300,000/yr
RN Turnover	A reduction in turnover of 4% equals savings of $60K per RN retained. *4% x 100 RNs x 60k/year	$240,000/yr
Turnaround Time	A reduction in average turnaround time of 60 minutes per patient creates room to see an additional 30 patients per day—virtual beds. If only 1/4 of those 30 patients (7) were realized x $300 per patient x 356 days per year it would increase revenue.	$757,000/yr

© 2001–2007 Studer Group
*Based on an ED seeing 36,000 pts/yr with average patient revenue $300

STUDERGROUP®

Figure 5.2 Return on Investment—Emergency Department

WHY LEADERS DON'T STANDARDIZE BEHAVIORS

Perhaps the reason why many leaders within an organization shy away from tracking and eliminating variances is that we're not sure what that actually means in real-life terms. (We don't all have a background in statistics!)

The term *variance* does indeed have several technical meanings. In statistics it refers to the square of the standard deviation. In chemistry it refers to thermodynamic variables necessary to specify a state of equilibrium of a system. In law it refers to the permission to engage in an act contrary to a rule or regulation.

For our purposes, the definition of a variance is simply the difference between what the results can be and what actually occurs. It might refer to an expense that exceeds plan or it might refer to high employee turnover. It could reflect an unacceptable customer service outcome or it could refer to a poor employee interview process.

Leaders may desire standardization for others, but want autonomy for themselves. (We want to provide leadership for our particular work area, *our* way.) We're all for leaders having their own individual style, but we still need to standardize certain procedures. The question for those who fight leadership standardization is this: Is personal autonomy more important than achieving the organization's desired results? And since organizational goals cascade from the organization's mission, is a single leader's autonomy more important than the organization's mission?

For many organizations, the prospect for achieving lasting results through standardized leadership behaviors remains little more than a dim, distant vision. The challenge of transforming an organization's culture is no small undertaking—somewhat like turning a battleship around on a river. It can be done, but not all at once.

It's up to our organization to figure out why our leaders aren't speaking in a unified voice. Here are some possibilities:

- Leaders don't have the training they need to be successful.

- There's no objective accountability system.

- The "dots are not connected" for employees regarding purpose, worthwhile work, and making a difference.

- We're not utilizing a sequenced approach.

- There's no process for managing high and middle performers.

- There's no system for addressing low performers.

Every organization must determine what could be holding it back from standardizing best practices. Which factors may be

What We Permit, We Promote

I first heard the phrase "What you permit, you promote" from Liz Jazwick, a presenter and respected colleague I've known for the past 10 years. I have found that it's very true.

When I became president of a hospital in 1996, 23 percent of employees had late evaluations.

This issue came to my attention when (in response to my questioning) an employee said, "If we are so respected, why is my evaluation late?" So I did a bit of digging and found that some of that 23 percent had been waiting for weeks, others for months. The problem was that no consequences befell the leader who did not complete employee evaluations by the deadline.

I guaranteed all staff that in 60 days there would be no late evaluations. Systems were put in place and consequences outlined, positive recognition went to leaders with no late evaluations, and dots were connected as to why an on-time evaluation is crucial to show respect and retain employees. Sixty days later, there were no late evaluations, nor were there any throughout my entire tenure. I believe the hospital's system of on-time evaluations and results is still strong.

In our travels, we find that many organizations are not fully aware of what they are permitting, and thus promoting. Here are some examples:

- When a leader who consistently fails to meet customer satisfaction goals is not dealt with—or worse, still gets a good review—we are promoting poor performance.

- When a vice president does not share information that others are sharing, we are promoting inconsistent communication.

- When a leader keeps blaming the data for results, we are promoting excuses.

- When a person types on his or her BlackBerry during a meeting, we are promoting a lack of attention and a lack of respect.

Ask yourself: "What am I permitting, and thus promoting?" At your next senior leader meeting, put on the agenda "What are we permitting, and thus promoting?" At the next department head meeting, take some time to ask leaders what they feel the senior leaders are permitting, and thus promoting. At your next staff meeting, ask staff what is being permitted, and thus promoted.

Yes, you may be disappointed in what you hear. But you will *not* be disappointed in the opportunities to improve the organization that will result from these efforts. And you certainly won't be disappointed in the outcomes that will be achieved. Even if you decide leaders need more training, you'll discover it's well worth the investment. Consistency in what gets promoted is a priceless attribute!

keeping the organization from going to the next level? There are ways to address that question. When thinking about the leadership within our organizations, leaders must consider:

- How many different interview systems does our organization use?

- When our leadership team exits a departmental meeting, how confident are we that the message we have given the supervisors to take back to their departments is actually delivered?

- When employees ask leaders tough questions, how confident are we that the leader will provide the answers senior leaders prefer?

- Do we notice that some leaders in our organization perform well while others do not, although they all work in the same environment?

- Does our leader evaluation process embrace a balanced approach that aligns each individual's accountability with organizational goals?

SIX WAYS TO REDUCE LEADERSHIP VARIANCE

Financial managers, by virtue of their professional training and experience, are uniquely qualified to help other managers reduce their leader variance by modeling standardization and consistency in their own leadership behaviors. Here are my top six suggestions for a strong start:

1. Use a common agenda. While we recommend that agendas are organized by the Five Pillars (People, Service, Quality, Finance, and Growth), the most important thing is that there is a standardized meeting agenda used by all leaders throughout the organization. First, this approach aligns all staff to the same organizationwide goals, thereby connecting to the vision and mission of the organization. Second, it provides a single mechanism to cascade communication to staff so all employees understand the critical success factors both in the organization and in their individual work areas.

2. Align the evaluation process to the pillars or the organization's critical success factors. Goals must be objective, measurable, meaningful, aligned, and focused on results.

3. Ensure that each leader leaves every department meeting with a packet of information he or she can share with staff so that every employee hears the same information. (Many organizations use "Flip 'n Tell," a tool widely available at office supply stores.)

4. Choose a single common selection method for hiring new staff. All applicants should be asked at least two or three of the same behavioral-based questions regardless of the job for which they are interviewing. Choose questions that are geared toward values and ownership.

5. Collect from leaders the tough questions they hear from staff. Work with leaders to develop ways they can respond uniformly across the organization when they receive these questions. If there are 100 leaders in an organization, there may be a multitude of different answers given to the same question, depending on the leader. This exercise provides leaders with skills to address these questions, which builds confidence and also provides evidence of the organization's desire that all leaders have the information they need to respond to staff questions.

6. Make sure leaders and supervisors have been trained in basic competencies to use the above five tactics. The most successful organizations annually provide significant hours of training in specific leadership competencies.

Great performers in any field do not tire of repetition; they thrive on it. As we become better at a learned skill, we become more efficient, and then get even better. The implementation of just a few of these tactics can reduce leadership variance in an organization. The rewards will be better and more lasting results, improved operational efficiencies, and greater innovation.

A PROCESS FOR TRANSFORMATION

How do we get that battleship turning on the river? A comprehensive, structured approach is the best way to move leaders from mediocrity or limited success to true excellence. The goal is to create a self-sustaining culture that has the energy and vision to achieve excellence for many, many years.

Over the next few chapters of this book, I will discuss the specific strategies for building lasting results through improved employee and customer satisfaction.

The table provides a detailed look at the overall direction our process requires:

Studer Group Process for Achieving Organizational Excellence					
Leadership Evaluation → Development		Key Tactics → Performance Gap		Standardization → Accelerators	
Align Goals		Align Behavior		Align Processes	
• Implement an organizationwide leadership evaluation system to hardwire objective accountability	• Create a process to assist leaders in developing skills and leadership competencies necessary to attain desired results	• Behaviors all leaders should follow	• Key words at key times • Re-recruit high and middle performers • Move low performers up or out	• Hardwire key goals and techniques	• Idea innovation • Technology • Process improvement

- *A method for evaluating and developing leaders.* Excellence starts when an organization's leaders commit to guiding their employees along the necessary path.

- *The application of key behaviors.* Leaders learn how to tap employee self-motivation to help their people attain higher performance levels.

- *The development of standardized processes for hardwiring excellence.* Cement the organization's alignment with the Five Pillars of Excellence.

When all leaders are "singing from the same choir book," the company's journey to results that last will progress much more quickly, smoothly, and effectively. In Chapter 6 you will learn more about the next important step: measurement.

KEY POINTS FOR HARDWIRING RESULTS

- Variances in how managers practice leadership across an organization can produce inconsistancies that make it harder to achieve excellence. Variances in practices within a single department can also reduce productivity and lower profitability. Align the practices of your managers and you can improve the quality of performance as well as enhance customer and employee satisfaction.

- Many leaders find it hard to standardize the behaviors of their managers. Leadership behavior can be difficult to quantify, and some managers fear intruding on another manager's autonomy. But, since organizational goals cascade from the organization's mission, any single leader's autonomy is less important than the organization's mission.

- A number of barriers can get in the way of standardizing leader behavior. They include lack of critical mass, lack of a balanced approach, untrained leaders, absence of objective accountability, dots not connected, no process for managing high and middle performers or for addressing low performers, and an inability to standardize best practices across the organization.

- Leaders should understand which organizational practices could be inconsistent and fragmented across their organization. They should consider factors such as variances in employee interview systems, inconsistent messages to employees, uneven leader responses to employee questions, varying leadership performance, and ineffective leadership evaluations.

- To reduce leadership variances, consider the following suggestions:
  - Use a common agenda format at all meetings.
  - Align the evaluation process to the Five Pillars.

- Give leaders information packets to share with their employees.
- Choose a single common selection method for hiring new staff.
- Develop ways leaders can respond uniformly to employee questions.
- Train leaders in basic competencies.

- The organization's goal is to create a self-sustaining culture with the energy and vision to achieve excellence for many years. This is best accomplished through revamping your leadership evaluation system, applying key leader behaviors that inspire self-motivation, and developing standardized processes for hardwiring excellence.

CHAPTER

6

MEASUREMENT 101

Why This Chapter Is Important

MEASUREMENT AND TRANSPARENCY DRIVE ACCOUNTABILITY. WHEN PEOPLE see the metrics associated with the work they do, they can easily adjust their actions to get better results. All levels of the organization are working together toward the same goals. Achievements get recognized. Excuses are taken away.

In this chapter, you will gain a clear understanding that objective measurement—the results of which are shared openly with everyone in your company—is a *must-have* for your organization. It is an indispensable part of achieving results that last.

Sometimes what appears to be a good thing can cost an organization dearly. I like to share the story of how I saved $84,000 and it cost my organization only $500,000. Basically, we had a manager leave. Another department down the hall was getting good results. My decision was to have that manager lead both departments. By not replacing the manager, we would save his $70,000 salary, plus benefits. At the end of the year, employee turnover was

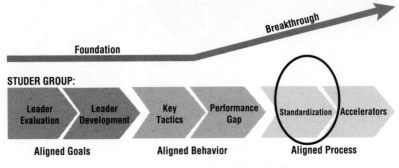

Figure 6.1 Evidence-Based Leadership

up in both departments, the area that had been doing well wasn't meeting its goals, and a leader's confidence was shattered. In the end, the turnover and reduced results added half a million dollars to expenses.

A good measurement system will prevent you from repeating my blunder. We know that what gets measured gets improved. This chapter helps you develop the metrics for each of your goals under the Five Pillars. It shows how a solid measurement system can motivate employees to achieve beyond your—and their—expectations.

In the bigger picture, how can you get other people in your organization—chief executive, management staff, or board of directors—to approve the extensive changes that may be required? The answers to this question can be found in this chapter.

MEASUREMENT ALIGNS BEHAVIORS

To achieve excellent results—results that last—organizations must be able to objectively assess their current status and then track their progress to the goals they have set. This chapter will demonstrate how outcomes-based measurement helps organizations define specific targets, measure progress against those targets, and align the necessary resources to achieve them. In this chapter, I use customer satisfaction as an example of how to align goals and measure progress. The same approach is used across all Five Pillars.

Measurement supports the alignment of desired behaviors. It excites the organization when goals are achieved. It also holds individuals accountable for their results and helps to determine whether things are working. Whether the numbers we are measuring refer to customers served, widgets produced, sales made, or profits earned, we won't know whether we've hit our targets without measurements. We *can't* know. *Never forget that we are not measuring just to measure.* We are measuring to align specific leadership and employee behaviors that cascade throughout the organization to drive results. The better an organization can align these behaviors, the quicker it will achieve desired results and create opportunities to recognize staff. Recognized behavior gets repeated, which turns the flywheel faster.

The ability to measure results is at the core of any organization's success. Measurement is the standard by which goals are set, progress is tracked, and results are calculated. It's the compass that guides our efforts and informs our judgments. The question is not "Should we measure?" The question is "*What* should we measure?"

MEASUREMENT AS A DIAGNOSTIC AND PROCESS-IMPROVEMENT TOOL

By looking at the data and adjusting the behavior, we can improve results. I find that if Finance people consider satisfaction data in the same way they would a profit-and-loss statement, then *they get it.* In fact, Finance people can be a great teaching resource for helping the rest of the organization understand how to use metrics. The same holds true for clinicians when they begin to review patient surveys in the same way they would the results of a diagnostic test:

- They evaluate the current results based on data.

- They take action to improve results.

- They closely monitor results.

- They report on what works and what doesn't.

Then they adjust the techniques they use and change prescriptions until they get the results they are seeking. Measurement is based on tracking and using indicators. As results improve, it ignites greater passion throughout the organization and turns the flywheel.

This data also leads to process improvement. When I arrived at Baptist Hospital, Inc., the food-service scores were in the high teens to low twenties. I met with the leader to find out what the plans were to improve. The key question to ask a leader is not "What happened?" but rather "What actions are you taking to move us in the right direction?"

We all have compelling reasons for why something has been difficult to achieve. In this case, the leader mentioned staff cuts and a smaller budget for nutritional snacks. But as I looked at the data breakdown by unit, I noticed that on 3 East, scores were higher. To this leader's credit, he became something of a "3 East student." It turned out that while 3 East had the same issues as other units, they had created a better process to pass out trays and explain diets. When all units adopted this process, food satisfaction scores increased all the way to the 99th percentile. So it's not about not having the financial resources, but about how well you can spot best practices and how quickly you can adopt and transfer them throughout the organization.

WHAT GETS MEASURED GETS IMPROVED

When we don't have solid, objective measurements of our organization's goals under each of the Five Pillars, evaluating employee performance becomes a fuzzy, mysterious process. Leaders are left speechless when the high performers ask them where they and the company will be one year from now if they exceed all the leader's expectations. If we as leaders don't know the answer to that challenge, we're doomed to give vague, uninspiring answers. To avoid that fate, we must ensure that our organizations have great measurement systems.

Accounting departments have traditionally been great about breaking down expenses (measurements) for individual leaders. However, companies rarely break down quality and turnover statistics for individual leaders.

One of our clients was plagued by complaints about employee turnover. As we began to break down the turnover to individual departments, however, we discovered that half of the employee turnover was found *only in one large department*, not everywhere.

This company focused on the turnover in that one department and saw nearly immediate improvements in its results.

Another client that operated a chain of restaurants was concerned because one of their locations was receiving very poor scores on its food service. The managers blamed the problem on a cutback in staffing. However, when we began to study the problem we found similar-sized staffs in other restaurants in the chain that *weren't* receiving complaints about the food service.

What was the difference? The more successful restaurants had instructed their staff to take out food to customers as soon as it was ready, regardless of who might be the server for that table. The troubled location was having the food sit until the table's server returned to the kitchen. Tables with busy servers got their meals served more slowly than those in less-busy areas, and the food was often cold. Many customers walked away vowing to eat elsewhere next time.

With one minor change in training and operations, the organization was able to dramatically improve the food-service processes of that restaurant.

We also know from experience that the only goals that are attained are those that are included in a manager's evaluation. You may say that you want turnover to decrease by 25 percent. However, if the manager doesn't see turnover tied to his evaluation—and ultimately to his compensation—then turnover won't decline. It becomes a nice idea, but not a must-do.

But, what do you think happens when you tell the same manager that employee turnover will be 15 percent of his evaluation? That's right: You'll see action on the turnover issue!

EMPLOYEE TURNOVER AND THE RIPPLE EFFECT

As mentioned earlier, employee turnover has an impact not only on the People pillar, but also on each of the other four pillars. Some organizations don't know how to measure employee turnover. And many that do measure turnover fail to examine *when* most turnovers occur.

Our evidence-based research tells us that if an employee leaves within the first 30 days, the company most likely has selection issues. Either job duties weren't what the employee expected, or training was lacking, or the actual job duties and hours were different from what was promised.

If the employee leaves after the first month but before the first 90 days, the organization probably has orientation problems, either with the job or with co-workers. If the new hire makes it past the first 90 days but leaves before his or first year is up, the organization probably has a teamwork issue.

Employees who complete the first year but leave within the first five years believe that they maxed out on their skill set and see no additional opportunity for career and personal growth.

But, we also know that if an organization can get its new hires to stay more than one year, it will cut its turnover in half. If the employees stay five years, turnover is reduced 80 percent.

What does reduced turnover mean to the other pillars? Financially, both hiring and orientation costs go down. Sales improve because the employees are more experienced and have better knowledge of the products. Under Quality and Service, less turnover means better continuity in production and service, less of a we/they problem, better alignment with goals, and better teamwork.

HOW OFTEN DO WE MEASURE?

Remember: What gets measured gets improved. One of the most important guidelines is to measure often enough so you can reward and recognize as soon as possible after the behavior occurs.

In my experience, tracking customer satisfaction quarterly isn't frequent enough. If I were trying to lose weight and someone told me I couldn't weigh myself for three months, I know I wouldn't be successful. I've got to see some progress quickly in order to stay motivated.

In 1993, a patient satisfaction survey company told me that if I wanted to measure so frequently, the data might not be statistically reliable and valid. But reliability was *not* my top priority. Changing behavior *was*. Trend data over many surveys will in fact be valid and reliable. But the most important reason to do frequent measurement is that it reinforces positive behavior. I am not suggesting you base big decisions upon a week's worth of data. But the data will add up, and trends will reveal themselves.

When you measure often, process improvement increases and your company becomes a better organization. Do you think the folks in accounting count the money once a quarter? No; they count once a day, and sometimes more often. Why? Because it's important that they have a good grasp on their ongoing gains and losses. It also allows staff to adjust focus as needed based on daily results. I think this is a good practice in all areas of business. Organizations should take a pulse frequently, whether for customers, financials, employee satisfaction, or other key operations.

The more often we *measure the important things,* the more we'll know about where we are making progress and where we are not. And the more we know, the more we can affect behavior.

While there are many questions on any given survey, some have more impact than others. It is important to find the *key drivers* or *correlating coefficients* on the measurement surveys that most powerfully drive results. Here is a focused approach that I recommend for leveraging results quickly from survey data: Choose one of the key driver questions and develop an action plan for improvement. This approach will not only lead to improvements in the particular issue that is being addressed, but it will also increase the overall results.

By creating a plan of action based on the highest impact questions for the department, leaders will maximize gains. Also, as staff members see the relationship between the actions they take and results they achieve, they will be ready to move to the next question. This is a great way to focus staff without overwhelming them with an exhaustive to-do list.

Remember to:

- Focus on opportunities to create desired behaviors—not just measurement.

- Act fast.

- Put the data to use.

- Push for results—not excuses.

GOOD TO GREAT: MOVING 4s TO 5s

Most companies have good service. Few companies have *great* service, however, and the irony of it is that being "good" is precisely what is holding them back from becoming great. In fact, the very first sentence of Jim Collins's bestseller, *Good to Great: Why Some Companies Make the Leap . . . and Others Don't* (New York: Harper-Collins, 2001), reads: "Good is the enemy of great."

Most service rating systems are done on a five-point scale: 5 is excellent or superior, 4 is very good, 3 is good or average, 2 is less than average, and 1 is very poor.

The mistake many companies make is quite simple: They focus on the 2s and 1s when they should be targeting the 4s. Most leaders are really bothered by low measurements. Believe me, I understand. But the reality is that there will *always* be 2s and 1s. We all know it's true: Some people will never be satisfied. It isn't unusual for the top-rated companies to have 1 to 2 percent in these boxes. (See Figure 6.2.)

We tell our clients to concentrate on moving the 4s to 5s. The 4s are quietly satisfied. They are content with their service from our company, but they aren't excited. The 5s are more vocal, and are so pleased with our company that they bring others to us.

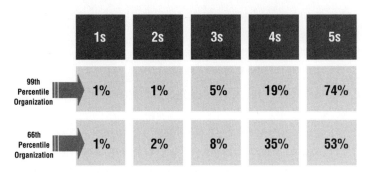

Figure 6.2 Sample Distribution of Customer Satisfaction Score Responses to Achieve Excellence: 4 versus 5

The more 5s we have, the more positive word of mouth we get, and the more positive word of mouth we get, the more business we get.

For example, my family recently enjoyed staying at the Wilderness Lodge at Walt Disney World in Orlando. We couldn't say enough good things about it. So, when a friend mentioned that they were taking their family to Disney World, I told him that they should stay at the Wilderness Lodge. My friend looked surprised and told me, "That's funny; you're the second person who's recommended the Wilderness Lodge." The 5s are your secret weapon and your most powerful marketing program.

Here's the thing: The 4s would probably go back to the Wilderness Lodge, but they wouldn't drag anybody with them. The 3s might stay again, but they will check out other options. The 2s will go back only if there aren't any other options. The 1s will never come back, regardless of how much it improves.

We have to change our expectations and work hard to move our 4s into the 5s box because of the high rate of return on the 5s. Don't fall into the trap of combining 4s and 5s into one score. A less experienced leader might have a combined 4/5 score of 93 percent and believe he's doing as well as someone with a similar aggregate score. In truth, it's only the 5s that matter because they are our best advocates in the marketplace.

Great companies must have at least 70 percent in the 5s. This book can help you achieve that goal.

TRANSPARENCY: HELPING PEOPLE UNDERSTAND THE METRICS

Today's leaders often find themselves "walking up a down escalator" in regard to performing well in an ever-changing competitive environment. They may wrap up a fantastic fiscal year only to find themselves starting in a hole the first day of the new fiscal year due to economic conditions beyond their control.

Not very long ago I was called in to consult with a large health care system that was facing a serious challenge. The CEO told me that he and his leadership team were headed for a breakeven year for the first time in history due to several major financial problems. For instance:

- Medicare and Medicaid cuts were going to result in $30 million *less* in collections, even if the same amount of care was provided. The patients would keep coming, but without the reimbursement.

- Pay raises that were scheduled to kick in were going to generate a $6 million cost increase.

- The projected increase in unreimbursed charity care was expected to top $8 million.

In short, the hospital was under serious financial pressure. Leaders would have had to improve the hospital's operation by $44 million just to reach the same results as the previous year (which was still a small margin).

The reality is that many managers do not understand how the organization can be okay one day and then face such fiscal challenges the next day or the next budget cycle. In our work, we have found that most managers and staff do not have adequate knowledge and understanding of the financial condition of the organization, how finances work for their industry, and the pressure the organization is facing from its shareholders, board, and the public. It is up to us, the leaders, to teach them.

FINANCIAL TRANSPARENCY IS A RELATIVELY NEW VALUE

Transparency, particularly in regard to financial matters, has not always been in vogue. For many years, senior leaders tended to believe that excellent strategy, tough negotiations, and tight controls could keep the company's financial situation from getting to an unmanageable point. They tried to prevent staff from noticing the financial issues, beyond the unavoidable pain of temporary hiring freezes, tighter purchasing requests, staff reductions, and impossible budget goals.

But now, times (and leadership philosophies) have changed. The days of a few senior leaders being able to pull, push, drive, or *will* an organization to success are over for most industries, especially health care. Today, we need all leaders and frontline staff to be well informed about company financials. The key steps are creating transparency of data and educating all leaders and staff about the organization's financial position.

For example, very few people realize that the cost of pay increases each year to retain staff puts more pressure on the organization to perform operationally. Yes, we must pay market salaries to attract and retain staff, but we must also improve operations to pay for the additional costs. Each year an organization must be *that much better* just to stay even.

Years ago a plant operations employee told me that he appreciated seeing the organization's monthly financials. It made him feel included and enabled him to get a good handle on potential overtime. The leaders who see and understand the financials and their impact simply do a better job of leading. They are also better communicators. Knowing what's going on within the organization makes it far less likely that leaders will take a we/they approach in their conversations with employees.

We encourage organizations to share monthly financials and implement educational sessions so all leaders and staff understand organizational issues. Employees should comprehend all key areas, including financial performance, beyond the sharing of results at monthly departmental meetings. Remember, *owners* know the data. *Renters* don't. Transparency in your financials creates the ownership behavior that we all seek from our workforces.

So, how can leaders develop transparency for various levels of the organization?

Senior leaders should:

1. Make sure all managers understand the financial pressures, the financial performances, and the steps needed to be taken—and *why*. Don't assume they automatically know. (Polling your leaders on their understanding of finances can be quite a wakeup call!)

2. Put a system in place that allows leaders to clearly understand finances and gives them the ability to take the information to their staff in a constructive way.

3. Design a way to verify that this system is being implemented. Follow the late President Ronald Reagan's philosophy: Trust and verify.

Frontline managers should:

1. Take *ownership* to learn the organization's financial operations, pressures, and next steps.

2. Make sure they have the skill set to communicate the financials or next steps, and to explain to staff why certain actions are necessary (without fixing blame, of course).

3. Ask senior leaders for information and education so they can do a better job.

4. Share information with their staff and work to create an environment in which employees expect to contribute their ideas and solutions.

Staff members should:

1. Provide ideas and solutions to help improve the organization's financial performance.

2. Take the time to read and listen to information on financial operations.

3. Role model their stewardship of resources for other staff members.

RETURN ON INVESTMENT

Proper measurement helps us calculate the return on investment from the tactics and process improvements we're trying to implement. Having a good grasp on ROI helps us get even greater buy-in from the board of directors, the senior leaders, and the employees.

In other words, leaders need to present the return on investment they expect their changes to produce. For example, if a particular department is understaffed, the board may look at the department's salary line item and think everything is fine. (As I'm sure you're aware, the first reaction to any request is, "No, there's no room in the budget.")

The department manager probably knows that the department is in a personnel spiral. The staff is tired of working long hours. There's less time for professional development and training. In fact, employees have started looking for other jobs because they don't see any relief in the future.

So how does the department head calculate the cost of not bringing her department's staffing levels up to standard? Well, overtime hours have a cost. The lost time in constantly having to train new staff also has a dollar figure. Within these frameworks the department head can calculate objectively what the staff shortages are costing the company.

Next, the department head must look at what changes the company must make in order to fill the staff vacancies. It may need to offer more flexible work hours or build in time for more professional development and training. It may have to make slight adjustments to salaries or benefits. Sure, these changes have an objective cost, too; but we're often surprised at how little the changes really cost the company.

One of our clients discovered that by investing $18,000 in staffing changes and training, they saved the company $45,000. What boss or board of directors would object to *that* return on investment?

The key is taking the time to objectively determine costs and financial benefits. One of our clients, a retail manager, discovered that his employee turnover was hurting his same-store sales. Whenever customers asked employees for certain items, the new, inexperienced employees told customers that they didn't know if they had them. Not surprisingly, customers went elsewhere—even though the store actually carried everything they were looking to buy.

The manager delved further and, from employee surveys, found people were quitting because of poor supervision and the lack of training. The company was spending nothing on training its employees or its supervisors. The manager computed what the training would cost and what the increase in sales would be if the employees had better knowledge of the store's inventory. Once again the benefits outweighed the costs.

Here's one more example of this type of cost/benefit analysis: I know of a car dealer that installed an automatic car wash on their lot to give all their customers free car washes for as long as they owned their vehicles. It was an expensive piece of equipment that might not appear to offer any return on investment for that dealership.

But my father bought his car from that dealer, and every time my dad gets his car washed (which is often) he walks around, reads the literature on the new models, and talks with the salesmen. Guess where he will purchase his next car? From the dealership that gave him free car washes, of course!

Some companies might see the car washes as an *expense* on the income statement. My dad's dealership sees the car washes as an *investment* that helps to maintain contact with satisfied customers.

That's the kind of thinking that gets real results for companies—results that last.

KEY POINTS FOR HARDWIRING RESULTS

- What gets measured gets improved. A lack of solid, objective measures of an organization's goals under each of the Five Pillars makes employee evaluations a fuzzy, mysterious process. Employees attempting to improve their performance without proper measurement will become demotivated and will most likely leave.

- Great organizations that have lasting results also have measurement systems because they support corporate goals and align desired behaviors across the company. Leaders, employees, and even customers get excited as measurements improve. And, most important, measurements hold people accountable.

- Measure frequently. Doing so allows you to quickly show progress, motivate employees, and reinforce positive behavior.

- In working to bring up customer satisfaction scores, it's better to focus on turning 4s into 5s than to try to bring up lower scores.

- Most managers and staff do not have an adequate understanding of the financial condition of the organization. They don't know how finances work for their industry, nor the pressure their company faces from its shareholders, board, and the public. Organizations should share monthly financials and implement educational sessions so all leaders and staff come to know and understand the larger issues.

- Employees should understand all key areas, including financial performance, beyond the sharing of results at monthly departmental meetings. *Owners* know the data. *Renters* don't. Transparent financials create the ownership behavior that we all seek from our employees.

- Measurement can help us calculate the return on investment on the tactics and process improvements we're trying to implement. Knowing ROI helps us achieve even greater buy-in from the board of directors, senior leaders, and employees.

CHAPTER

7

ALIGN BEHAVIORS WITH GOALS AND VALUES

Why This Chapter Is Important

WHEN WE ASK LEADERS WHAT THEY NEED IN ORDER TO BE BETTER LEADERS, they always say something along these lines: "I need specific goals, better direction on prioritization, and training to acquire the skills necessary for success."

If after reading this book you do only one thing aimed at taking your department or entire organization to the top, make it this: Establish an objective evaluation system to hold leaders accountable.

When we go into an organization, it's very common for us to see that the leaders are not achieving the results they would like—or at least, not achieving them consistently. However, when we audit their leadership evaluations, we find 94 percent or more of the leaders have excellent evaluations. This is the great disconnect.

Why would a leader feel an urgency to get better outcomes when he's already getting rave reviews? Implementing an objective evaluation system—one that includes weighted components, progress reports, and 90-day plans—is crucial to ensuring that

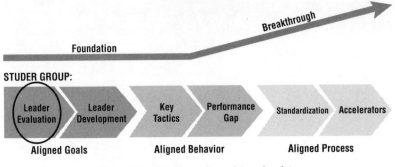

Figure 7.1 Evidence-Based Leadership

results last. It also helps in that your staff will see this not as just another program but rather as a way of life.

Objective evaluations set the foundation that moves leaders to the tipping point and creates the performance gap that leads to addressing low performers. In short, it gets your leaders and your organization over the wall.

Leader accountability is the most important lesson in this book. We can't address behavior properly without first setting goals and implementing an objective evaluation system. To do otherwise is to be like a ship leaving the shore without knowing the longitude and latitude of its destination. It can move efficiently but still end up in the wrong place.

It's leadership evaluations that give our hardwiring principles teeth—and drive the organization toward results that last.

• • •

The average employee probably faces her annual performance review with a sense of resignation and perhaps a touch of low-grade dread. It's not that she doesn't want feedback on how she's doing her job. She does. It's that she wants feedback that really makes sense—feedback that helps her improve her performance in a way that moves the company forward. And many performance reviews don't accomplish these goals.

Most, if not all, medium- and mid-sized organizations conduct this annual ritual. All probably believe that it's in the best interests of the organization, as well as useful for the employees' career development. Sure, some performance review systems succeed well enough. But far too often employee performance reviews deal with generalities and categories of behavior that bear little relation to the results that the organization is striving to achieve.

HOLDING LEADERS ACCOUNTABLE

Do we really believe that an individual manager's scores on "communication," "organization," "professionalism," or similar performance review categories are going to directly impact the bottom line? These qualities are too vague—too difficult to wrap one's mind around—to inspire anyone to change. Plus, typical performance review labels such as "Poor," "Average," or "Below Expectations" tends to label managers far more than it motivates them.

W. Edwards Deming took a decidedly dim view of performance appraisals when they were used as a substitute for effective leadership. He was not saying that reviews shouldn't be conducted at all, but that they should be conducted in the right way, with a clear message to the employee about what is truly important. Equally critical, we have to give those being evaluated clear-cut and *objective* measures of success—not subjective opinions about intangible qualities like "professionalism" or "organization."

After all, even if we restrict the appraisal to "quantitative measures," such as unit sales or expense management results, do we not still tend to ignore the long-term growth of the organization? That's why the system used for evaluating leaders is a vital component of our efforts to transform the organization. If we expect our leaders to promote and support the Five Pillars of Excellence, then we have to measure them on how well they perform on goals related to Service, Quality, People, Finance, and Growth. If we are trying to build a *results that last* culture, then we have to hold our leaders at every level accountable for the behaviors and goals that directly create results that last. It's as simple as that.

In our experiences coaching great organizations, we have found that we invariably have to revamp the organization's management appraisal system by implementing an objective, measurable leader evaluation tool based on the Five Pillars of Excellence.

In addition, an organization must also be prepared to:

- Reward its leaders based on those results.

- Demonstrate a sustained commitment to training and coaching leaders to achieve them.

- Deselect those individuals who are not achieving their goals, however painful this process might be.

As we discussed in the first chapter of this book, this last point is not for the fainthearted! For most of us, it is extremely hard to let go of an employee to whom we feel some loyalty, even if that person is not performing. But remember, it's the low performers who wear us out.

To be true to our organization's mission, we must *first* be loyal to achieving the goals we've set. That's how we create a great organization that strives for excellence.

Studer Group's evaluation tool, developed over years of trial and error, is being used successfully by many organizations around the country. While the tool is a simple one to use, it is not easy to implement because it forces senior leaders to ask some soul-searching questions:

- What are our top priorities?

- How do we weigh them?

- Which things should we stop doing or do less of?

- What do we do with leaders who are not hitting their targets?

This tool, because it is objective and focused, quickly separates performers. High and middle performers are motivated by knowing what's expected of them. They know exactly what they need to do to achieve results and, because they're high performers, they *want* to achieve them. It also makes low performers evident and visible, which means that if their behavior is not addressed by senior leadership, then senior leadership quickly loses credibility. Our experience tells us that most leaders and staff already know who these low performers are. The tool just makes it impossible to avoid taking action.

HOW DOES THE LEADERSHIP EVALUATION TOOL WORK?

The Five Pillars provide the foundation for setting and communicating organizational goals as well as the framework for the evaluation process as discussed in previous chapters. Once the goals for each pillar have been set for the organization as a whole, then they are cascaded from the division level to department or unit level to individual leaders through the development of aligned individual goals.

Figure 7.2 demonstrates how a department's goals can be aligned with the Pillars of Excellence. In this case, the example is from Avalex, a company that supplies flat panel displays, digital mapping systems, digital video recorders, and sensor pointing systems for the airborne surveillance and military markets.

Based on the organizational goals, each divisional leader sets division goals and *weights* them for each item under each pillar. Weights differ depending on the division and leaders.

In the above example, the department head's goal under the Growth pillar—"Achieve 25% growth in revenues"—may be more far-reaching than the goals posted under the other four pillars. Consequently, the department head's boss may assign that particular goal a weight higher than the other goals—say 30 percent to 50 percent.

This means that when all of the goals are evaluated this particular outcome will receive more relative value than other goals at review time. Bear in mind, though, that a leader does not necessarily need to have a goal under each pillar. The key is for the total weights to add up to 100 percent on each leader's evaluation. That way, the leader and his or her superior have a clear understanding of what is to be done, but have prioritized which goals have the most impact and significance.

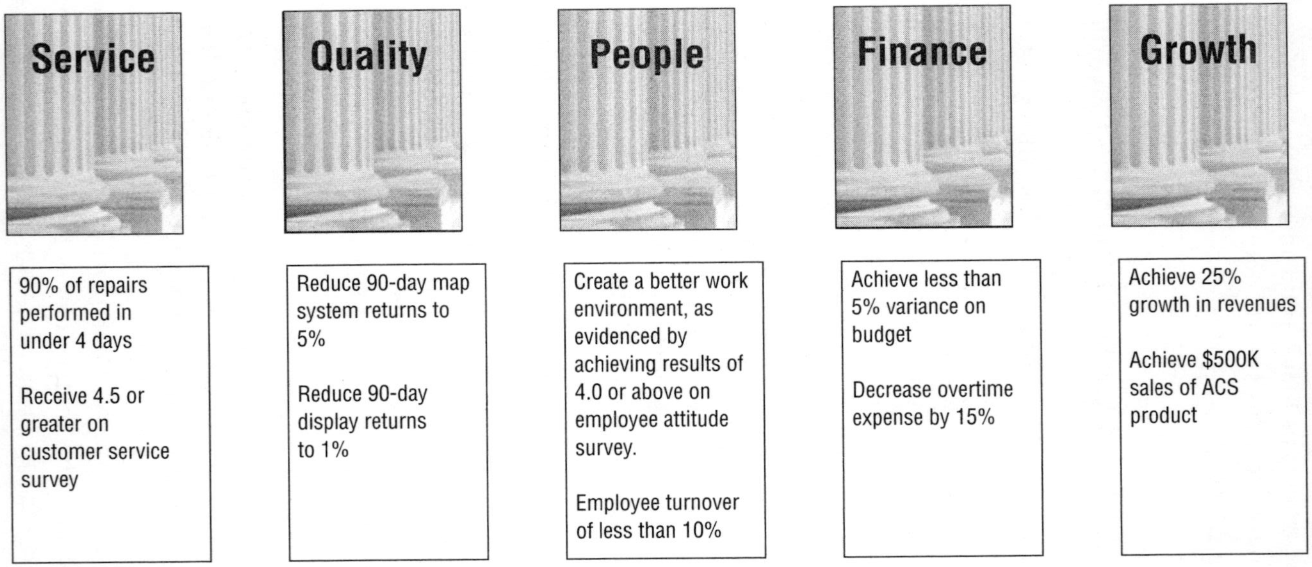

Service

90% of repairs performed in under 4 days

Receive 4.5 or greater on customer service survey

Quality

Reduce 90-day map system returns to 5%

Reduce 90-day display returns to 1%

People

Create a better work environment, as evidenced by achieving results of 4.0 or above on employee attitude survey.

Employee turnover of less than 10%

Finance

Achieve less than 5% variance on budget

Decrease overtime expense by 15%

Growth

Achieve 25% growth in revenues

Achieve $500K sales of ACS product

Figure 7.2 Avalex Pillar Goals

Once the weighting is set, we recommend a five-point scale (1–5) to rate results within each pillar, with 1 being the lowest and 5 denoting superior achievement. The same process is to be used for each leader, for each pillar. Our rule of thumb is not to have more than 10 targets for the entire evaluation—and if the weight for a particular goal is not at least 5 percent, it does not go on the evaluation at all.

Figure 7.3 shows sample goals and results.

HOW TO ROLL OUT THE LEADERSHIP EVALUATION TOOL

If an organization is committed to creating a results that last culture, it must commit to evaluating its leaders based on objective, measurable results. *This is so important to achieving and sustaining results that we agree to client engagements only with organizations that are willing to make this commitment.* It is the first step on the journey to excellence, and it must come from senior management. Once the commitment has been made, implementation timing for the leadership evaluation tool will vary depending on where in its journey an organization is starting. However, a clear plan must be developed on how the evaluation tool will be implemented and driven by senior management.

For example, some organizations already have organizational goals established and simply need to connect them to the pillars before they start rolling out the new evaluation process from the top of the organization on down, which we call the *cascading exercise.*

When we cascade, senior leaders roll out the goals to their divisions first. Then each manager takes historical data compared with the goals that were set and assigns metrics and ratings for their departments to ensure alignment organizationwide. (Note: Hitting a goal usually rates a 3 or 4 on a performance evaluation, with 5 for exceeding the goal.)

It's also important that leaders weight the goals appropriately under each pillar and create metrics for measurement that are significant enough for the organization to attain its goals. *This is the defining moment for ensuring sustained improvement.*

Name: CHO, CHO **Leader:** CEO, CEO **Department:** Administration **Division:** Administration **Year Ending:** 2007 Delete Evaluation

Pillar	Goals and Results	Scores	1	2	3	4	5
Service Weighted Value 30%	Goal: Achieve overall physician satisfaction rate of 75% Result: 75.0 through 10/2006 add goal remove above goal	Set Rating Type Percent 5 = greater than or = 77 4 = 76 - 76.9 3 = 75 - 75.9 2 = 74 - 74.9 1 = less than or = 73.9	15% Weighted Value	×	3 Score	=	0.45 Item Score
	Goal: Achieve patient satisfaction goal in the 73rd percentile as measured in the June 2007 in-patient quarterly report on Overall assessment Baseline 65th Percentile Result: 84 through 9/2006 add goal remove above goal	Set Rating Type Percentile 5 = greater than or = 95 4 = 80 - 94 3 = 73 - 79 2 = 65 - 72 1 = less than or = 64	15% Weighted Value	×	4 Score	=	0.6 Item Score
Quality Weighted Value 25%	Goal: Achieve reduction in falls by 30% overall hospital Result: 40.0 through 10/2006 add goal remove above goal	Set Rating Type Percent 5 = greater than or = 40 4 = 35 - 39.9 3 = 30 - 34.9 2 = 15 - 29.9 1 = less than or = 14.9	25% Weighted Value	×	5 Score	=	1.25 Item Score
Finance Weighted Value 15%	Goal: Achieve budgeted EBITA and margin target Rating Type 5 = x = 102, 4 = 101 - 101.99, 3 = 100 - 100.99, 2 = 99 - 99.99, 1 = x = 98.99 Result: 101.00 through 6/2007 add goal remove above goal	Set Rating Type Percent 5 = greater than or = 102 4 = 101 - 101.99 3 = 100 - 100.99 2 = 99 - 99.99 1 = less than or = 98.99	15% Weighted Value	×	4 Score	=	0.6 Item Score
People Weighted Value 20%	Goal: Achieve overall employee turnover of 12% Result: 12.0 through 10/2006 add goal remove above goal	Set Rating Type Percent 5 = less than or = 10 4 = 10.1 - 11.9 3 = 12 - 12 2 = 12.1 - 14 1 = greater than or = 14.1	20% Weighted Value	×	3 Score	=	0.6 Item Score
Growth Weighted Value 10%	Goal: Achieve 100% budgeted volume targets for deliveries per day. Result: 101.0 through 10/2006 add goal remove above goal	Set Rating Type Percent 5 = greater than or = 102 4 = 101 - 101.9 3 = 100 - 100.9 2 = 99 - 99.9 1 = less than or = 98.9	10% Weighted Value	×	3 Score	=	0.5 Item Score

Total Weight: 100/100 **Overall Performance Score: 3.90**

Figure 7.3 Sample Tools and Results

By cascading goals through the leadership evaluation tool, the organization sends a clear message to everyone that this is not the "program of the month" or "buzzword of the year." If it's on the evaluation tool, it's here to stay. And the challenge has always been how to sustain excellence—not just create it. The evaluation tool ensures that an organization will sustain the gains.

While some organizations have already established goals under the Five Pillars, they may not have hardwired the results yet by creating accountability. That's why the leadership evaluation tool is so important.

Regardless of your organization's timing, it is our recommendation that you don't attempt a *hybrid* approach. A hybrid approach occurs when some organizations try to modify current evaluation tools by adding this objective piece to a very subjective evaluation. In the end, it just creates confusion and provides a window of opportunity to derail the process. That is why the commitment to a purely objective leadership evaluation tool is vital.

When rolling out this process, communication and training become key. Let leaders know that this rollout is top priority. Senior managers frequently comment to me about their frustration that leaders are not hitting key targets. This evaluation creates the organizationwide alignment that is almost always needed and appreciated.

It is also important for senior leaders to be the first to establish their own goals and to share them with one another and with their managers. We have known highly committed senior leaders at several organizations who have taken this process quite seriously. Their senior management teams review not only their own goals but also the goals of all leaders to ensure organizational alignment.

Not only does this ensure that there are no conflicting goals, but the 1–5 rating scale guarantees fairness. And common goals will be uniformly defined. In addition, we recommend two tools to support strong communication about progress toward goals before leaders are evaluated: the *monthly progress report* and the *90-day plan.*

THE MONTHLY PROGRESS REPORT

Monthly progress reports are created for each leader within the organization and support the 90-day plan and leadership evaluation tool. The reports are set up to track the same metrics that are listed on the leader evaluations. Progress reports show actual progress made toward these goals on a monthly basis. Their purpose is fourfold. Monthly reports:

1. Help the leader communicate results to staff members who are critical in helping the leader achieve the goals.

2. Allow the leader to communicate progress to his supervisor on a monthly basis in between 90-day review sessions.

3. Hardwire a leader focus on results monthly (or more frequently).

4. Identify problem areas and the leaders who need assistance or coaching and those high performers they can benchmark based on their great results.

In essence, the monthly progress report shows the vital signs of the organization by leader. With patients, we know how critical it is to monitor their vitals. Based on the vitals, we treat them. By monitoring the vital signs of the organization, we can align behavior to what the vital signs are telling us we need to do. (See Figure 7.4.)

THE 90-DAY PLAN

Monitoring progress is one thing, but in modern organizations most leaders are "full-plate people." And those plates don't seem to get any less full, no matter how many responsibilities we try to remove from them! Somehow, that plate is always full; and once we accept that, it's not nearly as difficult to handle.

While we can't take things off a leader's plate, we can provide the leader with a system for understanding what needs to occupy

Monthly Report Card

Name: [▾]   Leader: Department: NURSING ADMINISTRATION   Division: 75 NBH   Year Ending: 2007

Goal	Rating Type	Jul 2006	Aug 2006	Sep 2006	Oct 2006	Nov 2006	Dec 2006	Jan 2007	Feb 2007	Mar 2007	Apr 2007	May 2007	Jun 2007	Summary
People Achieve budgeted turnover goal, or if not budgeted goal 15% department turnover.	*percentage* <= 13.99 = 5, 14.00 - 14.99 = 4, 15.00 - 15.99 = 3, 16.00 - 16.99 = 2, >= 17.00 = 1	15.50	15.20	14.80	14.20	14.10								Last 14.1 Nov 2006 ▾ Item Score: 30% × 4 = 1.2
Service Overall nursing patient satisfaction to be within the 75% percentile	*percentage* >= 90 = 5, 80 - 89 = 4, 75 - 79 = 3, 70 - 74 = 2, <= 69 = 1	85	88	86	91	90								Last 90 Nov 2006 ▾ Item Score: 25% × 5 = 1.25
Quality Achieve performance at the top 10% for 75% of the hospital compare indicators.	*percentage* <= 8 = 5, 9 - 9 = 4, 10 - 10 = 3, 11 - 11 = 2, >= 12 = 1	9	9	9	8	8								Last 8 Nov 2006 ▾ Item Score: 10% × 5 = 0.5
Finance Manage Labor Cost per unit of service to nursing budget	*percentage* >= 100 = 5, 90 - 99 = 4, 80 - 89 = 3, 70 - 79 = 2, <= 69 = 1	75	85	90	89	92								Last 92 Nov 2006 ▾ Item Score: 15% × 4 = 0.15
Growth Achieve 100% budgeted volumes targets for deliveries per day.	*percentage* >= 102.0 = 5, 101.0 - 101.9 = 4, 100.0 - 100.9 = 3, 96.0 - 99.9 = 2, <= 95.9 = 1	82.0	84.0	81.0	80.0	78.0								Last 78 Nov 2006 ▾ Item Score: 15% × 1 = 0.15
Community Participate in 4 NBH community sponsored or supported projects.	*number* >= 6 = 5, 4 - 5 = 4, 2 - 3 = 3, 0 - 1 = 2, <= (1) = 1	1	2	1	1	4								Last 4 Nov 2006 ▾ Item Score: 0% × 4 = 0
Monthly Eval Scores														**Overall Score:** 3.90

Figure 7.4 Leader Evaluation Manager—Monthly Report Card

the most space on his or her plate. Most people have too many things on their to-do lists, with no good way to prioritize them. By using the *90-day plan* in conjunction with the monthly progress reports, we help leaders know where to focus.

I first learned about 90-day plans as a teacher in special education. That industry calls them *individual education plans (IEPs)*. That meant that every 90 days, I sat down with the parents and talked about goals for the student in the next 90 days. If we waited for a once-a-year meeting at the end of the year, it would be too late. If we had only a beginning-of-the-year meeting, it also wouldn't work because there would be no way to adjust our plans based on how well they were working in practice to successfully meet our goals.

A 90-day plan is a tool to manage dialogue between a leader and his or her supervisor on progress toward goals and to put specific actions in place to achieve those goals. It is primarily a coaching tool, so that the senior leader can be kept current by his or her direct reports and provide valuable advice. (See Figure 7.5.)

It is also a planning tool for the leader to ensure that efforts to achieve annual goals do not become a last-minute scramble. The 90-day plan also facilitates the establishment of interim goals to create results and excitement to push to the next level.

A 90-day plan lists the annual goals, 90-day goals, and specific action steps (or tactics) to achieve results as defined by the goals. Ninety-day plans are created at the beginning of each quarter. At the end of the quarter, a meeting takes place between the leader and his supervisor in which the prior three months' progress is reviewed. From there, the 90-day plan is revised for the next quarter and the new 90-day goals and tactics are defined.

A unique component of the plan is a column with a rating system to help determine when to come to the supervisor for direction. Every supervisor has employees who bring too many issues to her. And every supervisor has employees who don't bring up issues that they should before they proceed. So, to help the employee know when to seek management advice and when not to,

Name: ▾

Leader:

Department: NURSING ADMINISTRATION

Division: 75 NBH

Quarter: 1st Quarter ▾

Year Ending: 2007

Save | Print | PDF | Completed

Pillar	Yearly Goal	Rating Type	90-Day Goal	Action Steps	Manage Up	Results
People 30%	Achieve budgeted turnover goal, or if not budgeted goal 15% department turnover.	*percentile* <= 13.99 = 5, 14.00 - 14.99 = 4, 15.00 - 15.99 = 3, 16.00 - 16.99 = 2, >= 17.00 = 1	**First Quarter Goal** Reduce turnover by 10% for 75% of direct reports	**First Quarter Action Steps** 1. Exit interviews with any RN requesting transfer or voluntary resignation. 2. Rounding to staff daily 3. Discussions with key physicians reasons they are aware of potential turnovers 4. Continue to work with Shan Largoza on environment, IT, and equipment 5. Thank you notes 6. Hire additional staffing coordination to ensure adequate staffing ratios 7. Work with Jana and Lori at regional to increase the LVN scope of practice 8. Work with Martha Stephenson to review CNAs getting to add responsibilities again like removal of foleys and IVs. 9. Bring on new Clinical Coordinators for IMC and Med/Oncology	**Level** 1	**First Quarter Result**
Service 25%	Overall nursing patient satisfaction to be within the 75% percentile	*percentile* >= 90 = 5, 80 - 89 = 4, 75 - 79 = 3, 70 - 74 = 2, <= 69 = 1	**First Quarter Goal** Increase overall nursing satisfaction to be within the 30% percentile.	**First Quarter Action Steps** 1. Hold directors accountable for sharing results weekly with staff. 2. Service recovery reports of dissatisfaction prior to discharge 3. Listen to again key physicians as to what their patients are telling them about care 4. Rounding by directors on patients daily 5. Again continue to work with Shan on any dietary or environment issues observed when rounding.	**Level** 1	**First Quarter Result**

Figure 7.5 The 90-Day Plan

Category			First Quarter Goal	First Quarter Action Steps	Level	First Quarter Result
Quality 10%	Achieve performance at the top 10% for 75% of the hospital compare indicators.	*percentage* <= 8 = 5 9 – 9 = 4 10 – 10 = 3 11 – 11 = 2 > 12 = 1	**First Quarter Goal** Increase compliance on pneumonia vaccine screening by 20% Increase compliance on smoking cessation education for CHF by 10% 90% of all nurses will participate in NDNQI survey	**First Quarter Action Steps** 1. Review with directors expectations of process at NEC 2. Include in Communication Letter what the process in and our compliance 3. Develop posters to be placed in lounges to remind nurses to follow process. 1. Review process with Admitting Director to determine gap in process that would lead to noncompliance 2. Implement action plan based on results of #1. 1. Post flyers throughout the nursing units. 2. Directors to encourage staff by reminding. 3. Reminder letters to go out to all nurses times 2.	**Level** 1 1 1	**First Quarter Result**
Finance 20%	Manage Labor Cost per unit of service to nursing budget	*percentage* >= 100 = 5 90 – 99 = 4 80 – 89 = 3 70 – 79 = 2 <= 69 = 1	**First Quarter Goal** Meet labor cost per UOS on 90% of direct reports	**First Quarter Action Steps** 1. Directors to receive daily report of last 24 hour labor cost 2. Review with directors outliers quickly 3. CNO to approve all contract and agency use 4. Hospital pool to be scheduled by staffing office before Bidshift 5. Hire additional staffing hours to better manage proactively staffing 6. Place staff on call before docking for shift.	**Level** 1	**First Quarter Result**
Growth 15%	Achieve 100% budgeted volumes targets for deliveries per day.	*percentage* >= 102.0 = 5 101.0 – 101.9 = 4 100.0 – 100.9 = 3 96.0 – 99.9 = 2 <= 95.9 = 1	**First Quarter Goal** Meet budgeted volume goals in areas assigned	**First Quarter Action Steps** 1. See June MOR	**Level** 1	**First Quarter Result**
Community 0%	Participate in 4 NBH community sponsored supported projects.	*number* >= 6 = 5 4 – 5 = 4 W – 3 = 3 <– (1) = 1	**First Quarter Goal** Become active in a community/civic organization	**First Quarter Action Steps** 1. Discuss with CEO possibilities even if it is in Seguin to reach rural areas. 2. Give blood 3. Attend SA Northside Chamber 4th annual Salute to Excellence luncheon.	**Level** 2 1 2	**First Quarter Result**

Figure 7.5 (*Continued*)

each action step is assigned a number. This is something the supervisor completes with each employee.

For example, if the action step has a *1* beside it, the employee knows he can go "full speed ahead" without talking to the supervisor. He is free to implement it.

A *2* means the employee can plan on implementing, but he needs to tell the supervisor about it before implementing anything.

A *3* means "Do not do this until your supervisor absolutely signs off." For example, if you are changing leadership positions or benefits, those would rate a 3.

Ninety-day plans are also a great way to communicate the amount of autonomy leaders want to give to the leaders they supervise. Here is a quick story: One time, Studer Group was coaching leaders within a large organization. Many of them felt that they were being micromanaged by Corporate. When we looked into it to see whether that assertion was true, it turned out that those who felt they were micromanaged were getting poor results. Those who felt they had a high degree of autonomy were getting great results. So we came to the conclusion that poor results often lead to micromanaging, while great results lead to more autonomy.

Sometimes, of course, supervised leaders don't realize how much autonomy they actually do have. The 90-day plan clears up their confusion. It helps them understand that they are, in fact, *not* being micromanaged across the board. With the rating system, it becomes clear that they have complete leeway on some actions and decisions and are requested to check in for approval in a few other areas.

Once a 90-day plan has been completed, the supervisor and the employee should discuss each item and action step and assign the numbers. The goal is to create clear 90-day plans. A warning comes with this tactic. The first time they are rolled out, most managers load up 90-day plans so that it's *not humanly possible* to accomplish the goals. We once saw an HR supervisor's 90-day plan that fit this category. It was so overloaded with to-do's that if she successfully completed her plan she would have accomplished more in 90 days in Human Resources than the entire organization had managed to do since 1951!

Let's concentrate on what is humanly possible so we can feel successful and get some good results. The 90-day work plan is a great coaching tool. Through clear measurement, it provides a regular format to discuss what an employee is doing well and which areas need development.

RETURNING THE ORGANIZATION TO A SENSE OF PURPOSE

We get phone calls like this: "This stuff worked for a while, but now we seem to be stuck." Then we ask whether an evaluation cycle has passed and whether the client used an evaluation process that was objective and geared to outcomes. They say *no,* and we instantly know that's *why* they feel stuck.

When an objective evaluation tool is not in place, things will slow down after about seven months of progress. Then the organization will get a few more months of slower movement. Then everything stops. And we begin to doubt whether we can sustain the gains. And we start to look for the Next Big Thing that will fix our organization, as I described earlier.

The evaluation tool is the glue that holds the entire system together and allows an organization to do just that—sustain those gains.

We have found that once the leadership evaluation tool, 90-day plans, and monthly report cards are in place, leaders appreciate them. They provide focus and clear priorities. They help leaders determine what their top priorities should be. They take politics and vagueness out of the evaluation process. Furthermore, they move results faster and make the learning needs in the organization more evident so leaders can align training to desired results. Finally, they hold leaders accountable for actual outcomes rather than mere effort.

The leadership evaluation tool is just one more way to help us refocus on the reasons why we care about our jobs in the first place—a sense of purpose and worthwhile work—after battling years of other, cloudy issues that have competed for our time and energy. By setting clear and objective goals, leaders create a pathway to once again recognize how their actions connect to results that make the organization a better place.

KEY POINTS FOR HARDWIRING RESULTS

- To build a results that last culture, we have to hold our leaders at every level accountable for the behaviors and goals that directly create results that last.

- Leadership evaluations are the first step in an organization's commitment to excellence. The evaluations must be based on objective measurable results. This principle is so important to achieving and sustaining results that we at Studer Group agree to coaching engagements only with organizations that are willing to make this commitment.

- Set goals for leaders under each of the Five Pillars. Make sure measurements for each goal are agreed on, particularly what will be determined above-average performance. The pillars themselves should be weighted for each leader according to his role in the organization. The weights will vary by department. The total weights add up to 100 percent and give the leader a clear picture of how to set his priorities.

- Senior management must create a clear plan on how the evaluation tool will be implemented and driven. We recommend a cascading approach in which the goals are first rolled out by senior leaders to their divisions. Then each manager takes historical data compared with the goals that were set and assigns metrics and ratings for her department to ensure alignment organizationwide.

- In addition to the leadership evaluation tool, Studer Group recommends monthly *progress reports* and a *90-day plan*:
  - Progress reports show actual progress made toward these goals on a monthly basis. They help us identify both the problem areas and leaders who need assistance or coaching

and those high performers we can benchmark based on their great results.

- A 90-day plan is a tool to manage dialogue between a leader and his supervisor on progress toward goals and to put specific actions in place to achieve those goals. It is primarily a coaching tool that allows a senior leader to be kept current by his direct report and enables him to give helpful advice.

C H A P T E R

8

CREATE AND
DEVELOP LEADERS

Why This Chapter Is Important

AFTER AN ORGANIZATION HAS AN EFFECTIVE LEADER EVALUATION SYSTEM in place, the next item on the to-do list should be helping leaders develop the skills they need to be successful. I call this the *value* domain. One can recognize an organization's values by the amount of training it provides its leaders.

Most of us leaders did not start out with the goal of being in a management position. Many of us accepted our first leadership role only after we were told it was merely interim. As we eventually discovered, "interim" can last a whole career!

I remember when I left my first leadership role to go to another company, I really believed that life would be better at my new post because I had learned so much in my previous job. Of course, I found out I still had plenty to learn.

My point is that training is a *must*. Once we realize this truth, we have to figure out how to make it work. Most organizations have tried more training in the past, only to cut back in

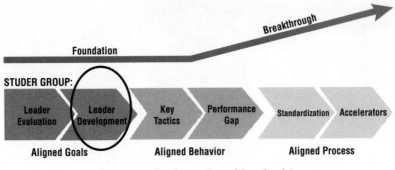

Figure 8.1 Evidence-Based Leadership

tougher times. So if training is a must, why don't we see better results?

In this chapter you will learn how to create leadership training that achieves organizational results. Just as we don't "measure to measure," neither do we "train to train." We train to achieve results that last. Let's find out how.

• • •

LEADER DEVELOPMENT IS A *MUST*

As was discussed earlier, most of us became leaders by default, not by choice. We filled in for someone who retired or quit and that temporary position became permanent. If we accept that postulate, then we have to admit that few of us were really trained to be supervisors. It isn't difficult to see why leadership training is so very necessary.

Most CEOs will say that leadership development *is* a priority at their companies. There are many reasons why this is so. But if one counts the hours of training a manager actually receives, the skimpiness of that number can be a wakeup call.

One reason—possibly the most frequently cited one of all— is that there's just no time to devote to it. When people are stressed to the limit and working nights and weekends just to accomplish their regular job, few companies are willing to pull them off task to attend a leadership retreat or a series of training sessions.

Another reason leadership development is given short shrift is that it's usually considered "a chief learning officer thing." Don't get me wrong; I am not implying that HR or chief learning officers aren't important. They are *vital* to the company's well-being. But the skills a leader needs to be successful in an organization need to come from more than one department and one leader.

Money is yet another problem. When budgets are tight, the "nonessentials" get cut. (That's in quotes for a reason, by the way! You'll see why momentarily.) It's just a fact of life.

Finally, leadership development just seems so random, vague, and, many times, soft. What courses make up a good leadership program? Is it the hot program *du jour* written about in the leading business magazines? What if it doesn't work within the corporate culture? And who chooses the curriculum? The Training Department? The CEO? Some outside consulting company? The whole subject is so confusing, so subjective, so hard to get a handle on, that many companies just throw their hands up and move on. (Lord knows there's plenty to do without it!)

All of these rationalizations illustrate the approach many companies take with their leadership training programs. That attitude also shows why, when training *does* happen, it rarely yields results that last. It is not a "nice-thing-to-do"; it is a *must.*

Leadership development must be treated as though it is the premium fuel that keeps your company's engine stoked and purring smoothly for the long haul. (See Figure 8.2.)

No organization can be great if it doesn't have great leaders. And we can't have great leaders—leaders who are aligned with our company's mission and goals—unless we invest in providing them the skill sets necessary to accomplish our mission and goals.

No matter how much progress we make in clarifying our values, setting goals under each pillar, and putting in place focused behaviors, tools, and techniques, gains will not be sustained if we don't continuously train leaders. They *cannot* be sustained. And the promise implied in the title of this book will go unfulfilled.

- Shares responsibility and creates ownership (Not just an HR job)

- "Tailor-made" for the organization and not "someone else's" program

- Improves results across the board

- Networking—builds relationships, trust, and support

- Creates a team that can adjust to environmental changes and a "built-to-last" culture

- Allows coordination and consistency within your leadership

Figure 8.2 Leadership Development Benefits

A CRITICAL KEY TO EMPLOYEE RETENTION

In my first book, *Hardwiring Excellence: Purpose, Worthwhile Work, and Making a Difference* (Gulf Breeze: Fire Starter Publishing, 2003), I shared this story:

In 1999, I talked to a CEO from South Carolina whose employee turnover was very high. He said, "Quint, our employee turnover is high, and you have very low turnover at your place. What are you doing that I should do?"

I said, "First of all, look at your exit interviews and find out why folks are leaving. We also find taking leaders off-site to train them on employee selection, new employee orientation, and retention is crucial."

He said, "How long should we take them off-site?"

"We do a couple of days, every 90 days," I replied.

"Just can't do it," he said. "We just can't get them away for that long. They're too busy."

"What's your turnover?" I asked.

"It's 33 percent."

I said, "They may be too busy interviewing new employees."

The truth is, leadership is at the heart of why employees want to come to work and why they want to stay. People don't leave their job. They leave their work environment. And work environment is directly connected to the relationships people have with their managers.

Employees want to come to a place where they feel that they have purpose, are doing worthwhile work, and can make a difference. They want to feel that they are a part of things. They want to be recognized and appreciated. Managers hold the key to all of these things. Therefore, they hold the key to employee retention.

Of course, employee retention is only one lens through which we can examine what we want to accomplish. From a broader perspective, I just don't believe any organization can truly succeed without investing in developing the necessary leadership skills.

I've talked a lot about the importance of providing employees with the tools to be successful at their jobs. *Leadership competencies* are the tools your leaders need. Consider the following:

- An organization might have the best benefits package ever, but if the managers don't know how to explain it, it is not fully appreciated.

  One organization we work with had very strong (above national and high-performing norms) employee survey results across all categories, except for one: benefits. Yet, when the organization did a comparison, it found it provided by far the best benefits in the community (see Figure 8.3).

Watson Wyatt data (see Figure 8.4) shows that effective communication raises employee perception of benefits, even when said benefits are "bad." And as you can see, our client's benefits were far from bad. This information allowed our client to create a big win simply by communicating the comparative value of the superior benefits already in place.

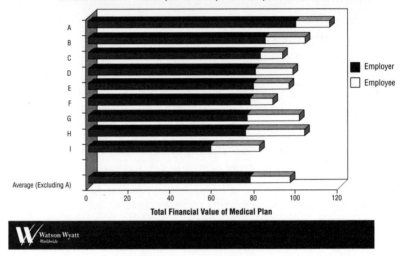

Figure 8.3 Comparison Study

- Effective communication can more than make up for below-average benefits

	Above-Average Benefits		Below-Average Benefits	
	Satisfaction with Health Care	Satisfaction with Pension	Satisfaction with Health Care	Satisfaction with Pension
Effective Communication	84%	81%	76%	78%
Ineffective Communication	26%	38%	22%	15%

Source: Watson Wyatt Work USA Study.

Figure 8.4 The Link between Communication and Benefit Satisfaction

An organization can adopt standards of behavior, but if managers don't know how to confront problem employees, it won't matter.

An organization can have great goals, but if a department leader doesn't know how to communicate these goals to employees, it won't matter.

An organization can have great certificates and prizes, but if a manager doesn't understand how to use reward and recognition to align behavior, it won't matter.

PRINCIPLES FOR DEVELOPING LEADERS

- *The CEO and other top executives must drive the training curriculum.* The CEO or some other high-level leader must take ownership of the leadership training and be there from day one to kick off the training, to observe it, to participate in it, and to wrap it up. It's that important.

- *All leaders must be trained.* Many companies send a sampling of leaders to training sessions, hoping they'll come back and somehow—by osmosis, perhaps?—pass along what they learned to others. This is *not* an effective way to approach leader training. First of all, it's unlikely that the 10 percent (or whatever percentage) of leaders you send to be trained will be able to sway the 90 percent you don't send. The untrained leaders won't have the benefit of having been inspired by the program. They'll simply stay in a state of inertia, continuing with business as usual, and the old practices and culture will prevail. To make matters worse, the trained leaders, frustrated with their inability to effect change, might even leave.

- *Leaders must help design their own training.* Imposing a canned training program on unwilling people rarely works. We must get the leaders' input up front. Leaders should develop an agenda of things they are concerned about, areas that they believe need changing, and they'll buy into the program much more readily.

- *Training must be linked to the company's overall performance goals.* Leadership training—at least effective leadership training—can't happen in a vacuum. When Studer Group does leadership training, we link it to our Five Pillars model. A company may or may not want to use this model, but the training framework must clearly tie into your company's goals and performance measures. Whether a leader works in accounting, in sales, or in product development, she needs to see how these new ideas and methods apply in her area—and how they advance her area's performance indicators *as well as* those of the entire organization. Training can't be abstract and generic. It needs a big-picture context that speaks to the organization and its future.

- *Leaders should understand the nature of organizational change.* Any time a company experiences change, it goes through a series of predictable phases. In the middle of this evolution is "the wall"—the point at which organizational performance begins to stall. Leaders need to know what the wall is, when to anticipate it, and—once they hit it—how to get themselves and their people over it. Therefore, leadership training needs to emphasize the Five Phases of Organizational Change (Figure 8.5):

   Phase 1: The Honeymoon. Everyone is fired up and excited. There is a feeling that things will get better and everyone is focused on the right to-do list. Hope reigns. During this phase:
   - Roll out behavior standards.
   - Provide more communication (information).
   - Acquire tools and fix issues.
   - Start to hardwire key behaviors (rounding/thank-you notes).
   - Implement a new accountability system.
   - Begin leader development sessions.

Figure 8.5 Phases of Change

Phase 2: Reality Sets In. Inconsistencies show up and the *we/they* mentality begins to assert itself. Some departments get it; some don't. Some leaders buy in; others don't. We begin to see differences between low, high, and middle performers. During this phase:

- Leadership training gets more focused.
- Re-recruit high performers—peer pressure sets in.
- Increase substance of communication to employees.
- Prepare to have high-middle-low conversations.
- Increase reward and recognition.
- Introduce key words.
- Hardwire the selection process.

Phase 3: The Uncomfortable Gap. The gap widens and the wall appears. High and middle performers begin to see the gap between themselves and the low performers as unfair and not consistent with the values of the organization. At this point, leaders need to focus on moving high and middle performers to a higher level and moving low performers either up or out. They must move

themselves and their employees over the wall. During this phase:
- Respond to tough questions and hardwire the answers.
- Complete high-middle-low conversations.
- Ensure the right people are in the right places.
- Hardwire agendas.

Phase 4: Consistency. The organization has moved over the wall and a team of disciplined leaders is in place. Leaders are seeing problems and suggesting solutions. Everyone understands the keys to success. All employees are aligned toward disciplined processes. During this phase:
- Push for innovation.
- Standardize and repeat key behaviors.

Phase 5: Leading the Way—Results. At this point, the organization has succeeded in hardwiring excellence at the core of your organization's culture. Results show across all the pillars of the organization. Employees have a sense of purpose.
- *Thoroughly train leaders in the art of high-middle-low conversations.* In my opinion, this is one of the most important skills leaders can possess. The high-middle-low conversations, described in detail in Chapter 1, are key to moving employees—and thus, the entire organization—to higher levels of performance. The training for leaders must also include how, when, and with whom to have these critical conversations.

LEADERSHIP DEVELOPMENT INSTITUTES (LDIs): THE SECRET TO HARDWIRING LEADERSHIP TRAINING

To achieve results that last, leaders must be constantly and consistently trained to develop the skills they need to (1) drive the achievement of organizational goals and (2) improve their own individual leadership performance. That's the idea behind Leadership

Development Institutes (LDIs)—a training program format that's designed for larger organizations but that may be easily modified for smaller companies. (In other words, any leader who thinks, "Well, that won't work for my company," should realize that she can take this basic idea and make it her own.)

Generally, Studer Group recommends that leaders be taken off-site for two days every 90 days to participate in an LDI. By doing so, the company can hardwire 64 hours of training every year. The 90-day period between LDI sessions allows for the feedback, coaching, and practice the leaders need to integrate their new skills into their daily work lives.

Of course, as stated earlier, we realize the ability to hold regular LDIs—not to mention what the LDIs look like—depends on the size of the company. A small company simply won't have layer upon layer of managers. While some of the directives in this chapter appear to be aimed at the larger, more complex organizations, they can't be skipped over. We have seen small companies initiate the LDIs in smaller increments (lunch meetings, weekend retreats, etc.). The key is a commitment to time and relentless follow-up with leaders to ensure implementation of tools and continuous coaching.

How do we design an LDI session? For our clients, the goals under the Five Pillars guide the framework for establishing the objectives and curriculum for each session.

For example, under the People pillar, a company has a goal to reduce its employee turnover. Therefore, it must develop leader competencies for retaining employees (Figure 8.6). Among other things, training might be centered on:

- Understanding how much employee turnover is costing your organization

- Conducting high-, middle-, and low-performer conversations

- Selecting the best applicants

- Improving productivity

- Using exit interviews to identify areas for improvement

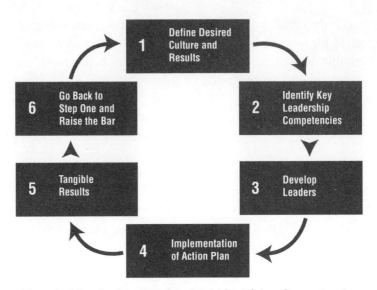

Figure 8.6 Leadership Development Identifying Competencies

- Reading a profit/loss statement

- Retaining customers to improve store sales

Remember, the curriculum needs to be tied to organizational goals, which means the CEO should be an active participant in the development and the ongoing activities of the Institute. He or she must articulate the vision and expected outcomes for the LDI and review and approve the objectives, curriculum, and "Leaders' Accountability Grid" (basically, an assignment sheet detailing actions to be completed) with the senior leaders.

Who Runs the LDI?

The LDI is led by a leader who is responsible for overall coordination. This individual is typically a manager in the company who agrees to take on this additional responsibility. He or she will facilitate agenda-setting with the CEO and senior leaders, lead team meetings, manage budgets, and work with individual LDI team leaders. This person is also responsible for reporting results and giving updates to senior leadership.

Senior leaders demonstrate their commitment to the goals of the company by actively participating in all sessions, modeling the behaviors they want the company to adopt, and holding their leaders accountable for attendance at all leadership development sessions and behaviors identified in the Leaders' Accountability Grid.

The LDI is generally designed, developed, and implemented by teams of middle managers. (The members of the team are voted on by other middle managers.) Leaders must design their own training so that it is relevant, practical, and focused on outcomes. These teams create the curriculum (based on the outcomes identified by senior leaders), manage the communication to attendees and the organization, select the venue, make sure all equipment is in place, and develop actions for the Leaders' Accountability Grid. The LDI teams we suggest (and again, these suggestions were developed for fairly large organizations) are:

- *Curriculum:* This team designs what is taught at each training session. Its main focus is to fulfill the learning objectives set forth by the senior leadership. Sample curriculum topics could include: how to run an effective meeting, how to deliver negative news, or how to address a specific challenge your organization faces. The key is to do *real work* at these two-day sessions that leaders can utilize immediately. In other words, the facilitator uses the organization's own data in any case studies presented.

- *Communication:* This team provides key and pertinent information to leaders and employees about the LDI. These individuals are responsible for keeping everyone informed of events and outcomes from leader learning and actions taken. They will communicate to leaders about their homework for the LDI and what will be taking place there and also share with employees what leaders will be learning at the LDI and how it will affect them. For instance, they might say, "At the LDI your leaders will be learning about peer interviewing and will present how this works at your next department meeting."

- *Social:* This team is responsible for setting the theme for each session, developing skits or role-playing activities, providing decorations, and creating other fun activities for leaders to participate in. A celebratory atmosphere fosters relationship building and a more cohesive team.

- *Logistics:* This team is responsible for providing the "nuts and bolts" of each session, including securing facilities for the training sessions and coordinating the provision of food and beverages, audio/visual equipment, and room setup.

Training the "Big Blue" Leadership Crew

The most successful companies have always recognized the vital importance of developing leaders internally, and some companies have become legendary for their leadership training and development. Under the guidance of Thomas J. Watson, International Business Machines (IBM) first became the world's leading manufacturer of office machines and later grew to become the world's leader in business computers. IBM was famous for promoting from within and for attracting the very best candidates from the nation's leading colleges and universities.

Legend has it that IBM's management trainees at the company's Armonk, New York, headquarters began their training by sweeping the floor of the factory. Eventually trainees were indoctrinated into the culture of "Big Blue," including a corporate style of dress (dark suits, white shirts) and a company songbook (a favorite tune went "We're Watson's great crew/We're loyal and true/We're proud of our job/And we never feel blue").

IBM's Human Resources Department once estimated that the company invested over $1 million training each manager. And when one of Watson's subordinates made a mistake that resulted in a $600,000 loss to the company, he refused to fire the individual. He said, "I just spent six hundred thousand dollars training him. Why would I want anyone else to have his experience?"

- *Accountability:* This team captures key learnings at training sessions for continued use by leaders, further organizational dissemination, or ongoing learning. The team turns learnings into specific assignments or behaviors that will be implemented in the next 90 days and identifies anticipated results to review at the next LDI that are based on reports about these actions. Early on, they might use an Accountability Grid. However, once an organization has implemented 90-day work plans, the Accountability Grid is no longer needed—the assignments are integrated into individual work plans.

In short, a Leadership Development Institute provides the tools and training leaders need to achieve the company's goals. It also goes a long way toward helping employees feel that they really *do* have a purpose, their work really *is* worthwhile, and they really *are* making a difference.

I'd like to share with you a letter that a leader shared with me:

My organization's commitment to training demonstrates to me how valuable I am as a person and as a resource to the organization. It affirms that senior leadership has confidence in my abilities to achieve and produce meaningful outcomes. That in return bolsters my self-esteem and reaffirms my commitment to the success of the organization.

A year and a half since the beginning of this journey, I now know that I can succeed, that I can contribute to successful outcomes, and that I can make a positive difference in the stressful world of health care for my patients, my organization, and my associates. While I still have 80-plus employees that report to me, my stress level has been reduced by at least half of what it was just 18 months ago. And for this I'm thankful.

Tim

Nurse Manager, Tennessee Hospital

Wouldn't we all like to get a letter like that? Of course we would! Commit to leadership training now, and you will hear such sentiments in the future—guaranteed.

KEY POINTS FOR HARDWIRING RESULTS

- We can't have great leaders—leaders who are aligned with our company's mission and goals—unless we invest in providing our leaders the skill sets necessary to accomplish that mission and goals.

- The CEO or some other high-level leader must take ownership of the leadership training and be there from day one to kick off the training, to observe it, to participate in it, and to wrap it up.

- All leaders must be trained. Many companies send a sampling of leaders to training sessions, hoping they'll come back and somehow pass along what they learned to others. This is *not* an effective way to approach leader training.

- Leaders must help design their own training so that they'll buy into the program much more readily.

- Training must be linked to the company's overall performance goals. It can't be abstract and generic. It needs a big-picture context that speaks to the organization and its future.

- Leaders should understand the nature of organizational change. Any time a company experiences change, it goes through a series of predictable phases:
  - Phase 1: The Honeymoon
  - Phase 2: Reality Sets In
  - Phase 3: The Uncomfortable Gap
  - Phase 4: Consistency
  - Phase 5: Leading the Way—Results

In the middle of this evolution is "the wall"—the point at which organizational performance begins to stall. Leaders need to know what the wall is, when to anticipate it, and—once they hit it—how to get themselves and their people over it.

- Leaders must be thoroughly trained in the art of high-middle-low conversations. This is critical for helping the organization deal with change and achieve results that last.

- We recommend that leaders be taken off-site for two days every 90 days for training. By doing so, the company can hardwire 64 hours of training every year. The 90-day period between the training sessions allows for the feedback, coaching, and practice the leaders need to integrate their new skills into their daily work lives.

EMPLOYEE TACTICS

CHAPTER 9

SATISFIED EMPLOYEES MEAN A HEALTHY BOTTOM LINE

Why This Chapter Is Important

EMPLOYEES WANT TO BELIEVE THEIR COMPANY HAS A MEANINGFUL purpose. They want to know that their own job is worthwhile. They want to make a difference. If all three of these conditions are accomplished, bottom line results will follow.

This chapter shows the correlation between satisfied employees and a healthy bottom line. Other chapters provide more details—you've likely already read some of them—but this one will show why we keep pounding the "employee satisfaction" drum. Keeping them happy is more than a nice thing to do. It's money in the bank.

• • •

Do you remember the story of George Bailey in the movie *It's a Wonderful Life?* At the beginning of the movie he is ready to end his life by jumping off a bridge as he faces the shame of "insufficient funds" with the police hot on his trail. He believes his whole life

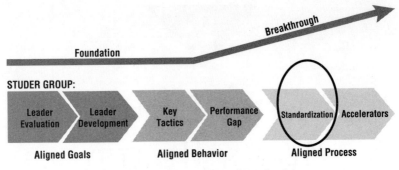

Figure 9.1 Evidence-Based Leadership

has been a waste. He has always wanted to get out of Bedford Falls, but events just kept conspiring to keep him there. He got stuck working at a Building and Loan that he didn't like. He got stuck in a house he wasn't happy with. And at the moment, he isn't too thrilled with his wife, Mary, and the decidedly large and noisy assortment of kids they have. George is discouraged.

Just as he's preparing to take the plunge, he's forced to change gears and fish his guardian angel, Clarence, out of the icy waters. It turns out that Clarence—who has been sent to earth to earn his wings—shows George what Bedford Falls would have been like without his life of service. It's a dreary picture, indeed. George is overwhelmed at the vision of what might not have been—and the important ways he touched so many in the town.

Near the end of the movie, when his life magically returns to normal, George runs through town, yelling, "I love you, Bedford Falls!" When he goes home he sees his wife and kids—and even the falling-apart staircase—in a joyous new light. And as Potter the miserly banker is preparing to have George arrested, the whole town shows up to bail him out of his financial crisis. His brother Harry, having just returned from the war and flown through a snowstorm, offers the following heartfelt speech: "I want to toast my brother George—the richest man in the world!" And of course, as the tinkling bell indicates, Clarence gets his wings.

What changed in those two hours? Had the town changed? Had the Building and Loan changed? Had Mary changed? Did the house change? Did the kids change? Did Potter change? No. What changed was George.

Somebody showed him that his life did have purpose, that his work was worthwhile, and that he made a difference in the lives of others.

THE POWER OF SATISFIED EMPLOYEES

At Holy Cross Hospital in Chicago, I learned that we could incite these same feelings in employees by showing a clip from that classic American film and then asking every department manager to answer the question, "If Your Department Didn't Exist, What Would Happen to Our Organization?" We wanted everyone in that hospital to know that they had purpose, did worthwhile work, and were making a difference.

Why? Because we knew that if these three factors were in place, our employees would feel satisfied in their jobs and that their satisfaction in turn would affect how they treated our patients. The same is true of employees at any organization.

Let's think about our own customer experiences. We know when we interact with satisfied employees. They're the helpful, cheerful, conscientious men and women who make us glad we stopped in at that particular store, or dined at that restaurant, or even chose that accounting firm to handle our taxes.

A workplace comprised of satisfied employees just feels different, and *better*. It feels better to employees and it feels better to customers. That's one big reason leaders should care about employee satisfaction. Satisfied employees tend to go the extra mile to please customers. Happy customers not only keep coming back, they refer friends, family, and business associates—and your company prospers.

BUILDING BLOCKS OF EMPLOYEE SATISFACTION

How do we get the chain reaction started? How do we ensure that our employees are fulfilled and motivated? Let's take a look at the three things that comprise the core of employee satisfaction:

1. *Employees want to believe the organization has the right purpose.* That's why the manager who makes himself look good at the expense of the senior leadership does a disservice to all the other employees. Senior leaders represent "purpose" to the employees. And if employees don't feel good about these men and women, then they don't feel good about the organization. Employees want to commit to a company they can trust and count on.

2. *Employees want to know that their job is worthwhile.* Every employee wants to know what she does is important to the company. Help her live up to this expectation and she'll want to do even more to serve customers and fellow employees. While it may seem evident, taking the time to explain to an employee the importance of what she does is time well spent.

3. *Employees want to make a difference.* The results of what they do fuel their passion. Success breeds more success. So getting results motivates people to persevere and constantly try to create better results.

Of course, knowing what employees want is one thing—you could have guessed that these elements were involved in employee satisfaction. But creating an environment where employees feel these results—a sense of purpose, worthwhile work, and making a difference—is another battle entirely. (If it were easy, every company would have mastered it by now.)

The good news is that while creating employee satisfaction may feel like a tall task, it gets much easier over time. When leaders get practiced at implementing the strategies and tools to make it happen, it becomes second nature.

Results-oriented leaders know that employees are the heart and soul of everything. They pay close attention to their wants and needs and take meaningful steps to address them. These leaders can transform an entire organization. When employees are happy,

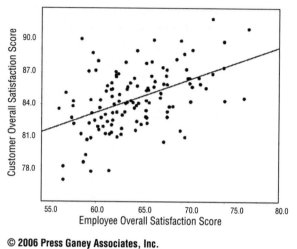

© 2006 Press Ganey Associates, Inc.

Figure 9.2 Customer and Employee Correlations

customers are happy—and many good results naturally fall into place.

Studies show, beyond the shadow of a doubt, a strong correlation between customer satisfaction and employee satisfaction. In other words, the happier employees in a particular organization are, the more satisfied the customers are with the service they receive. (See Figure 9.2.)

NINE WAYS TO GET STARTED

Like everything else involved in culture change, achieving employee satisfaction is an inexact science. People are complex. We can't follow a mathematical formula or implement a set of one-size-fits-all strategies. There are certain steps leaders can take that, overall, make most employees happy to be working for us most of the time. We can set goals and jump-start workplace habits that show our employees we care and want to help them to do a great job. Here are some of the ideas that have worked well for my clients:

1. *"Round" relentlessly.* As you've already read, rounding for outcomes is a critical leader behavior for achieving results that last. That's because it is a great tool that helps us communicate openly with our employees, allowing us to regularly find out what is going well and what isn't going well for them at the company. The process is similar to the one doctors use to check on their patients. In the business world, a CEO, VP, or department manager makes the rounds daily to check on the status of his or her employees. Basically, we take an hour a day to touch base with employees, make a personal connection, recognize success, find out what's going well, and determine what improvements can be made. The key, of course, is fixing the problems that come up. Rounding is the heart and soul of building an emotional bank account with our employees, because it shows employees day in and day out that we care.

2. *Build an emotional bank account.* Do your employees say communication could be better? Would they like more input into corporate decisions? Do they wish their contributions were more appreciated? Most leaders can probably safely assume that the answer is *yes*. If you're one of them, that means you must focus more of your attention on building an emotional bank account with your employees. Not only is it the right thing to do, it's good insurance for the future. Eventually, employees *will* feel let down—so leaders must ensure there's enough emotional capital in the account for that metaphorical rainy day.

Basically, building an emotional bank account means doing what we can to make our employees happy most of the time, in anticipation of those future times when they're sure to be unhappy. Yes, I know: As a leader you truly want to do the right thing *all* the time. You want positive, productive, trust-based relationships with your people. But let's face it: Perfection doesn't exist in leaders or in companies. We put in enough "deposits" so that when the inevitable "withdrawals" are made—let's say we forget to say *thank you* or we have to institute pay cuts—there's enough goodwill in the account to salvage those relationships.

3. *Diagnose employee satisfaction—and act on the results.* Use a proven, respected assessment tool to figure out where your

problems lie. Then commit to solving them. One of the biggest issues we see in our work with clients is that people say, "Well, they measured our satisfaction but nobody responded to what we said." We advise organizations to be open about the results and have everyone vote on the top three issues. Eventually, all issues need to be addressed, but start with the top three.

When used correctly, an employee satisfaction survey can be a valuable tool. The key to these surveys is not in the data itself. It's in how well the data is shared with the staff and how action is communicated based on their feedback. Let me explain how we help our clients handle employee satisfaction surveys:

Once the survey is complete and data has been collected, we train managers how to explain the results of the employee satisfaction survey. While survey vendors are excellent at helping an organization to interpret the data, it's also important to set leaders up for success as they communicate challenges and opportunities to employees. Our coaches recommend that the entire leadership team go off-site for a half day, roll out the survey results, and teach leaders how to develop key words and actions for the survey rollout meeting they will have with staff.

Step-by-Step Guide to the Employee Survey Rollout

Step 1. Survey is completed and data is collected.

Step 2. Leaders are trained on how to explain the results.

Step 3. CEO communicates the rollout.

Step 4. Leaders roll out results to the staff.

Step 5. Action plan is developed with staff involvement.

Step 6. Employees evaluate the rollout meeting.

Step 7. Ninety-day action plans are put into place.

Step 8. CEO communicates accomplishments back to the staff.

For example, if a manager got bad results, we'd urge her to share these results with staff by saying something like:

> "The employee satisfaction results are back. Thank you for completing the survey. I want to tell you I'm disappointed. Obviously I'm not the leader that I want to be. But I want you to know that I'm committed to being a good leader. In fact, I'm going to get additional training in the areas you identified where I can improve. I do want to tell you that I'm committed to making this a better department and to being a good leader. I hope you'll help me."

Once the manager says, "I hope you'll help me," they're on her side.

A big part of employee satisfaction discussions is the ability to be open about the results. For example, the same manager in a meeting with the department might say:

> "Here are the areas that you told me are the most important issues in this department, but I think some of you didn't fill out the survey, plus things could have changed. Let's read the five most important issues, based on the survey results. But I also want to give everybody a chance to add to this list. Sally, do you have anything to add? Nancy, do you have anything to add?"

So by the end of the meeting, there may be eight issues instead of just the top five from the survey. Everyone should vote on which ones they believe are the top three items. This helps individuals to see that their priority might not be the same as everyone else's priority, even though they assumed it was.

After the vote, focus on the top three issues. Eventually, all of them will be addressed, but start with the top three. These could range from work pressure and communication issues to cleanliness or storage needs. There will be some quick wins sitting there that leaders can address easily to build that emotional bank account with staff. Then vote on some actions to take and assign responsibilities. Finally, the employees will fill out an evaluation form for the rollout meeting itself.

When implemented correctly the employee satisfaction survey can be very useful. At Baptist Hospital, Inc., in February 1996, only 666 out of 1,700 people (39% of employees) filled in the first employee satisfaction survey. So this was the foundation for action when I arrived in1996. The second time we did the survey in 1997, 80 percent of employees completed the survey. And in 1999, 94 percent filled it out. We never changed how we did the survey. What changed was employees' perceptions about the impact their opinions would have on changes we would make in the organization. After seeing results, more employees *wanted* to have input.

Twelve Key Questions for Employee Retention and Development

In 1998 the Gallup Organization released the 12 questions (Q^{12}) developed from its landmark study of 80,000 managers to determine drivers for productivity, profitability, employee retention, and customer satisfaction. This book shares tactics that address every one of these questions. The charts given in Figure 9.3 shows each question and the tactic that is used to address it.

	Gallup	Studer Group
Q1	Do I know what is expected of me at work?	Selection and the First 90 Days Key Words at Key Times Leader/Employee Evaluations Performance Management Conversations (HML) Agendas by Pillars Employee Forums Communication Boards
Q2	Do I have the materials and equipment I need to do my work right?	Rounding for Outcomes Selection and the First 90 Days
Q3	At work, do I have the opportunity to do what I do best everyday?	Selection and the First 90 Days Key Words at Key Times Leader/Employee Evaluations Bright Ideas Program Service Team Involvement Employee Forums Employee Attitude Surveys

Figure 9.3 Twelve Key Questions for Employee Retention and Development

(Continued)

Twelve Key Questions (*Continued*)

Gallup		Studer Group
Q4	*In the last seven days, have I received recognition or praise for good work?*	Rounding for Outcomes Employee Thank You Notes Post Visit Phone Calls
Q5	*Does my supervisor or someone at work seem to care about me as a person?*	Rounding for Outcomes Employee Thank You Notes Selection and the First 90 Days Performance Management Conversations (HML) Communication Boards Professional Development
Q6	*Is there someone at work who encourages my development?*	Rounding for Outcomes Employee Thank You Notes Selection and the First 90 Days Leader/Employee Evaluations Performance Management Conversations (HML) Service Team Involvement Communication Boards Professional Development
Q7	*At work, do my opinions seem to count?*	Rounding for Outcomes Selection and the First 90 Days Key Words at Key Times Bright Ideas Program Service Team Involvement Communication Boards Employee Forums Employee Attitude Survey
Q8	*Does the mission of my company make me feel my job is important?*	Employee Thank You Notes Key Words at Key Times Leader/Employee Evaluations Post Visit Phone Calls Bright Ideas Program Service Team Involvement Communication Boards Agenda by Pillars Employee Forums Stories
Q9	*Are my co-workers committed to doing quality work?*	Selection and the First 90 Days Key Words at Key Times Performance Management Conversations (HML) Bright Ideas Program Service Team Involvement Communication Boards

Figure 9.3 (*Continued*)

	Gallup	Studer Group
Q10	*Do I have a best friend at work?*	Rounding for Outcomes Service Excellence Teams Selection and the First 90 Days
Q11	*In the last six months, has someone talked with me about my progress?*	Employee Thank You Notes Selection and the First 90 Days Leader/Employee Evaluations Performance Management Conversations (HML)
Q12	*This last year, have I had opportunities at work to learn and grow?*	Selection and the First 90 Days Key Words at Key Times Leader/Employee Evaluations Performance Management Conversations (HML) Bright Ideas Program Service Team Involvement

First, Break All the Rules, What the World's Greatest Managers Do Differently, Marcus Buckingham and Curt Coffman

© 2001–2005 Studer Group

Studer Group®: Taking You and Your Organization to the Next Level

Figure 9.3 (*Continued*)

If your employees are answering "Yes" to these questions, congratulations! You are doing your job as a leader to give them everything they need to be satisfied and efficient at work. If they are answering "No" to any of them, then there is still work to be done.

4. *Go for "quick wins" to establish credibility.* A quick win is an action that shows employees leaders are really committed to meeting their needs. If I were trying to establish an environment of fairness, for instance, I wouldn't pull rank as a senior leader and cut in line. Nor would I insist on having the parking spot nearest the door. (In this way I send a signal that I'm no more important than anyone else, and the longer parking lot trek gives me the opportunity to talk to employees and stay on top of what's going on in my company.)

Perhaps your quick win might take the form of getting a department a piece of equipment that employees have requested for years, or finally dealing with a low performer who's been dragging everyone down.

Sometimes you won't know what your quick win is until the moment it presents itself. And seemingly small gestures can have a big impact. During my first day as an administrator at a new hospital, I asked a nurse how I could make her job better. She said she was frightened walking to her car at night because of the tall bushes by the parking lot. While she worked that day, the bushes got trimmed and a small fence was built. It made the nurse feel safe and, more to the point, valued as an employee and as a person.

5. *Deal with low performers and understand the impact they have on your team.* Great employees want to work with other great employees and are extremely frustrated by low performers. Nothing makes employees as discouraged and resentful as having to coexist with people who don't pull their own weight. In fact, low performers have the potential to drive high performers right out the door. Leaders turning a blind eye to low performers can quickly turn high performers against their leadership and the organization as a whole. However hard it may seem, leaders must move low performers up or out.

6. *Harvest best practices.* If assessments reveal that a high number of employees cite "poor communication" as a problem, dig deeper. You may find that one department manager got great communication scores. Find out what she is doing right and reward her. Then, work to apply her communication practices throughout the organization. Most companies don't really have a problem with poor communication, just inconsistent communication. Take what people are doing right and expand it. It's much more effective than trying to start from scratch—and it builds goodwill.

In mid-2000, I was at a two-day Leadership Development Institute sponsored by an organization we coach. The topic was employee retention. At the break, I asked a leader who was being recognized for having low turnover what she did differently from others in the organization. After all, she had the same pay, worked with the same leaders, and worked in the same geographic location as the others did. She said, "Oh, nothing." This is the typical first response, so I asked more questions. Eventually, she told me that she met with all new staff at the 30th and 90th days of their employment. Since it worked so well, we helped hardwire this practice in all departments. The next year, employee retention skyrocketed organizationwide. Today, this organization has won many awards, including the Magnet Award for Nursing Excellence, and it can all be attributed to the fact that this organization was able to harvest a best practice of one of its leaders.

7. *Provide the tools that help your employees do a good job.* I really believe that when employees aren't performing, it's almost always because they don't have the tools they need. When I worked at a hospital in the 1990s that needed to improve some low patient satisfaction scores, I decided to ask the nurses what they needed to make the hospital a better place to work. One nurse, Valerie, told me that her unit needed its own copy machine instead of having to share one. So we got it for her. I heard similar things from other nursing units, and we got them what they needed. Soon, turnover decreased and financials improved, and yes, we got patient satisfaction scores up dramatically. It turned out that the employees wanted to do their best all along—they just needed the right tools to do the job.

8. *Embrace a "consider it done" attitude and empower your employees to do the same.* Your employees want to provide great customer service. If they're satisfied with their jobs and your organization, they will often do whatever it takes to make that happen. Consider this example from the health care industry: Sig Jones was a cashier in the cafeteria at the hospital. When anyone walked into the cafeteria, Sig's line was the longest. This was not because she was slow at her job, but because people so enjoyed talking with her, including me. She made both employees and patients feel good.

Anyway, Sig knew that some patients were admitted through our ER, and other patients might not have family to help them. She knew those patients would probably leave an inpatient stay in the same clothes they had arrived in. So Sig kept an eye out for those situations. She would take their clothes home with her and wash them and return them the next day. People left our hospital with clean clothes because Sig Jones, the cashier, chose to make a difference. She was an *owner*, not a *renter*.

If there is a Sig in your organization—someone who understands that ownership means thinking innovatively, making personal sacrifices, and sometimes bending (or even breaking) the rules to keep customers happy—praise her every chance you get. Reward her publicly. Hold her up as an example for others to follow. People like Sig get real joy and fulfillment from serving others. Do everything possible to empower them to serve even more fervently and to let their spirit rub off on other employees.

9. *Be open and truthful with your employees, no matter how difficult it may be.* Let's say you know that part of your organization is going to be outsourced in the next few months, or that there are going to be major cuts in benefits. Both scenarios can be very damaging to employee morale and obviously to satisfaction levels. Even if it doesn't directly affect your team, it certainly impacts them on an emotional level. Once the decision is final, you owe it to your employees to tell them. Don't wait for them to read it in the paper. They will know that you knew all along—and a huge amount of trust will be lost.

A Word About Trust and Transparency

Leaders of every type—from executives to generals to politicians—understand the importance of retaining the trust of their followers. At the beginning of the Great Depression in 1929, America's leaders, from Wall Street to the White House, continually painted the rosiest possible picture of the crisis to the public. "The downturn is temporary," they said. "Prosperity is just around the corner," they promised. But as conditions went from bad to worse, the public lost all confidence in their business leaders and the President, whom they turned out of office in 1932.

The new president, Franklin D. Roosevelt, understood the importance of leveling with the public. He told them, "The only thing we have to fear is fear itself." In speeches and radio broadcasts (called *Fireside Chats*), Roosevelt spoke in frank terms about the financial crisis and gave reassuring explanations about what had to be done to turn things around. He headed off a national state of panic and guided a slow but steady recovery for the next eight years. Roosevelt became one of the most beloved and trusted presidents, in large part because he leveled with the people when other leaders were misleading them.

Follow FDR's lead with your employees. Be honest, even when it's painful. Transparency builds trust. It is one of the hallmarks of a great company and it is an indispensable component of employee satisfaction.

Focusing on employee satisfaction is not a quick fix. It's a process. An organization can't wait for the perfect time to begin or to measure. Conditions are never perfect.

The longer employees' problems go unrecognized, the more they feel their leaders are ignoring them and the greater the disconnect between leaders and staff will become. Staff won't feel like owners but merely renters of space at the organization. And they won't feel the need to go out of their way to help customers.

I've heard it said that corporate culture is what happens when the boss isn't watching. So is customer service. No leader can be there *all* the time. No leader can monitor employees every hour of every day, making sure they're courteous and helpful, making sure they're "managing up" the company and its products and services. Ultimately, employees themselves are responsible for doing these things—and *satisfied* employees will happily accept that responsibility.

And here's one more reason to make employee satisfaction a top priority. Even more important than the bottom line (which, admittedly, is pretty darn important) is the fact that an organization comprised of happy employees is just a better place to work. It's the post-Clarence Bedford Falls—and beneath all the cynicism that surrounds us, isn't that what we all really want?

KEY POINTS FOR HARDWIRING RESULTS

- Satisfied employees tend to go the extra mile to please customers. Happy customers not only keep coming back, they refer friends, family, and business associates to you—and your company prospers.

- The building blocks of employee satisfaction are found in these three truths:
  - (1) Employees want to believe the organization has the right purpose.
  - (2) Employees want to know that their job is worthwhile.
  - (3) Employees want to make a difference.

- Leaders must *round* relentlessly. Rounding is the heart and soul of building an emotional bank account with our employees, which in turn helps us weather those tough days when things don't go quite as we planned.

- We recommend companies survey their employees to diagnose employee satisfaction. The key to these surveys is not in the data itself; it's in how well we share the data with the staff, and how we communicate action based on their feedback.

- Establish credibility with employees by going for "quick wins." A quick win is an action that shows employees that leaders are really committed to meeting their needs.

- Great employees want to work with other great employees. Employees can get discouraged and resentful if they have to coexist with people who don't pull their own weight.

- We can harvest best practices by recognizing those in our organizations who are doing well in meeting goals and then analyzing how they do it. Take what people are doing right and expand it. It's much more effective than trying to start from scratch—and it builds goodwill.

- Often when employees aren't performing well, it's because they don't have the tools they need. It's our job to find out from them what tools they're missing.

- Empower employees with a "consider it done" attitude. Our employees want to provide great customer service. We have to give them the freedom to do just that.

- Transparency is critical in building trust with employees. Leaders need to be open and truthful with their employees, no matter how difficult it may be. Most employees will accept any news if we explain it properly.

CHAPTER 10

KNOW YOUR
EMPLOYEES' *WHAT*

Why This Chapter Is Important

NOW WE'VE BUILT A CASE FOR AGGRESSIVELY PURSUING EMPLOYEE satisfaction and we've shared tools and techniques for improving it.

What is the one tool, reward, or benefit that would empower and inspire each employee to do a great job—an even better job than they're doing now—for you, your company, and your customers? In short, what is the *what* for your employees?

This chapter teaches how to answer that (often elusive) question. Once a leader discovers what the *what* is for his employees, he'll be able to deliver it—at least to the best of his abilities. And that's the real key to employee satisfaction.

Deliver on the *whats* and employees will be happier and more productive than ever. Performance will skyrocket. Customers will be happier. Employee turnover will decrease. Profits will increase. And another big step will be taken on the journey to achieving excellent results—results that last.

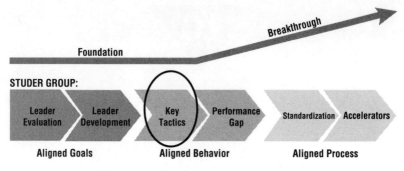

Figure 10.1 Evidence-Based Leadership

• • •

What *really* motivates employees? What makes them happy, inspires them to do their best work, and sends them home with smiles on their faces and enthusiasm in their souls? What one or two things do they need from their leader? What is your employees' *what*?

That's the million-dollar question. And of course there's no across-the-board, one-size-fits-all answer. (There never is!) A great leader is able to figure out the *what* for his employees and either give it to them or explain why he can't. Doing so is a critical part of moving your organization toward greatness.

WE ALL HAVE A *WHAT*

To understand what I mean by "the *what*," let's first apply the principle to you and your boss. (Customers have a *what*, too, but we'll get to them later in the book.) There are probably one or two defining actions or attributes that outweigh all others in your mind. Maybe your *what* is being punctual. You can't stand it when people aren't on time. Maybe your boss's *what* is that people should proactively tell her when something goes wrong, rather than leaving her to hear about it later. Everyone has a *what*.

Every leader should know what her own *what* is, first and foremost. If you don't know what motivates you, how can you tell your employees? Furthermore, you must know what your boss's *what* is. If you don't, how can you work with her in a productive way?

If you're a leader, you've probably already mastered these two *whats*. If you hadn't, you likely wouldn't be in a leadership position.

No leader can make everyone happy 100 percent of the time. It's not humanly possible. But when the leader knows what matters most to employees—and when she meets that need or desire—employees will forgive her when she can't meet some of their other (less important) expectations. The critical mass of staff support needed to achieve desired results is maintained.

Remember the emotional bank account mentioned in the previous chapter? Identifying employee *whats* is the key to making plenty of deposits!

YOUR EMPLOYEES' *WHAT*

If you know the *whats* of the men and women who work for you, they're more likely to engage at a deeper, more productive level. The *whats* I'm speaking of can exist on two levels—departmental and personal.

For example, a Marketing Department's collective *what* may be having free access to the ideas coming out of Product Development. (That way, they can have a hand in shaping the products to customer needs.)

Maybe your V.P. of Marketing's *what* is flextime so that she can take her sick niece to her weekly treatment sessions. (Make that concession and she'll gladly give you her best work, even if she has to do it on nights and weekends.)

It's true that understanding these *whats* takes a lot of attention and insight, but they're key in building strong working relationships. I want to tell you a story from my own career that illustrates how critical it is to get to the bottom of what truly motivates employees. As you'll see, discovering what the *what* is for employees can be an evolutionary process—one that unfolds on its own timetable and in sometimes humorous ways.

IN HOT WATER: A STORY OF *WHAT* DISCOVERY

Once upon a time, I was a new president of a large hospital. I had 1,700 employees. About once a week I would walk through the Surgical Intensive Care Nursing Unit.

We were a trauma center with three Intensive Care Units—a Cardiac Unit, a Medical Unit, and a Surgical Unit. The Surgical Unit was particularly stressful. It's where we treated accident victims, people with brain injuries and strokes, and so forth. Because events that brought patients to the Surgical Unit were often unexpected, the family waiting area was jammed with people worrying whether their loved one was going to live or die.

I would walk into the area and introduce myself and say, "My name's Quint Studer. I'm the president of the hospital. I'm so sorry you have a loved one in the hospital. We have a great hospital and a great medical staff."

I wanted these family members to know that their loved ones were in good hands. Then, I would tell family members that I was going back into the patient care area. *Can I get you anything?* I would ask. *Can I do anything for you?* Often, people would tell me to say "thank you" to the staff. (I was harvesting for reward and recognition.)

Usually, if there was an issue, it was about communication: *When can we go back?* or *Has the doctor been in?* I would find the answers for them.

When I went into the patient care area, the nurses would give me *the look*. I am quite familiar with the look. It's the one reserved for new CEOs or leaders, the one that translates into "What are you doing here? We're up to our elbows in caring for hurting patients!" (Believe me, I understand. The intensive care nurses are busy. Dealing with the CEO is not at the top of their list of priorities.)

After I fielded the look, we'd exchange hellos. "Some grateful families are out there," I might say. The nurses would nod. I could tell they were thinking, "This too shall pass," or "He's just coming through now to put on a good impression." Or "We save lives for a living; I wonder what *he* really does around here."

While I was on the unit, I tried to visit one patient room where at least one family member was present. Because the patient was often unconscious, I would say hello to the family member, shake her hand, and tell her who I was and that we wanted to make sure her loved one got the best possible care.

One day when I was talking to a family member, a nurse came in. I noticed that the nurse practiced a behavior that I wasn't doing. She touched the patient and immediately the family member looked like she just felt better. The nurse's touch conveyed compassion and empathy.

During this time I was desperately trying to improve the hospital's patient satisfaction results. When I saw the impact that this nurse's touch had on the family member, I thought, "Okay, if touch means so much to people I'll rub my body all over this department if I need to!"

So I added "touching" to my routine. Once a week I'd go into the unit, I'd touch patients, and I'd feel pretty darn good about myself. The nurses were still giving me *the look*. They were still in the getting-to-know-you period.

One day I went in and, for some reason, it caught my eye that there were four or five coffeemakers on the counter. I thought, *Hmmm, that's odd. Someone in here must really like hot drinks.* So I mentioned to a nurse, "You guys must like tea." She just gave me a blank stare. So I pointed out the coffeemakers. Another nurse said, "That's not for tea; that's for bathing patients."

She told me that the Intensive Care Surgical Unit—which was located in the oldest part of the hospital—didn't consistently have hot water. On extremely busy days, other parts of the facility would use it all up. Not wanting to be caught without hot water at a critical time, the nurses in the Intensive Care Unit had come up with a clever backup system.

Now, I'd been here for only three months. Thinking this had to be a temporary thing, I said, "Maybe there's construction going on. How long have you had trouble with hot water?" One of the nurses said, "I don't know; I've only been here for thirteen years." (Just as an aside, I find these kinds of jerry-rigged systems in organizations across America!)

Now I had a problem. The nurses knew I knew that they were having trouble getting hot water. I'd already come in and said we were going to make sure that employees had the tools and equipment to do the job, so we had to come up with a solution. Fortunately, the Plant Operations Department came up with a good idea—heat pumps to store hot water under each sink in the patient care area.

Anyway, after about two weeks, thanks to Plant Operations, the Surgical Intensive Care Unit finally had hot water. I was excited. I walked in, talked to the families, and went into the nurses' area. "How's your hot water?" I asked. To which they said, "Fine, thank you." Now, being a mature adult male who expects reward and recognition for taking out the garbage or changing the toilet paper roll, I was a bit disappointed in this lukewarm response!

Suddenly Maureen said, "I need to talk to you." Maureen is an intense ICU nurse. She takes her job seriously, which I admire. She talks briskly because she wants to get back to her patients. Anyway, I was a little intimidated. I was thinking I was about to hear a complaint, so I made sure my hand was close to the elevator button so I could push it quickly and make my escape.

Filtering Out the Positives

When I was in my early thirties, I couldn't shake the feeling of being a loser, no matter how hard I tried. I went to see a therapist with Catholic Social Services in Janesville. After several sessions, there was a revelation. Amy, the therapist, said to me, "Quint, when I provide positive feedback, you cross your arms and deflect the comment. When I give you negative feedback, you literally turn toward me, open up, and let it in. Maybe the reason you feel bad on the inside is because you are filtering out the positives." When I left therapy, I felt a weight had lifted. I needed practice but knew what I needed to do. As a leader, do you filter out the positives?

In a nonthreatening way, Maureen said, "You come in here a lot." For a moment I felt pretty good: Clearly, my visibility was paying off. Then she said, "You do a lot of touching." I beamed. She had noticed my compassion. I prepared myself for the forthcoming compliment. The words, "Well, thank you, Maureen," were poised on the tip of my tongue.

Then Maureen said, "Quint, there are a lot of infections on this unit." Immediately, my hair started sweating, my nose started itching, and the words of an infection control committee—"Anytime you put a lot of sick people in a hospital, infections are inevitable"—rang in my head.

Maureen continued, "Quint, we notice you don't wash your hands. It's important to wash your hands. You should wash your hands after every interaction. Hold them under hot water for six or seven seconds. In fact, if you can't find water, we now have these new devices on the wall that dispense antibacterial soap that'll kill germs." Maureen, who I now realized was the designated you-go-talk-to-him person in her department, turned and walked away. I couldn't help but notice that she'd forgotten about my compliment.

As I walked down the hallway, picturing germs crawling all over my body, I started wondering how long those infections had been there. Surely, they'd been there for the 12 weeks since I'd started my "touching" campaign. But why did it take so long for the employees to notice I wasn't washing my hands? It was a puzzler.

Today, after talking to thousands of nurses, I've come to the conclusion that at least one person probably noticed it the first day. Don't get me wrong. There's no one in the world I respect more than caregivers. But these nurses were only human. *Until they got their hot water, they didn't care if I lived or died.* Once I discovered and met their *what*—fixing the hot water problem that had plagued them for so long—they started to care about my well-being. Only then could I start building a productive relationship with them.

PURSUING THE *WHATS*

Sometimes, as in the hot-water story I just told, leaders stumble upon what the *what* is for their employees. But this is not the ideal method of *what* discovery. Here are four ways to get started:

1. *Do an employee satisfaction survey.* A good assessment tool will show you where most employees feel the problems lie—and the results invariably yield clues as to which *whats* are not being met. Review the previous chapter for more information on employee satisfaction surveys.

2. *Pay attention to what is learned during daily (or weekly) rounding.* When you round for outcomes, you're regularly asking employees what you can do to help them better do their jobs. Their answers will reveal their *whats*. In fact, if rounding had been hardwired into the hospital in which my hot-water story took place, the problem would have been solved years ago—and I wouldn't have needlessly risked my life (or at least my health) in the Surgical Unit!

3. *Send out a "What's your* what*?" e-mail to all employees.* At Studer Group, we like to ask our people "What is the best reward and recognition you've ever received? And, by the way, how would you *like* to be rewarded and recognized?" By asking employees about their past rewards and recognition, you discover what really matters to them. When you ask them how they would like to be recognized, they'll *tell* you what their *what* is.

4. *Finally, just ask.* It really is that simple. When I asked my administrative assistant what would make a good day for her, this is what she told me: "Quint, you're gone all the time. Sometimes I'm waiting for you to call so that I can help move stuff forward. When you don't call, I'm stuck in idle. If you could call me every afternoon, I could actually make progress. That would be my *what*."

Of course, once you figure out what the *what* is for your employees, you must fulfill it or connect the dots as to why it is not possible. Sometimes it may require buying or fixing a piece of needed equipment, as with the hot-water debacle. Sometimes it might mean giving people more responsibility. It might be something as simple and painless as saying *thank you* more often.

Regardless, it's always a good idea to deliver on employees' *whats*—or at least, to make every possible effort to do so. It will make their life, and yours, so much easier and more rewarding.

In fact, we can even bring the "what's the *what*" principle into our personal lives. I did it. I asked my wife what her *what* is and she quickly rattled off a list:

- If you're the last one out of the bed, make it.

- Take the garbage out without my asking.

- Pick your clothes up off the floor.

You see, for my wife these three *whats* show respect.

It's this pursuit of the *whats* that moves our organizations up. Because we know the *whats* of our customers, employees, and other stakeholders, we can begin to meet their needs. And when that starts happening, everything gets better and better.

KEY POINTS FOR HARDWIRING RESULTS

- In order to maximize our company's potential, we must find out what the *what* is—for our customers, our employees, our bosses, and even ourselves. It's the discovery of the *what*— that is, what is truly important to each party—that moves the organization toward greatness.

- Every leader should first and foremost determine his own *what*. A leader can't tell his staff how to work with him unless he knows what motivates him. Furthermore, he must know what his boss's *what* is.

169

- To figure out what employees' *whats* are, sometimes a survey will do the trick. Alternatively, simply ask them.

- It's this pursuit of the *whats* that moves our organization from good to great. Because we know the *whats* of our customers, employees, and other stakeholders, we can begin to meet their needs. And when that starts happening, everything gets better and better.

CHAPTER 11

IMPROVE EMPLOYEE SELECTION AND RETENTION

Why This Chapter Is Important

OUR GOAL IS ACHIEVING RESULTS THAT LAST. THOSE RESULTS PLAY themselves out through the men and women who sit in our cubicles, work our front desks, and sell our products. So the logical question is: *What good are all of these ideas and tactics—rounding for outcomes, managing up, and so forth—if we turn around tomorrow and hire the wrong people?*

Once we establish a high-performing culture, we have to hire people who fit that culture. Otherwise, the wheels fall off the wagon and we quickly find ourselves back where we started.

This chapter reveals how to make sure the new people brought on board will keep all the hard-won results going strong in the months, years, and decades to come.

• • •

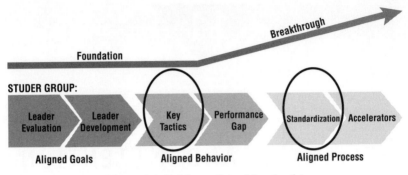

Figure 11.1 Evidence-Based Leadership

The Long Goodbye

The following essay is excerpted from my interactive blog at www.studergroup.com. I include it here because even though the bulk of this chapter is about the hiring process, you may have employees who've been quietly dissatisfied for many years. Some of them may be planning their exits even as you read these words. Learn to detect their discontent and you can salvage these valuable old relationships while you're forming new ones with new people.

When an employee announces his or her departure, the decision to leave is made months and years before the actual resignation occurs. Because health care is a small world, the departing employee will usually say that the resignation is due to family, pay, or opportunity. The real reason for the departure is more than likely tied to some event or action that occurred months or even years ago. Usually it's something that a leader either missed or saw as inconsequential at the time.

People work in health care primarily because they enjoy the work relationships and have a strong desire to do their job well. Thus, when leaving a job, an employee knows she'll have to develop new relationships and will experience those difficult feelings of not being at one's best as she becomes acclimated to her new position and company. So why do people leave? Most likely it comes back to reasons such as an unfulfilling relationship with their supervisor, frustrating systems, a lack of tools necessary to do their job, a lack of development or training, having to work with low performers who are not being dealt with, and a lack of appreciation. The following story is an example of what happens when that loyalty knot gets loosened.

Not long ago, I ran into a nurse while grocery shopping with my wife. The nurse was disappointed with her current employer. Why? She had applied for a nursing instructor position at her hospital. Someone else got the job.

That hurt, yes, but what hurt even more was the lack of respect she felt because of the way the communication was handled—or more accurately, the way it was *not* handled. It wasn't until she read the announcement on the staff bulletin board that she learned she didn't get the job.

She said to me, "I've worked there for years and they didn't even have enough respect for me to call and explain that I wasn't chosen or why."

Will she walk out right away? No, she is too professional. Will she leave tomorrow? No, again she doesn't want to leave her teammates and patients in a bind.

Will she return calls from another organization if called? Yes. Will she look online for openings at other organizations? Most likely. Will she leave? Yes, if something doesn't happen to retighten her loyalty.

So how does a leader become aware of such disconnects and either prevent them or intervene sooner? Here are two possible ways:

1. Hardwire communication with people not selected for positions. Clarify the next steps of the interview process, particularly *when* the decision will be made and *how* people will be notified.

2. Consistently round on staff. In the story above, I feel that if the manager had rounded on this person with some basic questions, the leader would have been aware of the situation. If an employee quits and the leader is surprised, there are two issues: the employee's departure and the fact that the leader is unaware of the employee's feelings.

(Continued)

The Long Goodbye (*Continued*)

A new leader told me that he once asked a nurse how she was doing. The nurse mentioned a particular supply need on the unit. The leader followed up and got the supplies. A few weeks later the leader was walking through the unit and saw the same nurse. The nurse told the leader that when she had mentioned the supplies, she had already written her resignation letter and planned on turning it in that day. However, she had decided to wait just to see how the leader handled her request. She then thanked the leader for being so responsive and said she was staying. Never underestimate the impact of such actions!

Love to hear your comments on this and your own life's lessons. Thanks, Quint

THE IMPACT OF SELECTION AND THE FIRST 90 DAYS

A critical skill for leaders and staff is to ensure that an excellent staff selection system is in place. If you are married, look at your spouse. Now, ask yourself how good you are at selection. That's the biggest selection you are ever going to make! How did you do?

Hopefully, you're happy with your choice. But if you had to choose a spouse for someone else, well, that someone else might be less than thrilled. It's usually best to let the person who has to live with, eat with, sleep with, vacation with, and bank with someone actually *choose* that someone!

And that's why I'm such an advocate of peer interviewing. In peer interviewing, we essentially ask the employees to hire their co-workers. We are saying, "We're an adult organization. Everybody has the data. We have well-trained leaders. Everyone has the tools and equipment to do the job or knows why not. Now step up to the plate."

In other words, we're saying to hire your co-workers. Train your co-workers. Orientate your co-workers. Role model for your co-workers.

At Studer Group, employees volunteer to be *peer-interview certified*. This means they've gone through training on the interview process and behavioral-based questions. Leaders select which certified employees they want to interview their candidates. Not surprisingly, they always select the highest-performing team members to be part of the interview process.

They are selecting a co-worker. We want to make sure co-workers agree they are the best people for the job and will assimilate well within the department. And we'd rather know before we hire them than afterward. Peer interviewing is a good way to ensure that new hires fit the company's culture and that their relationship with current employees starts off on the right foot.

PEER INTERVIEWING: A VITAL SKILL FOR HIRING THE RIGHT PEOPLE

The idea of peer interviewing was gleaned from physicians. In a group practice, several physicians interview a doctor for a potential spot. If six doctors interview a physician and one of them doesn't feel good about the physician, what happens? The doctor doesn't get hired. Why? They need to share calls and thus patients. One bad decision can bankrupt a group practice. We can learn a lot from physicians about selection. They know what it costs if they don't make a good choice.

Peer interviewing for a company is very similar. It's going to make for a good beginning—the first step in reducing high turnover. First, every individual who peer interviewed the new hire already knows the new person. Second, they're going to take a personal interest and ownership in that person's success.

Who in the organization should make up the "peer interview team"? It depends on the size and structure of your company. A human resources representative should screen the candidate's skill set and share Standards of Behavior with her. The candidate should also be interviewed by the leader in the department where she'll be working. The leader makes the decision to pass (or not pass) a candidate to be interviewed by peers. Peers are selected from high performers who will interact with the person hired. It's this peer team who will determine whether the candidate is a good cultural fit.

We usually get two main objections from leaders about peer interviewing:

1. *What if they hire somebody I don't want to hire?* Don't let them interview these people. Screen people first. The leader of the department should lead the way in screening out those applicants he can't live with before peer interviewing begins.

2. *I don't want people I might hire to meet the staff they might be working with.* In other words, if they met their co-workers, they might not want the job? If this is the case, there are other existing problems in the department that need to be recognized and addressed.

THE STEP-BY-STEP PROCESS OF PEER INTERVIEWING

The first step in the employee selection process is to ask the potential employee to read and sign the Performance Standards agreement even before completing the employee application. We want on board only employees who agree to align their behaviors with our values. (See Figure 11.2.)

Next, we want the leader, in conjunction with the employees, to have a shared understanding about the skill set and attitude they are seeking. We recommend that leaders and employees put together a matrix that captures key attributes an employee should have for that particular position. The peer interview team will then use the Decision Matrix during the interview process. (See Figure 11.3.)

The matrix is important because it:

• Makes evaluation of all candidates more objective and consistent.

• Ensures the interview team selects the right questions for the attributes that are identified.

Application process includes a signed agreement and commitment to the standards and values of the organization.

```
┌──────────────────────────────────────────────────────────┐
│                  PERFORMANCE STANDARDS                      │
│                                                             │
│  A set of performance has been developed by the employees   │
│  of _____ to establish specific behaviors│
│  that all employees are expected to practice while on duty. │
│                                                             │
│  By incorporating these standards as a measure of overall   │
│  work performance, _____ makes it clear that     │
│  employees are expected to adhere to and practice the       │
│  standards of performance outlined in the Standards of      │
│  Performance handbook.                                      │
│                                                             │
│  I have read and understand the Standards of Performance    │
│  handbook and I agree to comply with and practice the       │
│  standards outlined within.                                 │
│                                                             │
│  _____        _____           │
│  SIGNATURE OF APPLICANT                DATE                 │
└──────────────────────────────────────────────────────────┘
```

Figure 11.2 Application Process

Desired	Wt 1–3	Candidate 1	Candidate 2	Candidate 3
Experience: Minimum 3 years experience in accounting, finance or health care	3	3/9	2/6	4/12
Diligence: Tell me about a time when you had to work on a project that did not work out the way it should	3	5/15	3/9	3/9
Integrity: Describe a situation in which you felt it might be justifiable to break company policy or alter a standard procedure	3	4/12	3/9	4/12
TOTALS		36	24	33

WEIGHTS: 1. Preferred, but not necessary
2. Moderately necessary
3. Essential

SCORE: 1. Very Poor 4. Good
2. Poor 5. Excellent
3. Fair

Figure 11.3 Decision Matrix Completed

- Facilitates the decision-making process and helps companies avoid emotional decisions.

Prior to the actual interview, the peer interviewing team will select the best behavioral-based interview questions that speak to the attributes described in the Decision Matrix. These questions fall under categories such as:

- Competency

- Integrity

- Flexibility

- Decision-making ability

- Organizational skills

- Ability to follow through

- Dependability

- Creativity

Each position requires different skill sets. This is why the Decision Matrix and behavioral-based questioning are so important. Using the right interview questions will increase the chances of selecting the right candidate and choosing a high performer. There are specific behavioral-based questions listed by category on our web site at www.studergroup.com. (Just search on Behavioral-Based Interviewing Questions. See Figure 11.4.)

Once the interview has been completed, the leader collects the interview matrix and, based on the objective evaluation from the interview team, makes a decision. Of course, there will always be challenges in this process. For example, a leader's top candidate may not be the top candidate as decided by the peer interview team. If this occurs, I recommend that the leader choose the candidate the team recommended. (And as mentioned, the leader should have put forth only candidates that he or she felt comfortable with initially.)

Studer Group has helped companies all over the country install this selection process. We use it at our company, too. It works.

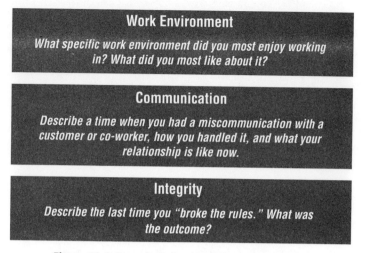

Figure 11.4 Sample Behavioral-Based Questions

However, remember I said that good selection is only the first step in filling your organization with the right kinds of employees.

What you do in the first 30 and 90 days is crucial to keeping the employees you just hired. Also remember that if you can keep them for 12 months, then your turnover is cut in half. So let's look at how we make the most of the new employee's first weeks and months with the organization and ensure he or she stays.

THIRTY- AND NINETY-DAY NEW-EMPLOYEE MEETINGS

An organization has spent months remedying a major staff shortage. After reviewing countless applications, conducting peer interviews, assessing performance skills, and completing all the other necessary processes, a leader has finally hired the "cream of the crop" for his department. He pats himself on the back and takes a moment to feel pride in how he, his team, and the company have attracted and hired such superstars. But he takes only a moment, because there is still work to be done. Attracting the best and the brightest is only part of the equation. Now that he has them, what will he do to keep them? It's simple: He must hit the ground running by opening up the lines of communication.

More than 25 percent of employees who leave positions do so in the first 90 days of employment. *This first 90-day period is critical.* To retain this new team member, the leader needs to build a relationship. We have found that scheduling two one-on-one meetings, the first at 30 days and the second at 90 days, has an enormous impact on retention that directly turns into savings for your organization. Look at the chart in Figure 11.5 to see how 30- and 90-day meetings impacted one organization.

If these meetings are handled successfully, new employee turnover is reduced by 66 percent. Again, leaders should schedule these meetings at the 30- and 90-day marks. It is important to let the employee know that these meetings will be taking place and which questions will be asked. This heads-up reduces anxiety and gives the new employee time to think about her answers. To make the most of these meetings, we have the leader use a structured list of questions to discover not only what's *not* going well, but also what *is* going well.

	Terminations		Cost		Difference
Using 30/90 Day Questions (Checkpoints)					
	2003	2004	2003	2004	
Leader 1	29	4	$580,000	$80,000	$500,000
Leader 2	10	7	$200,000	$140,000	$60,000
Leader 3	50	40	$1,000,000	$800,000	$200,000
Leader 4	2	0	$40,000	$0	$40,000
Not using 30/90 Day Questions (Checkpoints)					
Leader 5	15	8	$300,000	$160,000	$140,000
Leader 6	10	13	$200,000	$260,000	($60,000)
Leader 7	3	3	$60,000	$60,000	Even
Leader 8	1	5	$20,000	$100,000	($80,000)

Turnover Reduction During the First Year of Employment Recommendations for the Vice President of Human Resources Tammye L. Kaper April 2005

Figure 11.5 Impact of 30- and 90-Day Meetings

Here is one thing to keep in mind: We can be certain that our new employee is comparing her *first* few weeks of work with our company to her *last* week at her previous job. And what usually happens to an employee during the last week? Her former co-workers throw her a going-away party that includes a cake and a card signed by everyone with their well-wishes and fond memories of how great she was to work with. She's wistfully comparing that experience to this new place where nobody knows her, no parties have been thrown, and very few well-wishes come her way. In fact, very few people actually call her by name. It doesn't take a rocket scientist to see that our company is getting the short end of an unfavorable comparison.

That's why it's very important to have the supervisor ask key questions during the 30- and 90-day meetings. (For the purpose of this exercise, let's pretend that you are the supervisor conducting the interview.)

Four Key Questions for the 30-Day Meeting

Question #1: How do we compare to what we said we would be like?

You're asking how your company's behaviors have stacked up against what you said those values were when she took the job.

You may hear about a perceived discrepancy. Perhaps, for example, you'll hear about hours: "When I was hired, I heard the job was from 8 to 5. But now you're asking me to work different hours."

If the employee brings up a question, the key obviously is to listen and talk about it. It's much better to hear and discuss an employee's frustrations than to let them fester. If you don't, you'll have an unhappy employee who may quit.

It's critical that you not accept "fine" or "okay" as an answer to your questions. Dig deeper. Ask for specifics. You must also demonstrate concern, responsiveness, and appreciation for the new employee. This will also increase employee satisfaction and retention.

The three main issues that come up are that the hours, training, and/or duties do not align with the new employee's expectations. Be prepared for them.

Question #2: Tell me what you like. What is going well?

It's important to move into this realm because your new employee may have already started focusing on things that are not good.

As a part of this question, you can also harvest wins by asking your new employee, "Who are some people who have been very helpful during your first days at the hospital?" And when she names Nancy, ask her how Nancy was helpful. That helps you create a template for helping new employees. It also allows you to go to Nancy and tell her the good things the new employee said. Now, how does that cause Nancy to treat the new employee? She treats her even better.

And when a new employee says, "The Sales Department here is the best I've ever seen," and you pass that on to the sales staff, how is the new employee treated in the Sales Department the next time he shows up? He's treated pretty good. The employee has just learned that when he rewards and recognizes staff, he gets treated better.

Notice that this technique works well with all new employees regardless of their department or vocation.

Question #3: I noticed you came to us from ____. Are there things you did there that might be helpful to us?

Ask that question early on in the new hire's employment—before she gets too ingrained in the new system—so she doesn't forget those best practices you can learn from. This is a great way you can benefit from the person's past employment. Let's harvest all opportunities for process improvement that walk through our doors.

But in doing so, be sure not to sell out the employee. Don't run back and tell everyone in the department, "Paula says we should do it this way!" That might not go over very well. Instead, you might go to the department and say, "Here's something we're struggling with. Paula, how did they do it at your former organization?"

It's standard procedure in many industries to harvest intellectual capital from new employees. If I worked at General Motors and hired someone in project design from Ford, the first thing I'd ask about is what he was doing at Ford that we should try at GM.

Whatever your industry, you likely have wonderful new employees walk into your organization with fresh eyes. You really should ask their opinion about what they notice you could do better. Especially be careful that you don't send the message that you don't want to know. If an employee offers, "This is what we did where I used to work," do not, under any circumstances, say, "Well, you don't work there anymore, so this is how we do it here." To do so is to miss big opportunities for process improvement.

Question #4: Is there anything here that you are uncomfortable with? Anything that might cause you to want to leave?

Typically, employees bring up misunderstandings about scheduling or perhaps a question about training they thought they would receive but haven't yet. Or they might be confused about whether they are making good progress—especially if they've had multiple instructors. In any case, this is a great opportunity to reassure them.

By the *90-day meeting*, new employees have a better understanding of the company, their co-workers, and their leader. It is important to re-ask the four questions you asked at their 30-day meeting. They may have new insight now. There are two additional questions that should be asked during this meeting.

Additional Questions for the 90-Day Meeting

Question #5: Is there anyone you know who might be a valuable addition to our team?

At this point, your new employee is still likely to be in touch with former co-workers. If she is having a good experience with your organization, encourage her to let former co-workers know. This is a very effective recruiting measure.

Question #6: As your supervisor, how can I be helpful?

Those are the six questions that make for a productive 30- and 90-day meeting with new employees. Using them will help you reduce the large employee turnover that typically occurs within the first quarter of employment.

Close the meeting by telling your employee that the lines of communication are always open. Simply say, "We realize having the right people is the key to having the best place to work and providing the best service for our customers. I want to make sure we are doing everything we can to assist you in being successful. My door is always open for you to share your questions or concerns. We want this to be the best place you ever work."

Peer interviewing and 30-/90-day new-employee meetings are the tools necessary to reduce turnover at your organization. In turn, bottom-line savings from higher retention will really add up. Take a look at this example from the health care industry: One hospital we coach reduced employee turnover from 20 percent to 12.6 percent in two years for a savings of $1.2 million, based on an "average" hourly rate per employee they determined.

Not only will we save money and time because we won't constantly be training new employees, but we'll be creating an environment filled with employees who feel like their voices are being heard. And employees whose voices are being heard and who see the results of that open communication with their leaders are satisfied employees. I can't say it often enough: Satisfied employees foster satisfied customers. A satisfied employee is one who is happy to be at work and happy to go the extra mile for the customer. Employees like that are invaluable.

When an organization decides to tackle its problem with employee retention, it is making a commitment to excellence. I believe that a core focus on employee retention (rather than recruitment) serves organizations best. Organizations will ensure that they keep their top performers and also attract the very best new job candidates. And new employees will want to be a part of the team *because* of the organization's commitment to excellence. It's a win-win for both sides.

Trump Organization: A Surprising Example of Employee Retention

The man who occupies the center seat in the boardroom of the reality series *The Apprentice* is better known for firing people than for retaining them. But privately, Donald Trump is also well known for his ability to build high-performing employee

---

teams that are hard working, successful, and, above all, loyal. The best way to avoid employee problems, says Trump, is to "make all your employees feel like part of the team. If they all feel as if they have a vested interest in the overall success of your business, then most likely these [problems] won't happen." As a result of this high-level teamwork, Trump's various enterprises are collectively worth several billion dollars and his employee turnover is relatively low.

In his blog, Trump frequently writes about teamwork and employee loyalty and how they impact turnover. Recently he said, "When employees and employers, even co-workers, have a commitment to one another, everyone benefits. I have people who have been in business with me for decades. I reward their loyalty to the organization and to me. I know that they'll always be dedicated to what we're trying to accomplish. The reason I have so many loyal people in the Trump Organization is that the loyalty is reciprocated. A lot of companies feel that dedication is a one-way street, but I think that's an easy way to lose good, talented people."

KEY POINTS FOR HARDWIRING RESULTS

Once we get our corporate culture the way we want it, we have to hire people who fit. Otherwise, the wheels fall off the wagon and we quickly find ourselves back where we started.

- Peer interviewing helps reduce turnover. Because they are intimately involved in the hiring process, the staff takes a personal interest in and ownership of a new employee's success.

- We recommend every potential employee read and sign the Performance Standards agreement even before completing the application. We want on board only employees who agree to align their behaviors with our values.

- We also recommend that leaders and employees put together a Decision Matrix to determine the key attributes an employee should have for a particular position. This matrix is important because it:
  - Makes evaluation of all candidates more objective and consistent
  - Ensures the interview team selects the right questions for the attributes that are identified
  - Facilitates the decision-making process and helps companies avoid making emotional decisions

- We recommend leaders schedule new-employee meetings at the 30- and 90-day marks. To make the most of these meetings and to ensure a leader is hitting on the right areas of concern for the new employee, we have the leader use a structured list of questions to discover not only what's *not* going well, but also what *is* going well. This can reduce the new employee turnover by 66 percent.

BUILD INDIVIDUAL ACCOUNTABILITY

Why This Chapter Is Important

FEW BUSINESS OWNERS WEAR ONLY ONE HAT IN THEIR COMPANIES. THEY manage, market, sell, build, and sometimes even clean up. Forty-hour work weeks don't exist. They don't shut down for the day at 5 P.M.

Chances are you have employees with the very same attitude, even though they don't own stock. They believe in the mission of the company and want to make a difference. Such employees are worth their weight in gold. Besides them, there are others in your company whom you may be able to transform into "owners."

An organization that achieves lasting results must have a staff characterized by this strong sense of individual accountability. Follow the strategies in this chapter to help build that critical attribute in all of your employees.

• • •

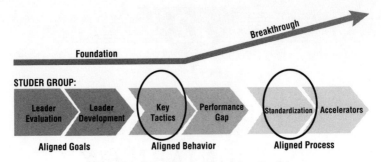

Figure 12.1 Evidence-Based Leadership

At some time in our lives, most of us have lived in a rental property. We may have loved the apartment, condominium, or house that we rented. Perhaps at the beginning we even treated the place like it was ours, but gradually over time our care wasn't quite what it was in the beginning. After a while, we started calling the landlord to fix problems that we could have done ourselves with minimal cash outlay—but why should we? We weren't the owners, and the problems really were not *our* problems.

When we became homeowners, everything changed. The yard, the garage, the plumbing and heating system all became our responsibility. Suddenly, any problems with them *were* our problems. We learned how to repair and replace things in the house that, months before, we never knew existed. We even bought tools and how-to manuals to be sure we took care of our investment. Now that we were owners, *everything* was our problem.

Likewise, organizations are filled with renters and owners. The *renters* are those who have decided what their responsibilities are, and everything that falls outside that realm is "someone else's problem." *Owners* see the big picture. They know that tasks that fall outside their realm of responsibility (as defined, perhaps, in a job description) affect the health of the entire company—and at some point will affect *them* as well.

THE RICH BENEFITS OF EMPLOYEE OWNERSHIP

One day in 1933, a young college student and part-time employee named Ralph Wiley was busy cleaning the lab at Dow Chemical

Company when he came upon a glass vial that he was unable to wash. It seems the vial had become coated with a green substance that was a byproduct of some chemist's experiment. The youthful janitor could have easily dropped the ruined vial in a trashcan and continued with his work. But he knew the scientists at Dow were investigating the properties of various chemical formulations and he suspected they might be interested in a substance that could cling so tightly to a glass container.

Indeed, they were—and subsequent experiments with the chemical resulted in the invention of polyvinylidene chloride film, better known in today's kitchens as "cling wrap" or "plastic wrap." Thanks to a young employee who held himself accountable for more than just pushing a broom, the world has benefited from an invaluable invention. But Wiley's story—individual accountability—isn't that rare.

It's also the story of a secretary who grew tired of scratching out her typing mistakes and invented something with which to "white them out" in order to more efficiently complete her assignments. It's the story of a factory worker who thinks up a way to speed up production or cut waste. It's the story of a computer programmer who finds a faster way to debug a program.

In short, it's the story of thousands of employees who do much more than go through the motions. It's about workers who see themselves as co-owners of the company's mission and goals and who develop a sense of individual accountability to see that the right things get done, and that their company is more efficient, less wasteful, or better at customer service.

As leaders we can set goals, develop plans for reaching them, and help our organizations implement them. We can set up systems that recognize and reward good efforts. However, we don't hit that home run until each employee assumes responsibility for improving the organization. When individual accountability becomes the norm, then companies are poised to move from good to great.

At Holy Cross Hospital in Chicago, our patient surveys told us that the patients had trouble moving around the hospital complex and finding various departments. We were too poor to afford new signs throughout the facility. Instead, we decided to have employees walk the public to wherever they needed to go. It was a big hit with the patients and their families. Our patient satisfaction numbers moved up. As we rewarded their behavior and shared how much it meant to the patients and visitors, the employees, too, became excited about walking people to their destinations. When you saw an employee with visitors, you knew that he was helping them find their way. It became a source of pride to be known as the hospital that cared enough to personally guide visitors. Everyone became accountable for living up to that reputation.

Building individual accountability isn't easy. The rewards aren't always evident to the employees. In the past generation, when a person went to work for a large, well-known company, he saw his job as a lifetime job. He focused on being good at his job and making the plant successful. Today's employees figure that they will have five or six jobs throughout their life. Some are just filling positions until something better comes along. Even if he won't be there forever, the employee still needs to own his own performance and understand how it impacts the organization.

THE DIFFERENCE BETWEEN RENTERS AND OWNERS

Have you ever driven to a store only to arrive seconds after closing time? You knock on the locked door hoping to get the attention of the person sweeping the floor. An *owner* will look up and see if he can help you. A *renter* will keep his head down and act as if he can't hear your knock, or he will point to the clock on the wall and mouth the words, "We're closed."

The renters may be good middle performers, but there are limits to their commitment. As I mentioned before, they have a tendency to divide tasks into "my job" and "not my job."

What we need are more owners in the workplace. Owners care about what is happening around them. They understand their jobs and responsibilities, but they also willingly help others—both fellow employees and staff members. They feel they are part of a team and relish that sense of working together for the common good. They are high performers and solid middle performers who take responsibility for their careers.

Owners connect the dots between what they do and the company's goals and mission, and also see the connection of others' jobs in the organization. Owners seek solutions as problems surface. They answer the phone and care whether the caller gets the answer she needs. They follow up to see if any more can be done to help.

Owners focus on the end result and push past obstacles and barriers. They realize it may take more than a phone call, e-mail, or fax to reach someone. They work smartly and efficiently and don't confuse effort with accomplishment. They figure out how to make things happen.

Owners take things off the leader's desk. They prioritize their work based on the company's goals. They may like some tasks more than others, but you can't tell by their daily work. Owners make things happen in your company. They are never victims.

How can we shift more of your employees from the renter mentality to that of an owner? Sure, we can institute profit-sharing plans and even stock options, but that isn't always practical and it doesn't necessarily change people's attitudes.

However, there are certain initiatives you as a leader can start that will help shift more employees toward the owner attitude and build individual accountability.

STRATEGIES TO TRANSFORM RENTERS INTO OWNERS

We have found that companies that have employees with a strong sense of individual accountability have two things in common: Management shares information openly with the employees, and employees get involved in the hiring and selection process.

There are four strategies a leader can use to build an ownership mentality and individual accountability within a company.

Strategy 1: Transparency/Sharing of Information

As leaders, to act like owners we need to share information with our employees. Rumors and gossip thrive in a vacuum. We've found that openness is the best remedy:

- Hold regular quarterly employee forums with posted agendas.

- Have departmental meetings that review all the pillars and focus on the key behaviors you may be emphasizing that month or quarter.

- Set up communication boards throughout the company where you post newsletters, reports, and announcements.

- Send written communications to the employees—such as regular e-mails or newsletters enclosed in their paycheck envelopes—that let them know what is happening in the company. In the beginning, leaders may have to take time to explain reports and data given to the employees, especially financial information.

Strategy 2: Selection and Hiring

- Let the employees be involved in the hiring process. This technique of peer interviewing builds teamwork and ownership very quickly. It also makes the staff feel more responsible for a new hire's success with the company. Organizations where employees are involved in the selection process outperform others.

- Let employees be a part of the orientation process for their new co-workers.

Strategy 3: Explaining the *Whys*

- We must constantly remind the employees of why a task, job, or even company policy is important. Help them connect the dots so they understand the reasons for leadership decisions.

- In the beginning, we may have to take extra time to explain reports and data given to the employees, especially financial information. We ask open-ended questions to ensure they understand what we tell them.

Strategy 4: Performance Management

We find the biggest holes in most organizations are their lack of both an employee training program and an objective employee evaluation system.

- *Employee training program:* We too often hire bright people and expect them to learn jobs through osmosis. We may give them an employee manual and expect them to read it, but no one helps them beyond giving a few brief details about their job. Good employees need more. We need to establish training programs that go beyond just the regular tasks they perform and look at the professional development of the entire person. Training must take into consideration not only the goals of the company, but the goals of the individual employees.

- *Objective evaluation system:* Evaluations must be based on objective data, individual goals should be set, and the employee's compensation should be tied to those goals.

These initiatives foster an environment that promotes individual accountability, but, of course, they won't be effective unless the employees themselves buy in. As leaders, we need to let them know what our expectations are for them. Don't allow them to adopt "victim" mentalities.

SETTING REASONABLE EXPECTATIONS

What is reasonable to expect from your employees? Where does that dividing line fall between renters and owners, those who do the minimum expected and those who take responsibility for the organization's overall success? Naturally, reasonable expectations will vary by individual business and industry. But there are some common benchmarks for what any dedicated employee should be expected to know and do in the performance of his or her job.

In general, it's reasonable to expect employees to:

1. Acquire and comprehend the information they are given, by:
   • Attending employee forums and departmental meetings
   • Reading communication boards and organizational information.

2. Take an active role in employee selection, by:
   • Participating in the peer interviews
   • Helping with the training and orientation of new hires

3. Learn the *whys,* by:
   • Asking questions to better understand information given
   • Avoiding gossip and helping to combat misinformation.

4. Improve job performance, by:
   • Taking ownership of personal/professional development and seeking out courses and materials that will help with this development.
   • Coaching other employees

Owners do these things without thinking. Others need to be reminded. We need to empower all employees with the information they need to be owners.

The question of encouraging individual accountability among our employees is really nothing other than making sure they know what is important. Regardless of the type of business or number of employees, it is possible to let employees know what's most important in order to make them accountable for the organization's overall success.

An excellent example of this can be seen in the car-rental business. Enterprise Rent-A-Car places a high priority on creating a sense of ownership and customer service among all employees. This is no small feat, considering that Enterprise employs approximately 57,000 people in more than 6,000 offices worldwide. They manage a fleet of more than 700,000 vehicles and generate around $7.4 billion in revenue.

How does a company that large create a universal sense of employee ownership? Enterprise did it by developing a comprehensive system for measuring customer satisfaction on a continual basis. Feedback from nearly 2 million customers is used to rate the performance of *all* office managers and is the cornerstone measure that determines which managers get promoted and which don't. Enterprise's leaders know that no matter how large their sales volume, no matter how high their profits or how tight their expenses, they aren't going to advance in the company if their customers aren't satisfied. That understanding creates a big *why*, which keeps their managers accountable and maintains a strong sense of ownership in the company.

Helping Staff Members Achieve Ownership

At Studer Group, we employ a number of talented organizational coaches, and one of our best is Lucy Crouch, RN. I recently invited Lucy to answer three questions on how staff members can show a sense of ownership. The three questions and her responses to them follow:

1. How can someone who works in the trenches effectively promote change?

One of the best ways to effect change is by our own behavior—role modeling the excellence we would like to see in others. For example, we can demonstrate teamwork, like offering help to co-workers when we are caught up with our own work, or when it appears a co-worker is overwhelmed. We can be sensitive to a co-worker who is having personal problems and maybe not functioning up to par. We can model excellence by not engaging in gossip or enabling others to gossip by listening. We can be willing to confront peers *in a positive way* when we see behavior that is not consistent with the organization's values.

(Continued)

Helping Staff Members (*Continued*)

In addition, this means that when we do not understand why a decision was made, or when we find ourselves wondering about the *why*, we need to go to the appropriate person and ask questions. Instead of complaining that we never get told anything or making up our own reason for the *why*, going to the appropriate source and asking questions models ownership, engagement, and maturity.

Often I find that when staff members are not told everything it is because the assumption was made that we already knew more than we actually did. If we do not ask for the *why*, it is easy for leaders to think that assumption is valid.

Every day when we wake up we have choices. I believe that the most important choices are, first, to have a good attitude, second, to stay connected to purpose, and third, to live by personal values, no matter what. I also believe that adults learn best by example and we do tend to mirror the behavior of those around us.

2. How can employees hardwire excellence in their leaders?

Ultimately, the best way to hardwire excellence in the leader is to take ownership of the leader's success. No leader is perfect. Some leaders are better than other leaders, but I have not met the perfect one yet.

As staff members, it is easy for us to see the leader's faults. Often what we do is tell others about our dissatisfaction with the leader—so our peers know about it, or our spouse knows. But, the one person who can fix the problem is the one person we *do not* tell. Then we wonder why the boss doesn't get better. I was on-site a couple of years ago at a partner hospital and several managers who reported to the same senior leader pulled me aside to complain about their boss. They cited a couple of specific issues with this leader. When I asked them if they had brought these issues to their leader's attention, they all said no.

One leader a bit angrily said to me, "I should not have to tell my boss how to be a good boss—she is the leader. She should know." I then asked her, "If one of your employees was unhappy with something you were doing and had some suggestions for how you could be a better leader, would you want that employee to tell you?" Her response was a quick *yes*. My response was, "Why should it be different for *your* leader?"

In all fairness, the reason we do not tell the boss is that this is a very hard thing to do. It is very uncomfortable and, frankly, it is easier to take the victim's way out by complaining to others. But when we do that, the leader misses an opportunity to improve.

Try rounding on your boss. At Studer Group, we teach leaders to round on staff for the purposes of increasing employee satisfaction by harvesting wins, seizing recognition opportunities, and identifying system and equipment issues. We know that over time if a leader rounds well it results in the building of a good relationship—one that has a wealthy emotional bank account.

Rounding on your leader helps you develop a positive relationship with him that makes open communication easier. Give your leader some recognition by commenting about something he has done well. Then ask your leader if there is something you can do for him. Over time, this should result in a relationship strong enough to allow you to more easily give feedback to your boss.

3. Don't we have the right to have excellent leaders who really listen to us?

Yes. However, I think leaders need help to achieve excellence; no leader can do it single-handedly or alone in a vacuum. Leaders need help from their boss, from their peers, and from their employees. I do not think there is a leader in this country who gets up in the morning and, as she is getting dressed for work, is thinking about how she can be mediocre or how she can fail her staff. We all want to be successful, and the reality is that we all need each other to achieve excellence.

KEY POINTS FOR HARDWIRING RESULTS

- To improve individual accountability at your organization you must do all you can to create an ownership mentality throughout your organization. Owners not only focus on their jobs and responsibilities, but they take the time to help others as well, creating a team environment in the company.

- We can foster more owners in our organization by sharing information and allowing employees to take part in the selection process. Four strategies can be used to help them make the transformation from renter to owner:

  1. *Transparent communication:* Keeping lines of communication open between employees and leaders helps reduce the spread of gossip and rumors.
  2. *Selection and hiring:* Using hiring processes such as peer interviewing helps build teamwork and ownership among all of your employees.
  3. *Explaining the* whys: Help your employees connect the dots so they understand the reasoning behind leadership decisions.
  4. *Performance management:* Provide necessary employee training and evaluation.

- To help your employees reach high levels of individual accountability, it's important that you provide clear expectations. Responsibilities vary from organization to organization, but, in general, employees should be expected to:
  - Acquire and comprehend the information they are given.
  - Take an active role in employee selection.
  - Learn the *whys*.
  - Improve job performance.

CHAPTER 13

HARVEST INTELLECTUAL CAPITAL

Why This Chapter Is Important

IN THE PREVIOUS CHAPTER INDIVIDUAL ACCOUNTABILITY WAS DISCUSSED.
This chapter is about harvesting employee innovation—a natural
outgrowth of employee ownership.

Employees are an amazing source of untapped ideas. They are
the ones who—metaphorically speaking—make the widgets, package the widgets, ship the widgets, and deal with the customers who
sing the praises of (and sometimes complain about) the widgets.
Why *wouldn't* they see more clearly than anyone else how to make
the widgets more quickly, more efficiently, more attractive to a
wider marketplace—or just plain *better?*

They would. It's just that they're so busy doing their jobs that
they don't think about making your company more efficient, productive, and profitable. They may not have been asked to think
about it. It's up to you, the leader, to remedy that.

In the article "Double Loop Learning in Organizations," written by Chris Argyris and published in *Harvard Business Review,* they

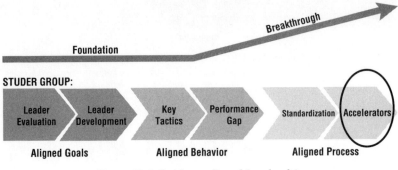

Figure 13.1 Evidence-Based Leadership

call this single-loop and double-loop communication. Single loop is "leader to employee." Double loop is "leader to employee and employee back to leader." The article showed that sometimes leaders don't ask employees for ideas, when in reality employees want to provide input.

In this chapter are some practical ideas for harvesting the kinds of bright ideas that can come only from the people who are intimately involved with the day-to-day nitty-gritty of providing products and services to customers.

• • •

Employees have great ideas. After all, they do the hard work of the company day in and day out. Who could possibly be better positioned to come up with ideas on how to improve that work? Intellectual capital is the richest and most plentiful natural resource a company possesses. It's a leader's job to harvest that resource. Doing so drives individual accountability, fosters a culture of ownership, and can have a significant impact on your bottom line.

This means more than a suggestion box where employees may submit ideas (if the spirit moves them) or (and this is more likely the case) may *not*. We have found that having suggestion boxes scattered throughout a facility doesn't work very well. It's too passive an approach. For suggestion boxes to actually yield workable results, leaders must drive the program.

When I was working at Holy Cross Hospital, we were deeply focused on improving patient satisfaction results. Many of the ideas we implemented during this effort came from the staff. Making sure the wheels on our food carts were changed regularly and taking care not to overuse the hospitalwide public address system are two examples that come to mind. After a while, we began calling these suggestions *Bright Ideas*.

After Holy Cross won the American Hospital Association's Great Comeback Award in 1995 and began to get national media exposure for its service excellence, people from other hospitals would visit to learn how we turned around our operations. Invariably, these visitors would zero in on a tool or technique that they wanted to bring back to their own organizations. Our Bright Ideas program was one of the more popular initiatives they tried to adopt.

I say *tried* because, frankly, many of these efforts to replicate Holy Cross's successes fell short in the implementation phase. (We kept track of their progress.) While these hospitals might benchmark a program and roll it, they often missed some critical (and obscure) detail upon which the whole plan hinged. This is not to criticize them or brag about us but to illustrate how complicated these seemingly simple ideas really were.

One of the organizations whose leaders came to visit us in the spring of 1995 was Baptist Hospital from Pensacola, Florida. It had been struggling with high employee turnover and low patient satisfaction. The Bright Ideas program was one of the management tools these visitors brought back to Pensacola to implement.

Later, when I became president of Baptist Hospital, I spoke with the program coordinator about her experience with this program. She told me she had placed suggestions boxes in the employee areas, had printed Bright Ideas forms for the employees to fill out, and had coffee mugs screened with lightbulbs as giveaways. When I asked how many bright ideas Baptist was actually collecting, she replied, "That's the problem. We aren't getting many."

MOVING BEYOND THE SUGGESTION BOX

All of the tangible tools were in place, so what was missing from the program? It was proper leader training focused on outcomes and accountability for results. The leaders at Baptist Hospital simply hadn't been trained in how to harvest quality ideas from their employees. Such training needs to include details such as: how to garner enthusiasm for the program and encourage participation, how to help employees focus their ideas on the organization's goals, how to say no to an idea without saying no to the employee, and how to tweak an average idea so that it truly shines. Proper leadership training makes the difference between a Bright Ideas program that truly fosters innovation and one that consists of a dust-covered suggestion box.

To emphasize the importance of driving the Bright Ideas program, we recommend that an organization build it into their leadership evaluations. We tell leaders: "Unless every employee in your department has implemented a bright idea, it will be impossible for you to get a good evaluation." When this is done and you properly train your leaders on how to seek ideas, then your bright ideas will be successful.

Please note: This program won't necessarily unleash a flood of brilliant ideas from day one. Progress will be incremental. At Baptist, an early bright idea from a lab employee centered on reducing the size of a bag that held a particular product. It saved us $2,000.00. No, this idea didn't have a huge financial impact, but it paved the way for employee ownership and greater individual accountability. After we trained our leaders better, our Bright Ideas initiative worked so successfully that we budgeted for $1.2 million in cost savings each year from the program.

To further encourage submissions, employees who participated were publicly recognized. Big barrels were placed in the cafeteria with names of all employees who submitted ideas. Once a month, we drew names from the barrel and awarded prizes to those whose names were chosen.

Even though the prizes were small, the drawings were big events. Afterward, we listed all the ideas that came in, along with the names of who submitted them, so employees could be inspired by the thought processes of others. After all the ideas had been reviewed by the oversight committee, those who suggested the ones that were most feasible and that offered the most significant savings were honored at our quarterly and annual employee meetings.

These Bright Ideas programs centered on improving efficiency and cutting costs. That's appropriate in a hospital setting. But bright ideas needn't be limited to "belt-tightening" suggestions. What if a company, say, packages organic foods and distributes them to grocery stores? A Bright Ideas program at that company might draw suggestions that relate to breaking into new markets— for instance, creating a division that markets its healthful foods to upscale day-care centers and retirement communities.

A Bright Idea with Sticking Power

Even for an innovative company like 3M, the creation and successful marketing of Post-It Notes took a concerted effort by many dedicated individuals. In 1968, 3M scientist Dr. Spence Silver developed a new adhesive whose most distinguishing characteristic was that it didn't stick very well. For years, 3M struggled trying to come up with uses for the slightly sticky glue, but with limited success. Then, in the late 1970s, Art Fry, a new-product researcher at 3M, came up with a novel concept. Fry was frustrated that the scraps of paper he used to keep places in his hymnal during choir practice at church kept falling out whenever the hymnal was opened. Could Silver's adhesive solve the problem?

It could, and it did, but Fry's new-product idea was met with plenty of skepticism. Who would want to pay for a product that merely replaced scrap paper? But Fry and a few dedicated individuals persisted. They distributed Post-It pads throughout 3M headquarters and created numerous fans among professionals and clerical staff. At the same time, other Post-It advocates aggressively test-marketed the product with potential customers. Finally, internal resistance to the new product was overcome and Post-It Notes became one of 3M's best-selling products. In 1981, 3M named Fry's brainchild "Outstanding New Product" of the year.

To hardwire bright ideas into the company—and thereby foster individual accountability and a sense of ownership across the board—we recommend telling employees they must come up with one *implemented* bright idea in order to receive a good evaluation. This will motivate them to take the program seriously. Leaders can further champion bright ideas at departmental meetings by saying, "Please share something that's working well in your department that could help others."

Here are some practical steps for implementing a Bright Ideas program for an organization:

1. *Set clear goals for the Bright Ideas program.* This will provide overall direction for the program. The company might want to focus initially on a particular pillar. Or it might encourage participation by insisting that every employee submit at least one bright idea to kick off the initiative. Later, as the program gains momentum and the organization matures, leaders might ask employees to contribute ideas that will improve operational efficiency in their own departments.

2. *Communicate Bright Ideas goals.* This is done in two stages: first in the department head meetings and then in "town hall" meetings for all employees. How the program will work should be explained. The initial goals and the overall direction of the program are also communicated clearly. Leaders should tell the employees how ideas will be recognized and implemented.

3. *Establish a process for reviewing bright ideas.* All ideas should be collected and sent to one center where they are reviewed and assigned for appropriate follow-up. Senior leadership should receive copies, too.

   At the Cleveland Clinic Foundation, the CEO reads every idea that's submitted. Because of his level of commitment, 65 percent of the CCF's 14,000 employees have submitted bright ideas, resulting in over 9,000 ideas in the first 10 months of the initiative.

4. *Reward and recognize for innovation.* An employee is recognized upon receipt of an idea, upon its implementation, and after a number of his or her ideas have been applied. This three-phase approach to recognition continually communicates the importance of employee contributions. All employees learn that their ideas are important and that they will be rewarded when positive, constructive change has occurred.

5. *Train leaders how to respond to bright ideas.* Leader response is a critical element in your program's success. A leader needs to learn how to acknowledge and thank staff members for their ideas and how to evaluate ideas based on objective criteria. Focus on ways to say *yes,* rather than rejecting a bright idea. Seek to reinforce all sincere efforts in this arena whenever you can. In fact, if even a so-so idea is budget neutral, might improve efficiency, and might encourage the employee to submit more ideas, implement it on a trial basis.

   Leaders also need to know how to go back to an employee and help her further tweak an idea that has promise or use a weak idea as an opportunity to transform a reactive employee into a proactive, problem-solving employee. Whether a suggestion is accepted or rejected, the leader must be comfortable communicating his decision to the employee in a way that encourages more ideas.

   > At Holy Cross Hospital in Chicago, we had very little money for marketing. An employee came up with the following bright idea aimed at publicizing our hospital: We should give every employee a windbreaker with our corporate logo on the back. I immediately saw two glaring problems with the idea: (1) We had no control over what someone might do while wearing a "Holy Cross" windbreaker (i.e., what if Joe from Radiology got busted for a crime and ended up, emblazoned with our logo, on the evening news?), and (2) we had far more pressing needs (e.g., basic hospital equipment) for the money the windbreakers would cost.
   >
   > I thanked the employee for her suggestion and for thinking about using word of mouth to market the hospital. Then I

asked, "What are some other ways employees might carry the message about the hospital?" That question led to the employees brainstorming ways of creating positive word of mouth. Later, when Holy Cross was ready to launch a new health care program, we gave each employee two door hangers. First, we explained the new program described on the door hanger. Then, we asked each employee to go out and hang two door hangers in his or her neighborhood. This accomplished three things:

1. Since we had about 1,000 employees, 2,000 community members learned about our new program very quickly.
2. The employees learned about the new program so they could tell their family and friends about it.
3. We got the employees to feel more a part of the hospital by taking a positive action.

So a rejected idea—buying windbreakers—ultimately led to Holy Cross employees going out in the community *en masse* and serving as our marketing company.

6. *Establish an oversight committee to rescue bright ideas that are rejected too quickly by the immediate supervisor.* Leaders are only human. Sometimes we fail to see the true, positive impact of an idea. We suggest that an oversight committee be put in place designed to either give all rejected ideas a quick once-over, or serve as a second-chance committee to which an employee can appeal if he thinks his bright idea was unfairly passed over.

A graphic designer at a community newspaper suggested that all designers be allowed to speak directly with advertisers about their ads. At the time, the ad sales representative was the only contact with the clients. The production manager rejected this idea, fearing the advertising director might object. However, the paper's oversight team approved the idea and created service teams comprised of a graphic artist, an ad sales rep, and an accounting staff member for each advertiser. The number

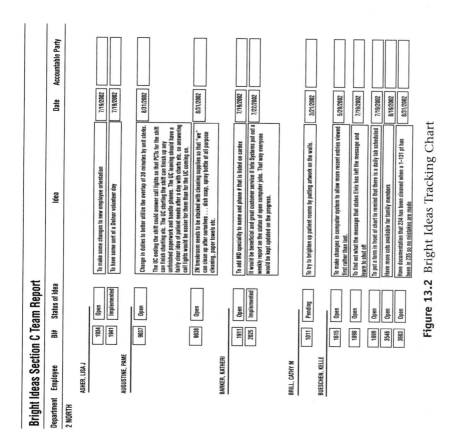

Figure 13.2 Bright Ideas Tracking Chart

of complaints about ad designs was reduced by one-third, and contract renewal increased by 25 percent.

7. *Define methods for tracking and accountability.* As we build individual accountability within our organizations, leaders must realize that the principle applies to us as well. We must also be accountable to our employees. That's why we must put in place a solid tracking system for the Bright Ideas program. An employee should hear within 30 days of submittal whether his idea has been accepted or rejected so that he will be motivated to offer more suggestions. In fact, make adhering to this policy part of the leader's 90-day plan and annual leader performance evaluation in order to give it teeth.

Assign someone to maintain a tracking log (Figure 13.2) that identifies ideas being reviewed by the oversight committee, how many have been approved, rejected, or sent back to the leader for improvement, when the employee was notified, how the ideas have been implemented, how much money has been saved, and how the organization has allocated awards.

Once this groundwork is in place, the company is ready to launch its Bright Ideas program and begin harvesting the intellectual capital of the organization. Its employees will become stakeholders in the company's success as their ideas and suggestions are implemented. The company will eventually be able to budget the cost savings from their ideas. Many of our clients have enjoyed successful Bright Ideas programs that yielded (and continue to yield) measurable results. The concept has worked for countless organizations. It can work for yours, too.

KEY POINTS FOR HARDWIRING RESULTS

- Take advantage of your employees' intellectual capital and the bright ideas they produce. Implementing a program that allows you to harvest this important resource helps drive individual accountability, fosters a culture of ownership, and can have a significant impact on your bottom line.

- For a Bright Ideas program to work better than the antiquated suggestion box method, your leaders will need to be on board, driving the program and encouraging employee participation. To garner great ideas from the program, leaders will need to help employees focus their bright ideas on the company's goals and will need to learn how to say no to ideas that won't work without saying no to the employee.

- To successfully implement the Bright Ideas program at your organization, here are some practical steps to follow:
  1. Set clear goals for the Bright Ideas program.
  2. Communicate Bright Ideas goals.
  3. Establish a process for reviewing bright ideas.
  4. Reward and recognize for innovation.
  5. Train leaders how to respond to bright ideas.
  6. Establish an oversight committee to rescue bright ideas that are rejected too quickly by the immediate supervisor.
  7. Define methods for tracking and accountability.

C H A P T E R

14

RECOGNIZE AND
REWARD SUCCESS

Why This Chapter Is Important

RECOGNIZED BEHAVIOR GETS REPEATED. WHAT WE REWARD, WE GET MORE
of. That's why it's so critical that leaders recognize and reward employees who are doing all the right things: bringing in new business, pleasing customers, and generally taking ownership of problems that come their way.

However, reward and recognition isn't easy for many leaders.
We don't realize that we need to do it as often as we do, and furthermore, we're not trained in the art of catching people doing
something right.

This chapter explains how to overcome the barriers that keep us
from rewarding and recognizing people who deserve it. But most
important of all, it sets forth guidelines for hardwiring a reward and
recognition system that motivates more employees to practice—
and *keep on practicing*—the behaviors that lead to results that last.

• • •

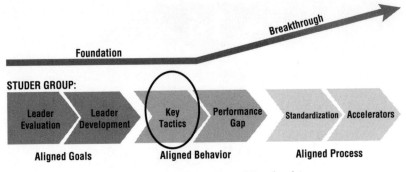

Figure 14.1 Evidence-Based Leadership

Are you chronically overrewarded in life? Do you receive too much recognition on the job? If your boss calls you and says, "Come down to my office. I want to see you," is your first thought, "Here comes more reward and recognition"?

If you laughed at the opening paragraph, pretend your employees were asked the same question. Guess what? In all likelihood, you'd hear the same laughter. Why? Because providing recognition is not a natural talent; it must be taught.

You could be thinking, "I'm not going to recognize people for what they're paid to do. They are *supposed* to be nice to the customers. I am not rewarding anybody for being nice. The next thing you'll be telling me is to recognize employees for smiling." (Read on to see why this "smiling" example isn't a wild exaggeration!)

Recognized behavior gets repeated. When what's supposed to be happening isn't happening, leaders must get employees to change their behavior or start over with a whole new crew. (Yes, some likely will have to go). Leaders might have to start recognizing success at a level that they'd rather not, but they have to start somewhere. Besides, recognizing and rewarding success feels good to leaders and employees alike.

When I was in a hospital administration, many of our departments were in the process of improving their patient satisfaction. However, one department was dragging. After about six months, we made a leadership change. The new leader came in and began giving out *WOW* awards. The WOW awards (Figure 14.2) were little

WOW!
CARD

Name _Cindy S._
Dept. _Marketing_
Date _12/5/04_

TODAY YOU "WOWED" ME WHEN YOU _Oversaw the BKD_
Quality Award Billboard on I-65. It blew me away
when I first saw it. You live Commit to Excellence and
Communicate at all levels and I appreciate it.

Submitted by _James M._

THANK YOU! Department _Quality Resources_

Figure 14.2 The WOW Award

pieces of paper that said, "Wow, you did a good job!" If you got
five of them, you could go to the gift shop and exchange them for
a gift.

Well, like all organizations, this hospital had a tendency to take
something simple and inadvertently make it complex. Friction began to develop between the leaders over the WOW awards. Some
supervisors felt other managers gave them out too easily. If you
worked in Department A, the WOW awards were handed out like
candy. In Department B, you'd have to cure a disease to get a WOW
award.

All the leaders were brought together and asked to outline examples of good employee behavior and then vote on whether each
hypothetical person warranted recognition. So we brought in the
supervisors. We had some good examples that clearly highlighted
the differences in leaders' approaches.

Suddenly the new leader of the one department that had lagging
results stood up and said, "Please don't do this to me. You're way
ahead of me, so unlike me, you don't have to recognize daily behaviors that seem like common sense. I'm in the second percentile in
the entire country in patient satisfaction. So if an employee comes
in and smiles the whole day today, I will tell her, 'Nice job smiling
today.' And I'll give her a WOW award. Please don't make it too
hard for employees to get recognized."

The bottom line is that the administrative team walked out of
the meeting with the agreement that we would trust the leaders to
recognize and reward their employees on their decision. My point
is that if employees are at a place where being rewarded for smiling

makes sense, then fine—go ahead and reward them! You've got to start somewhere.

Small Prizes Can Have a Big Impact

Sometimes even simple awards can take on a "larger-than-life" significance. The following story, reported by *Inc.* magazine, proves the amazing impact of reward and recognition. At the Phelps Group, a Santa Monica, CA, marketing firm, the last item on the agenda of the organization's weekly meetings is the bestowing of an "Atta-Boy/Atta-Girl" award in recognition of excellent effort. The original award was a two-foot-square wooden plaque, but over the years recipients began adding personal touches to the plaque by gluing quirky items to the award, including a Pez dispenser, pennies, pictures, and so forth. Each week the previous winner selects the new winner and passes the award on at the end of the team meeting. The highly decorated plaque has become a powerful incentive for employees both to work well and to recognize others who work well.

REWARD AND RECOGNITION CHANGE AS YOU MATURE

Of course, the behaviors you reward and recognize *do* change as the employees and the organization improve. When I was at Holy Cross Hospital in Chicago, we started out with very low patient satisfaction. When we reached the 40th percentile, the hospital had a huge celebration in the cafeteria. We gave out charts showing that we were at the 40th percentile and discussed what we'd have to do to get to the 75th percentile. A year later, after we had hit the 99th percentile in patient satisfaction, we dropped down one month to the 72nd percentile. You would have thought the roof had caved in. We were 32 percentage points above what we had rewarded with a big celebration just a year ago, but now we were asking the department heads for action plans. Why? Because the hospital had matured. It now had higher standards.

Reward and recognition doesn't mean accepting poor performance. There's a world of difference between accepting poor performance and recognizing good performance that isn't yet perfect. Here is one of my favorite analogies that illustrate this point:

In my seminars I often ask the audience how many people have a little girl between the ages of three and nine. There's a show of hands and I'll ask one mother her daughter's name. For this example, let's say that the girl's name is Katye. I'll ask, "How old is Katye?" The mom will reply that she's four. "Is Katye completely potty trained—poo-poo, pee-pee, both?" The audience laughs. The mom looks at me like I'm crazy and says, almost indignantly, *of course!*

Here's an aside. If you're wondering why I don't ask for examples of boys, it's because I've tried this before and the answers were quite different. I'd ask, "How old is Billy?" The mom would say eight. "Well, is Billy completely potty trained—poo-poo and pee-pee?" The reply, after a moment's hesitation, would always be, "What do you mean by *completely?*"

[Note: From this admittedly less-than-scientific survey performed before hundreds of audiences, I've finally come to the conclusion that no human male is ever completely potty trained—no matter what age!]

Now, let's get back to little Katye. I'll ask the mom, "So what happened when Katye went poo-poo on the potty for the first time?" Now, the mother may be a little shy, but then she'll start describing how the family celebrated this momentous occasion. They cheered. They clapped. Maybe they took snapshots of the kid on the potty chair. They called Grandma. One time I asked, "Oh, what'd your mom say when you told her your daughter poo-pooed on the potty?" She said, "Don't flush it. I want to come look at it."

People go quite wild the first time their child poo-poos on the potty. And then, of course, when I ask, "What happens after a few months when Katye goes poo-poo on the potty?" And the mom says, "I remind Katye to flush." So we move recognition to flushing. In other words, there's no reward and recognition then. Why? Because we've moved on to other, more advanced behavior.

So with reward and recognition, we've got to realize that where we're starting—meaning the behavior we initially reward—*isn't* where we're going to finish. However, as I said before, you have to start somewhere.

WHAT HOLDS US BACK?

Most people have no idea how much we need to reward and recognize in order to change behavior. Psychologists tell us that it takes three compliments to counterbalance every criticism. Many

---

Why Leaders Don't Compliment: Some Common Myths and Excuses

People really need recognition and specific feedback, and a good compliment provides both. But too many leaders resist giving them, for a variety of reasons. Ask yourself: *Do I harbor any of these beliefs and attitudes about complimenting my employees?*

- *Big Head:* "If I compliment them too much, they'll get a big head!"

- *Complacency:* "If I tell them they did a good job, they'll get complacent!"

- *Martyrdom:* "I don't need a compliment; why should they?"

- *Another Day, Another Dollar:* "They should just be happy with a day's work for a day's pay—in fact, they should be grateful to have a job at all!"

- *Scrooge Mentality:* "I can give out only so many compliments a week!"

- *Pride:* "This is hokey!"

Remember, recognized behavior gets repeated. It's okay if you feel uncomfortable as you begin to compliment. Just do it . . . and know that it will feel more natural with time.

of us grew up in the 1960s and 1970s, an era when the ratio between positive and negative statements was one-to-one, so achieving three-to-one balance means overcoming a lifelong habit. By the way, we're very good with the one negative. I find most leaders do not need a lot of practice in criticism, except in how to do it in a more professional manner without an ugly confrontation.

Why don't we give more compliments? For one thing, you've got to really watch for what someone is doing right and most of us haven't mastered that art. My work as a Special Education teacher really helped me hone this skill.

We had a 14-year-old girl who was profoundly challenged. When it was snack time, she'd get so excited about Popsicles that she'd put the frozen treat in her mouth without unwrapping it. The first day she pulled the paper off the Popsicle before she put it in her mouth, it was like an Olympic gold medal celebration.

In Special Education, you get very good at looking at little incremental improvements, because they are deeply important to the parents and child. In the workplace, leaders need to develop the skill sets for noticing incremental improvement, because rewarded and recognized behavior gets repeated.

THE AMAZING POWER OF REWARD AND RECOGNITION

I could write a whole book just on stories of people telling me how it felt to be recognized. I've got story after story about people getting thank you notes from their boss and framing them or carrying them to work in their purse. One employee shared that at a baby shower in her home, her mother-in-law saw a thank you note from her boss on the refrigerator and passed it around the room for everyone to read. Everyone said, "I wish I worked where you work."

Steve, who is president of an organization, had an employee die in an auto accident. The employee's mother called him after she found a thank you note from her daughter's leader in her daughter's mail. She told the leader how much all the thank you notes had meant to her daughter and urged the leader to keep writing them to other employees.

Recognition cannot be minimized. It is a motivator—recognized behavior gets repeated. When we compliment a child on potty training, she moves to something else. When we compliment an employee on finishing her work on time and in a professional manner, she keeps on doing it and even improves.

Here is one example I use when I visit organizations and discuss reward and recognition:

> Let's say I have two employees, Sam and Larry. I approach my first employee and say, "Sam, I was walking through your work area today. I noticed it was really clean. The shelves are all stocked so professionally. I looked at your latest customer satisfaction feedback and it was just excellent. I really want to thank you for keeping your shelves so nice and clean and for providing great customer service. You really set an example of professionalism."
>
> Now, next to Superb Sam sits Less-Than-Superb Larry. To him, I simply say, "Hi."
>
> How long will it take Larry to move his behavior to a level resembling Sam's? For 90 percent of employees, it happens almost immediately. The other 10 percent will miss the point entirely and you will have to take more direct action to align and adjust their behavior. (A story for another chapter!)

When you recognize behavior, it's important to be specific. Nobody wants to hear, "Hey, you're doing a good job." Tell the employee specifically *why* he's doing a good job. Not only does it encourage him to keep up the good work, it increases the odds that other people will follow suit because they now understand exactly what the boss is looking for.

HARDWIRING THANK YOU NOTES

We at Studer Group are big advocates of sending thank you notes to employees who do an excellent job. Our work with organizations has taught us that hardwiring a thank you note system—in which leaders send and track a specific number of notes in a given time frame—has a profound impact on employee retention and customer satisfaction.

At first, A company should literally *mandate* a specific number of thank you notes for its leaders to send based on the number of people they supervise. At first glance, you might assume that being systematic about thank you notes creates another meaningless layer of bureaucracy. But thank you notes don't just happen. If they aren't hardwired into an organization, they won't get written. And thank you notes are just too powerful a tool *not* to use. I have found that people love receiving thank you notes. They cherish them. They carry them around in purses and briefcases. They even frame them.

Of course, thank you notes must be done right to be effective. Impersonal "generic" notes—or worse, fill-in-the-blank templates—don't make anyone feel rewarded or recognized. Furthermore, they can't be randomly sent via a lottery system (i.e., *I drew Bob Smith's name out of a hat so he gets a thank you note this month*). They must be merit-based. (See Figure 14.3.)

I have found that the best thank you notes are:

- *Specific, not general.* A thank you note that focuses on something specific the recipient has done is far more effective than one that says "Hey, nice job!"

- *Handwritten if possible.* There's something authentic and special about a handwritten note. I've been told by countless employees that they'd rather receive a three-sentence handwritten note than a two-page typed letter.

July 15, 2005

Dear Amanda,

John Smith wrote me the nicest note about the number of positive comments you have been getting on the patient satisfaction surveys. He also told me you are helping interview staff for the unit. This is very important. Thank you for being at our organization!
Sincerely,
Quint

July 16, 2007

Dear Mike,
Thank you so much for all of your hard work. We enjoy having you as part of our team.

Sincerely,
Quint

Figure 14.3 Sample Employee Thank You Note

- *Sent to the employee's home.* When an employee receives a thank you note at home, it somehow feels more personal than one laid on her desk along with a stack of reports and memos.

Over time, sending thank you notes will become an ingrained habit with your leaders. You will be able to do away with requiring a certain number of thank yous—they will occur consistently and spontaneously.

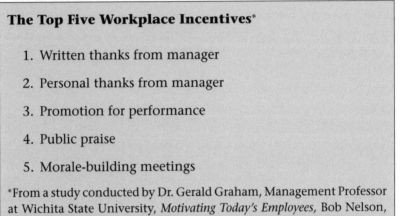

The Top Five Workplace Incentives*

1. Written thanks from manager

2. Personal thanks from manager

3. Promotion for performance

4. Public praise

5. Morale-building meetings

*From a study conducted by Dr. Gerald Graham, Management Professor at Wichita State University, *Motivating Today's Employees,* Bob Nelson, Talent+, 1998.

HOW TO SCHEDULE AND IMPLEMENT REWARD AND RECOGNITION

You have to schedule reward and recognition. People sometimes balk at this, but it's necessary. Spontaneity doesn't work. If spontaneity did work, then we'd probably be bringing our spouses cards and gifts a lot more frequently than just on birthdays and anniversaries.

1. *Hardwire it into your rounding.* Rounding is a management tool you read about in Chapter 2. It involves visiting departments with specific goals in mind. One goal should be to reward and recognize good performers. Enlist the supervisor's help to create a rounding log that tells you who deserves to be recognized and what's going well.

2. *Put your recognition system in writing.* Set up a system whereby managers report on a regular basis which employees deserve to be thanked and recognized and specifically *why*. You must have a hardwired system in place that consistently gives you feedback on individual employees.

3. *Encourage group celebrations.* I'm not advocating group compliments, but find creative ways to celebrate team accomplishments. Here's an example from my own career:

> At Holy Cross Hospital in Chicago, we were broke. We were trying to collect money that was owed us. The Finance Department put a bell in their department. Whenever they hit their weekly goal for collections, they'd ring this bell. And they'd always have cookies sitting beside the bell to (literally) sweeten the celebration.
>
> After a while the whole floor got programmed that when the bell rang it meant the Finance Department had had a good week and it was time to celebrate. We'd all join them in the cookie-fest and let them know what a great job they had done. See? You can literally hardwire celebrations when you put systems in place.
>
> TGI Friday's restaurants also keep a bell by the bar, which bartenders ring every time someone makes a tip. While ringing the bell may help to motivate customers to "dig a little deeper," it's really intended to keep the service team focused on delivering excellent customer service.

4. *Be consistent with your reward and recognition.* At Studer Group we had a client that had a small department with only 12 employees. The manager started an Employee of the Month (EOM) award, but was worried that it might seem hokey. She had a new employee, Susan, who won the EOM award. Susan was later diagnosed with cancer and eventually died. At her funeral, that award was in her casket. We underestimate the impact of reward and recognition, and we shouldn't.

We've all gone into restaurants and department stores and seen plaques honoring employees, but so often they aren't maintained. Maybe the last entry is March 2002. I think that's sad. We as leaders sometimes rationalize that they don't mean much to the employees . . . but they do.

> In Sarasota, one organization enhanced the EOM program by adding a box in the break room where employees could leave congratulatory notes for the winner. When one of the winners, Dave, passed away, the manager and the nurses attended the wake. The manager saw that Dave wore the Employee of the Month pin on his lapel. Dave's wife hugged her and said, "Dave talked about you all the time. He kept that box of notes at his bedside and read them every day." Reward and recognition are never hokey, especially if we take care in how we give them.

Here's the bottom line: Reward and recognition isn't natural for leaders. If it were, everybody reading this book would feel appreciated. Do you? When he was discussing his religious experiences, William James wrote that one of the things people want most in life is to feel appreciated. Abraham Maslow believed that for people to be self-actualized they must feel that they are doing meaningful work.

The fact that you can help people feel appreciated should make you realize what a high calling leadership really is. Reward and recognition not only tells employees that their work is worthwhile, but the very act of providing it gives our own jobs meaning. By elevating the people we lead, we elevate ourselves.

KEY POINTS FOR HARDWIRING RESULTS

- Recognized behavior gets repeated. Reward and recognition ensures that employees make the effort to keep up the good work.

- When recognizing behavior you must be specific. You can't simply say, "You're doing a great job!" By being specific, you encourage the employee to keep doing what he's doing and you communicate to your other employees the kind of behavior that you think is important for your organization.

- Hardwire a thank you note system in which leaders send and track a specific number of notes in a given period of time. thank you notes should be based on merit and recognize a specific behavior or accomplishment. Ideally, they should be handwritten and sent to the employee's home.

- By having a plan in place you will ensure that you regularly give employees who are doing a great job the recognition they deserve. Spontaneity doesn't work. Here's how to schedule reward and recognition:
  - Hardwire reward and recognition into your rounding.
  - Put your recognition system in writing. This ensures managers will report on a daily basis who needs to be recognized and why.
  - Encourage group celebrations when your employees do well as a team.
  - Be consistent with your reward and recognition. Employee of the Month programs are a great way to achieve this goal— just be sure to maintain them over time.

CHAPTER 15

FIND AND RECOGNIZE
DIFFERENCE MAKERS

Why This Chapter Is Important

HUMAN BEINGS NEED STORIES. PARTICULARLY, WE NEED STORIES ABOUT people who make a difference. These stories prove to us that we can be better than we are now, and that we can improve the lives of others. Stories about "difference makers"—also known as *heroes*—inspire us. By showing us someone who did something great, they give excellence a human face.

In particular, I've always been intrigued by the power of employee stories. Every organization we've worked with has had those standout employees everyone talks about. These heroes embody your highest values. They give people an ideal to rally around. They bring co-workers together and motivate them in profound and powerful ways.

In this chapter, you'll learn how to find the difference makers in your organization and spread the good news about them. These stories will become your culture—and it's your culture that drives your organization to achieve results that last.

• • •

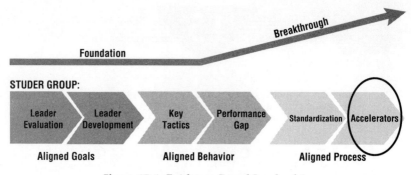

Figure 15.1 Evidence-Based Leadership

The word *hero* is both overused and underused in our society. We often call athletes and Hollywood celebrities "heroes." We buy their books, flock to their (often violent) movies, and purchase the products they endorse. By doing so, we send a message to our children that they should strive to emulate these larger-than-life figures. Yet what truly heroic things have they done? Some deserve the applause, while others may not.

Meanwhile, we may miss teachers like Jacci, who for the past 24 years has taught at Hallmark Elementary School in the poorest neighborhood in Pensacola, Florida. Jacci recruits mentors for her students. She goes out into the community, talking face-to-face to struggling parents and teaching their children lessons about pride and self-esteem.

I think difference makers are the world's real heroes, the people who are working to make things better. You know who they are: those men and women who give extra effort without thinking of themselves. They may not get a lot of glory, but they are deeply appreciated by the people whose lives they touch.

Look around. There may be a difference maker working tirelessly in your organization—an executive who works late to help a client meet a critical deadline or a store clerk who lovingly comforts a crying child who has somehow gotten separated from his mother.

All organizations have difference makers—people who do more than what is in their job descriptions. Their actions embody the purpose, mission, and positive culture of your company. It's important that you recognize these difference makers and share their stories with others both inside and outside the organization.

THE POWER OF HERO RECOGNITION

Recognized behavior gets repeated. Sharing the stories of the organization's difference makers goes a long way toward giving employees a sense of purpose. I had a CEO client share this story of one of his company's difference makers:

> The CEO heard that one of his hospital's patient transporters, Steve, had been invited by the family to attend the wake of a former patient. It piqued his interest so much that he asked around and discovered that everyone had an incredible story about Steve. For instance, Steve carried socks with him to put on patients' cold feet as he wheeled them from room to room.
>
> The CEO shared this story at an Employee Forum and invited even more Steve stories.
>
> Three weeks later, Steve's father, who lived in a distant city, died. The employees took up a collection and bought Steve a plane ticket so he could be at his father's funeral.

Sharing Steve's story with his fellow employees not only encouraged them to imitate his extraordinary personal care for the patients, it also built a stronger sense of team so that they all wanted to help him in his time of crisis.

Difference makers also are those employees who know when to bend the rules for the right reasons:

> At Baptist Hospital in Pensacola, we instituted a program where nurses called patients after they had been discharged. One nurse called a patient who said she was doing fine. However, the patient, who needed a wheelchair to get around, wished she could go outside. Her husband was older and had health problems, too. They couldn't afford a ramp.

The nurse was so moved that she called the Plant Operations Department and told them the story. The Plant Ops people were also touched and they went out and spent an afternoon building the lady a ramp.

Neither the nurse nor Plant Ops told me about the ramp—probably because they weren't sure whether it was the wrong or right thing to do. I might never have known about if I hadn't gotten a wonderful letter from the patient telling how our staff had built her a ramp. You could just picture the workers from Plant Ops watching the lady use the ramp after their efforts and thinking, "We're doing worthwhile work today."

Needless to say, we did not reprimand the employees who bent the rules to help this patient. Actually, we made a big deal out of it and made sure others knew about it. About a year later, I was giving a speech at a national conference. The number-one question I got from the attendees was, "How did you get the purchase order so quickly?"

It's a sad fact that, when instituting "use your own judgment" policies, managers worry more about abuses than positive outcomes. Yes, it's true that no system is perfect. There may be abuses, but I can just about guarantee that you will have many more wins that will outweigh the losses.

I am an optimist. I truly believe life rewards action more than inaction. When you go for the gusto, you usually don't regret it. I mean, Hall of Fame pitcher Nolan Ryan struck out more batters than any other pitcher in major league history. Ryan also walked more batters than any other. But still, he's a Hall of Famer (not a Hall of Shamer).

My point is this: You have to focus on the wins that will be harvested from the employees' efforts and stop worrying about what might go wrong.

At Holy Cross Hospital we created an avenue whereby every employee could get up to $250 from a cash fund to fix a customer issue on the spot. When we implemented it, the number-one concern we heard was that someone might abuse the system. For instance: "Let's say I have a buddy come to the ER and act like he's hurt. When he complains about the service, I will give him a couple hundred bucks that we split later."

Sure, that could have happened. But I don't think it did. And *even if* we were scammed once or twice, we felt that it was a small price to pay for the good that it could potentially do. When we ran this program, we didn't spend more than $5,000 in a year. Frankly, if you have a problem with employees abusing such a customer service program, then you've got bigger fish to fry.

Alaska Airlines has been recognizing employee difference makers since 1991. The 70-year-old airline, which serves destinations in the Pacific Northwest, annually names a selection of employees for delivering outstanding levels of customer service. The employees who are being recognized, called "Legends of Customer Service," have their names etched on a pillar at the company's corporate office in Seattle. A tribute to the honorees is posted on the airline's website, along with their pictures and profiles, and a dinner is held at the Palace Ballroom in downtown Seattle. Since the program was implemented, 134 of Alaska Airline's 10,000 employees have been named Legends of Customer Service.

HOW TO FIND DIFFERENCE MAKERS

Finding and harvesting difference makers takes a conscious effort by senior management and supervisors. Yes, you have to make a commitment to do it—and relentlessly follow through on it—but the results will be well worth it.

- *Harvest examples of extraordinary employee behavior from your managers' notes.* Be sure to get the complete story and all the facts.

- *Look at customer feedback.* Some retailers give customers cards when they walk into the store and say, "We want to meet your expectations. As you walk through our store, if you notice that anyone is particularly helpful, please write down their names." These customers become more active shoppers and they help you recognize your top employees.

- *Just ask.* I'm a big believer in calling our customers and inquiring about our level of service. Again, just ask them if anyone was particularly helpful or if anyone exceeded their expectations. You might be surprised by how helpful people will be.

- *Develop a consistent program for recognizing your organization's heroes and their stories.* Good tools include newsletters, bulletin boards, and employee forums. Your recognition should not focus solely on who's providing direct customer service, but also on who's managing expenses and who's excelling in other, less-visible areas of the company. Behind-the-scenes people are just as important, and they often get overlooked!

All of these management tools will help you accumulate stories about those employees who give that little bit of extra effort and who know when to break the rules to make a difference. Gradually, an organization's stories become its culture. The better the stories, the better your culture—so get started story sleuthing!

KEY POINTS FOR HARDWIRING RESULTS

- Every organization has those employees who go above and beyond the call of duty and on occasion even bend the rules to make sure they are keeping customers happy. These are your organization's heroes, or difference makers, and their behavior should be recognized. Share their stories with others, both inside and outside the organization.

- Sharing stories about difference makers goes a long way toward giving employees a valuable sense of purpose.

- Don't shy away from "use your own judgment" policies because you're worried about abuses. No system is perfect, but you'll almost certainly have more wins than losses.

- Finding your heroes and recognizing their behavior is key because (as I've said in Chapter 14) recognized and rewarded behavior is repeated. Here's a quick breakdown of how to find your heroes:
  - Harvest examples of extraordinary employee behavior, making sure to get the complete story and all the facts.
  - Look at customer feedback.
  - Ask your customers about the level of service they receive at your organization.
  - Develop a consistent program for recognizing your organization's heroes and their stories. Make sure no one gets overlooked!

Customer Tactics

CHAPTER 16

BUILD A CULTURE AROUND SERVICE

Why This Chapter Is Important

IN A GLOBAL ECONOMY, NOTHING MATTERS MORE THAN SERVICE. You might have hundreds, even thousands, of competitors—and that means your customers have hundreds, even thousands, of alternatives to doing business with you. Ultimately, the way customers are treated will make or break an organization.

Service is hard. Getting everyone on the same page and practicing the same behaviors may be the most difficult challenge a company faces. Those that succeed dominate their markets.

Simply instructing your employees to "provide great service" isn't good enough. You need to discover what great service looks like to your customers and get 100 percent of your team to provide it. Eventually, the building blocks of great service are infused into your company culture, and it's then that your *results that last* efforts really take off.

• • •

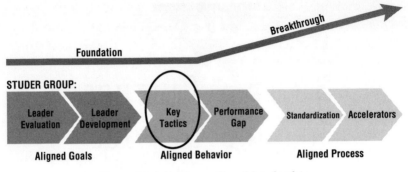

Figure 16.1 Evidence-Based Leadership

If I had told you in 1987 that I was going to start a new business selling brewed coffee for $4 per cup, you would doubtless have told me I was crazy. But, if I also told you that little coffee shop was Starbucks, and that 20 years later there would be more than 35 million customers buying coffee at more than 7,000 stores in 37 countries, you probably would have asked, "Where can I buy some stock?"

Is Starbucks coffee really *that* much better than the competition or are there other explanations for their success? Well, it *is* good coffee, but Starbucks' success is actually based on a culture of service that the organization has instilled in employees from the very beginning.

Starbucks' CEO Howard Schultz says,

> We believed very early on that people's interaction with the Starbucks experience was going to determine the success of the brand. The culture and values of how we related to our customers, which is reflected in how the company relates to our employees, would determine our success. While we are a coffee company at heart, Starbucks provides much more than the best cup of coffee—we offer a community gathering place where people come together to connect and discover new things. We are always looking for innovative ways to surprise and delight our customers.[1]

---

[1] Howard Schultz and Dori Jones Yang, *Pour Your Heart Into It: How Starbucks Built a Company One Cup at a Time* (New York: Hyperion, 1997).

What Schultz is talking about is a culture in which all employees are committed to creating an experience for customers that they can't find anywhere else. How does Starbucks maintain that culture of service? First, by giving each partner (which is what they call each employee) a small pocket-sized booklet that reminds them to always be "welcoming, genuine, considerate, knowledgeable, and involved" with customers.

Starbucks partners are encouraged to always be on the lookout for ways to surprise and delight customers. They're also strongly encouraged to give back to the communities in which they live. This constant employee focus on the customer experience has made Starbucks one of the most visible brands in the world. Surely Starbucks has to be one of the few businesses in the world that can open a new store in direct competition with one of its own, older stores and wind up increasing business at *both* locations within a year, a feat that the chain accomplishes regularly.

You might be thinking, "Okay, Quint, but building a culture of service is easier if you're in the business of serving coffee to customers in the first place."

Service *is* an integral part of a retail operation like Starbucks, but service is also central to the operations of *all* organizations, whether it's an airline, a manufacturer, a bank, an accounting firm, a consultancy, a hospital, or even a government agency.

For example, the city of Gulf Breeze, Florida, is a beautiful town. Not only is the city's Maintenance Department committed to keeping the streets and sidewalks swept and clear of litter, all city employees are encouraged to make the city's tidiness a personal priority. So, how do the city's personnel *know* that keeping the streets clean is important? Every Saturday morning the city manager, Buz, and his son walk the main streets picking up trash. The message to the public, and to Buz's 50 employees, is, "I care about the appearance of my city." Thanks to this practice, city employees and even citizens are more likely to pick up trash as well. When the leader demonstrates the behavior, then no one is entitled to overlook it. Needless to say, the city of Gulf Breeze is known for its cleanliness and small-town charm.

Just setting a personal example isn't usually enough, particularly in large organizations whose employees don't have daily contact with the senior leadership. What drives a great service culture, such as Starbucks Coffee, is an organizationwide dedication to a specific set of behaviors that embody great customer service.

A POWERFUL TOOL FOR BUILDING A SERVICE CULTURE

At Studer Group we've helped numerous clients to build a culture of service through the process of developing official *Standards of Behavior* and having everyone, from the CEO to the front-desk receptionist, sign a pledge to uphold the standards.

In short, this document sets the rules by which employees are held accountable. It can address any and all aspects of behavior at work: from interaction with clients (never taking cell phones or BlackBerries into meetings) to phone etiquette (returning voice mail messages within 24 hours) to basic good manners (knocking on doors before entering) to "positive attitude" markers (smiling or saying *thank you*).

One organization we worked with wanted its Standards of Behavior to improve efficiency and show respect for co-workers. Its document included a standard that required employees to ask, "Is now a good time?" when they walked into a co-worker's office. Yes, it's a very simple courtesy, but that standard had a huge impact on the entire organization.

Another client of ours had problems with its policy for public-address announcements. Whenever someone from corporate headquarters called the local division, the receptionist would get on the PA system and announce that corporate was on the phone and somebody better pick up the line. Thanks to the low-level panic that ensued, the poor division manager was always out of breath when he spoke to the corporate headquarters. He was running all over the place to get to the phone. We suggested that they add a standard requiring that the receptionist first ask the caller whether there was an emergency. If the answer was no, she would take a message. I'm sure this new policy added to the life expectancy of the division manager!

CREATING YOUR OWN STANDARDS OF BEHAVIOR

There are seven steps necessary to create a viable set of Standards of Behavior that will help you to develop a culture of service within your organization:

1. *Seek input from all employees in creating the standards.* Form a *service team* to spearhead the initiative and create a first draft. *Don't* have Human Resources write it and impose it on everyone else. You want to create buy-in, and that requires companywide participation.

2. *Align desired behaviors with corporate goals and desired outcomes.* Make sure the content of your Standards of Behavior supports and promotes organizational goals. You must be able to measure the success of your standards by seeing an impact in many of the key metrics of your operation, whether those are increased customer satisfaction, reduced rejects, or other measures.

3. *Be crystal clear and very specific in your wording.* Don't write, "Display a positive attitude." Instead, write "Smile, make eye contact, and greet customers by name." Don't worry about insulting people's intelligence. Sometimes people really don't know what is appropriate behavior and what isn't. For instance, if you don't want common "slang" phrases used with customers, you need to identify them right up front. One Standards of Behavior document created by a Studer client contains the phone etiquette directive: Avoid words and phrases like "Okay," "Yeah," "Hold on," "Honey," and "See ya."

4. *Hold a ceremonial Standards of Behavior rollout.* Once you have finalized your Standards of Behavior document, it's time to implement it. Hold an employee forum or companywide meeting in which you introduce the standards and distribute pledges for everyone to sign. Create an event around your CEO and leadership team signing the pledge. You may even hold activities designed to educate employees about some

of the points. Make it fun. But do have everyone sign a pledge—it's amazing how much more seriously people take rules when they've signed on the dotted line.

5. *Hold people accountable when they violate a standard.* Make sure all employees know they'll be held accountable for the behaviors outlined in the Standards of Behavior document. Then, just do it. How you hold them accountable is up to you. Sometimes a simple meeting in which you show an employee the signed pledge and point out her error is sufficient. Other times, you might need to write her up or take more drastic disciplinary measures. But one thing is clear: The Standards of Behavior pledge gives you something to hold people accountable *to.* It's worth implementing for that reason alone.

6. *Create a designated "Standard of the Month."* Every month, highlight a specific standard. This will boost awareness of the standards in general and will get people thinking about how that specific one applies to their daily lives. For example, you decide to focus on your policy for dealing with disgruntled customers. At the beginning of the month, a reminder e-mail detailing the policy is sent out. Next, you ask employees to write up real-life or hypothetical scenarios in which they must deal with angry or dissatisfied customers. Finally, you might hold a companywide forum in which you recruit people to act out both sides of a conflict: the disgruntled customer and the employee trying to soothe her. Not only is this fun and often hilarious, it can be a valuable learning tool as it forces people to see both sides of an issue.

7. *Update the Standards of Behavior.* The standards are dynamic and will need to be updated from time to time. One or two directives may not work as intended and may need to be changed. You may also discover new standards that need to be added as your company grows and evolves in new directions. Make changes as necessary. Your Standards of Behavior should be a living document that serves your company—not the other way around.

Have new applicants sign the Standards of Behavior right up front. Before you even interview prospective new employees, have them read and sign your standards. You will be able to eliminate undesirable prospective employees if they visibly balk at conforming to your corporate culture. But more important, when you do hire someone, there will be no doubt in his or her mind what you expect. If the employee is going to have trouble meeting your standards, you will probably know during the initial probationary period.

Sample from Pensacourt Health, Racquet & Fitness Club

Developed with Studer Group

STANDARDS OF BEHAVIOR

#1 Respect

Show respect for yourself and others:

- Park in designated areas, so members have parking closest to the facility.

- Display body language that is attentive and a facial expression of interest.

- Remember at all times that we are here to serve members and other staff members—that is the core of what we do.

- Adjust the volume of your voice to the environment; be considerate of others.

- Give sincere compliments to co-workers and members.

- Take pride in keeping our environment clean and safe.

- Our members and staff have a right to be treated with dignity and respect at all times.

(Continued)

Sample from Pensacourt Health (*Continued*)

#2 Professional Conduct

Choose to come to work with a positive attitude. Live this by:

- Making eye contact

- Smiling

- Being optimistic, positive, cheerful

- Anticipating needs

- Having relaxed body language, stopping to talk

- Walking people where they are going (never point)

- Treating others in a caring, sincere manner

- Seeing problems or complaints as opportunities to create wins

- Being aware of what you say and how it could be interpreted

- Being aware that *how* you say something is just as important as *what* you say

#3 Greeting and Interacting

Greet/interact with members and co-workers so as to create a feeling of belonging so they look forward to coming back:

- Have a smile on your face and in your voice.

- Use appropriate friendly greeting including member name.

- Create special greetings for "your" members.

- Practice *service recovery* (apologize, correct, track/trend).

- Have fun!

- Learn interests, hobbies, likes, and dislikes.

- Engage members to promote feeling of belonging.

- Be emotionally "present" when interacting with a member; don't get distracted.

#4 Appearance

Dress with pride; appearance reflects our respect for our members and ourselves:

- Wear expected attire for your job.

- Clothing should be clean and wrinkle free.

- Shirts should be tucked in.

- Name tags should be worn at all times above the waist.

- Practice good hygiene.

#5 Staff Meeting Attendance/Participation

Staff is expected to attend all required meetings and participate positively:

- Be a good adult learner.

- Pay attention.

- Relate information to your job and overall goals of Pensacourt.

- Take notes.

- Bring suggestions.

- Be prepared.

- Be on time.

- Share experiences and support co-workers.

- Maintain all certifications required.

(Continued)

Sample from Pensacourt Health (*Continued*)

#6 Promotions/Participation

Each staff member must participate in two events per year:

- Arrive at assigned time to participate.

- Have fun, play, and represent Pensacourt positively.

- Act as host or guide.

- Offer refreshments.

- Encourage participation.

#7 Communication/Listening

To promote an inclusive culture, employees are expected to participate in interactive communication by:

- Being responsible for reading the communication book in your area at the beginning of each shift

- Listening to other staff for their input and opinions

- Reading the Pensanote

- Listening to clients for needs and possible opportunities for better service

- Communicating in an honest, sincere manner, and never allowing the conversation to erode into gossip or negative talk

- Being sincere, honest, and "meaning what you say, and saying what you mean"

#8 Ownership

Take responsibility for resources and be a part of our great team:
- Submit two Bright Ideas or cost-saving ideas per year for implementation.

- Use supplies efficiently; don't waste.

- Work with a sense of pride; you are making a difference.

- Allocate human resources efficiently.

- Give 100% when on duty; your actions are the keys to success.

- Keep the environment clean and safe.

At Pensacourt, loyalty rules!

- Show you are proud of where you work.

- Refrain from speaking negatively about your organization.

- Be part of the solution, not part of the problem.

- Have empathy (understanding, being aware and considerate) for the owners.

WHY STANDARDS WORK

For most employees, just knowing that a Standards of Behavior document exists—and knowing that their signature is affixed to a pledge to uphold it—is enough to keep them on their toes. It creates an extra boost of awareness that really does affect day-to-day behavior. A Standards of Behavior document forces people to do their best and to *be* their best.

You may worry that enforcing Standards of Behavior will create a company of robots—a company in which human differences are discouraged in favor of mindless conformity. That is not true! An office unified by agreed-upon standards is a far more pleasant place to work. Plus, individual responsibility flourishes, because it's clear what everyone's responsibilities are. That contributes to an environment of fairness, cleanliness, and good manners—and happy customers who keep coming back for more.

THE POWER OF KEY WORDS

Have you ever wondered why large businesses began investing in those maddeningly complex call-answering systems? You know the ones I mean—"press one for customer service, press two for technical support, press three for billing questions," and so on. Were automated phone systems really cheaper than letting customers speak with live employees? Or was it because large businesses wanted to standardize the customer experience?

I'll concede that it's a little of both, but I think many businesses fear the havoc that ill-informed, misguided employees can create while trying to interact with customers. Better to let a recorded voice handle problems and complaints, they believe, than risk letting a live employee really mess things up.

A case in point occurred just a few months ago. A customer of a well-known Internet service provider phoned to cancel his account because he hadn't been using it. For some reason this customer also tape-recorded that phone call, which was quite unfortunate for the Internet service provider. Their problem was an overly zealous customer service rep that caused a national sensation by doggedly attempting to talk the customer out of canceling. The strained conversation, in which the customer can't persuade the rep to process the cancellation, led the man to post the recording of their exchange on the Internet.

Apparently, many people found the incident to be both funny and all-too-typical, because the transcript wound up making appearances all over the media, including national television news and morning talk shows. A "red-faced" company leader ended up apologizing publicly for the incident and the poor customer service rep ended up on the unemployment line.

I say "poor" customer service rep, because I suspect he was fired for merely doing what he was taught to do in the first place. Redirecting a customer's decision to discontinue a service is simply good business policy. Even if you don't succeed in saving the customer, a few well-phrased questions can be a valuable source of information to improve service for future customers.

The problem with this situation was that the employee clearly hadn't been provided with the right language, the correct *key words*. These carefully chosen words that leaders teach their employees to say at key times in a business transaction are an important part of building a culture around service.

Key Words at Key Times has long been a cornerstone of a successful business philosophy. Key words are important among employees to demonstrate the culture. They are vital among customers, and you'll learn much more about this subject in Chapter 19. For now, suffice it to say that a heartfelt apology, a sincere expression of understanding, or a well-timed question can often make all the difference between retaining and losing a valued customer.

THE LOYALTY FACTOR

By creating Standards of Behavior and key words that focus an organization on providing excellent service, you create lasting customers. In Chapter 18 we go deeper into providing service on an individual level. Here is an example of great service that has made me a loyal customer:

> I use a bank in Pensacola, Florida, called Peoples First Community Bank. Over the years, I've been impressed with the service Peoples provides. Every summer they even hold a cookout for all Studer Group employees. But the thing that put them over the top may surprise you: It was a call from an employee regarding the ATM I used.
>
> Branch manager Donna called me to explain that because of the hurricane that had just struck, they needed to rebuild the bank we visit and the ATM would not be working. She said she didn't want to inconvenience me and informed me that I could use any ATM and Peoples would reimburse me for the service fees.
>
> Over the years I've had other banks approach me and I've explained the relationship. They have understood why my loyalty is with Peoples. This doesn't mean my loyalty will never shift. It does mean that the stronger my loyalty is, the harder it will be to convince me to switch. Even if a ball is dropped, I am willing to stick by an organization that has earned my loyalty.

This story is a good illustration of the loyalty factor. It is a tremendously valuable force in keeping customers around for the long haul. Instill loyalty in the men, women, and companies that ultimately pay the bills, and you've taken a big step on the path to lasting results.

KEY POINTS FOR HARDWIRING RESULTS

- Everyone in your company should adhere to a specific set of behaviors that embody great customer service. We call them *Standards of Behavior*. These standards set forth rules that address any and all aspects of behavior at work—from interactions with clients to phone etiquette to basic good manners to positive attitude markers.

- To create a viable set of Standards of Behavior—and ensure that everyone is on board with the requirements—do the following:
  1. Seek input from all employees in creating the standards.
  2. Align desired behaviors with corporate goals and desired outcomes.
  3. Be crystal clear and very specific in your wording.
  4. Hold a ceremonial Standards of Behavior rollout.
  5. Hold people accountable when they violate a standard.
  6. Create a designated "Standard of the Month."
  7. Update the Standards of Behavior as needed.

- Not only should current employees sign the Standards of Behavior, but the document should also be part of your hiring process. By having prospective employees read and sign the Standards, you'll let them know right up front what is expected of them at your organization.

- Emphasize the importance of *Key Words at Key Times*. These are carefully chosen words offered by your employees at critical points in a business transaction. When used in the right way, they'll help you build a culture of service and operational excellence.

- Do everything you can to instill loyalty in your customers. The loyalty factor will keep customers coming back, even if you occasionally drop the ball.

Zappos.com—a Company That Truly "Gets" Service

Zappos.com, a company that started out in 1999 as an online shoe retailer, has one of the best *service attitudes* I've ever seen. It's known for its lightning-fast delivery times, tremendous selection, and helpful staff—attributes that add up to outstanding customer service. Its web site is packed with heartfelt testimonials from delighted shoppers. Even its e-mails to customers shout, "We care about you!" This one is a prime example:

- - - - -Original Message- - - - -
From: shipping_notify@zappos.com [mailto:shipping_notify
    @zappos.com]
Sent: Tuesday, March 27, 2007 10:35 AM
To: Kennedy, Bekki
Subject: Your Zappos.com order #53973609

Dear Bekki Kennedy,

Hope you're having a great day! :)

We wanted to let you know that we've been working around the clock and that we've just finished picking and packing your order:

Order #53973609
French Connection Rio Cotton Shirt—Black—2/Apparel
DC Kids Kids Court Graffik (Toddler/Youth)—Carbon/White—1
    Youth/M
Charles by Charles David Neat—Navy—6/M

(Continued)

Zappos.com (*Continued*)

Since we are shipping your order with Free Overnight Shipping, your expected delivery date for this order is:
Wednesday, March 28th 2007

(UPS and FedEx will only pick up from our warehouse on business days, and they will only deliver on business days.)

We will be emailing you your tracking number later today, when our computer systems are finished processing all of today's transactions.

While most companies spend a lot of money on marketing in order to grow their business, our philosophy at Zappos.com is a little different. Instead of spending a lot of money on marketing, we would rather work on improving the customer experience (running our warehouse around the clock, super-fast free shipping, free return shipping, 24/7 customer support, etc.), and rely on repeat customers and word of mouth to grow our business instead.

So if you enjoyed your experience with us, please be sure to tell your friends and family about Zappos.com!

We are constantly striving to improve our service. If there is anything that we can do to help improve your experience, please don't hesitate to let us know. We like to think of ourselves as a service company that happens to sell shoes (and now handbags, sunglasses, watches, and apparel).

Thank you for all of your support—we really appreciate it!

Zappos.com Customer Loyalty Team
cs@zappos.com

CHAPTER

17

IMPLEMENT PRE- AND POST-CUSTOMER-VISIT CALLS

Why This Chapter Is Important

PRE- AND POST-CUSTOMER-VISIT PHONE CALLS PROVIDE A LOT OF BANG for very little buck. The two minutes you spend making one of these calls can translate to vastly increased profits and results for your organization.

First and most obviously, pre-calls help ensure that customers will show up. Post-calls help you gather valuable information you can use to make your service even better. Both types of calls inspire referrals and beneficial word of mouth. They enable service recovery and even allow you to defuse potentially litigious situations.

What's more, the positive feedback often received from the calls provides real-time reward and recognition for employees. It proves once and for all that your employees really *do* make a difference in their customers' lives. Both pre- and post-customer-visit phone calls really get the flywheel spinning, which generates results across every pillar of excellence in your organization.

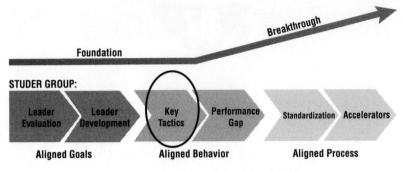

Figure 17.1 Evidence-Based Leadership

In this chapter you will discover the measurable benefits of pre- and post-customer-visit calls—and learn how to implement them in your organization.

• • •

Customer-driven service is more important than ever. It's easy to see why. The global economy has created so much competition for business that *every* organization must provide superior service. Adequate service won't keep the doors open. An organization may coast along for a while, but eventually some other bank (or real estate firm or spa or carpet cleaning company) that really *gets* the customer-driven service concept will put it out of business.

The good news is that leaders want to provide superior service. Quite simply, we know it gets results. Basically, leaders want two things from our organization's customers: (1) We want them to show up and buy our products and services, and (2) we want them to be happy enough with the experience to keep coming back and enthusiastically recommend us to their friends, family, co-workers, and acquaintances. Pre- and post-customer-visit calls greatly increase the likelihood that your customers will do both of these things.

These techniques are exactly what they sound like. An employee calls a customer before her scheduled appointment to remind her to show up and bring any information she'll need. Then, after the appointment is over, the employee calls the customer again to follow up and ask a few strategic questions.

Pre- and post-visit calls originated in the health care field, where they not only improve clinical outcomes but give patients a more satisfying service experience. Yes, just like all organizations, hospitals and medical practices have found that it's not enough to provide a good "product" (clinical outcome)—they must also provide excellent service.

That said, it's not surprising that pre- and post-visit calls translate smoothly to other industries. Here are just a few of the ways we've seen them employed:

- A local mortgage lender calls customers before an appointment to remind them which important documents to bring.

- A lawn service worker calls a homeowner before his weekly appointment and says, "It's time to aerate and reseed your yard. Do you want me to do that this week?"

- A weight loss center representative calls a customer after her regular appointment and says, "It's wonderful that you lost two pounds this week. You've lost 25 pounds to date! Do you have any questions about the new diet plan we gave you at Tuesday's meeting?"

Now, imagine what a pre- or post-visit call might look like for your company. If you're thinking, "Well, that's fine for mortgage lenders, lawn services, and weight loss centers, but these kinds of calls won't work for *my* business," then I urge you to *relate*, not *compare*. Even if you have to modify them to fit your business model, pre- and post-visit calls will work for almost everyone.

PRE- AND POST-VISIT CALLS EXCEED CUSTOMER EXPECTATIONS

At Studer Group we've helped many organizations hardwire these calls into their daily operations and, as you'll see later in this chapter, the results are amazing. These calls can completely change the way your customers view their interaction with you—and given the high expectations of today's consumers, you need every possible edge!

Take an informal poll of your friends and family and you may walk away feeling that customer service is a lost art. You'll hear stories about indifferent store clerks, rude ticket agents, surly food servers, and impenetrable call centers. You'll leave the conversation feeling that customers today are feeling ignored, insulted, misunderstood, and generally underappreciated. In fact, you probably even have a story or two of your own!

When companies go out of their way to provide great customer service, customers *really* notice it. What's more, they really appreciate it.

Pre- and post-customer-visit calls help give customers exceptional service (which they appreciate), and exceptional service leads to bottom-line results (which *you* appreciate). Instituting them is a win-win for everyone involved.

CUSTOMER SERVICE AND THE BOTTOM LINE
(PROOF THAT THESE CALLS WORK)

Before we get into the measurable benefits of pre- and post-customer-visit calls, let's look at what happens when we provide poor service. Businesses that take customers for granted are suffering very real monetary losses as a result. Just consider these statistics:

- Sixty-five percent of a company's business comes from existing customers.

- Ninety-one percent of their dissatisfied customers will *never* again buy from that company.

- It costs five times more to attract a new customer than to satisfy an existing one.

It should simply make economic sense for an organization to attempt to improve customer satisfaction, yet too few seem to try. If you haven't created a culture of service, your employees may not realize the vital role that customers play in your organization's success.

The Cleveland Clinic Foundation's business is driven by appointments. In order to achieve many of its operational, financial, and patient satisfaction goals, it needed to make sure that patients kept the appointments that were scheduled for them.

To increase the ratio of appointments that were kept by patients, leaders instituted a policy of phoning all patients prior to their visit to confirm the time and date. These calls were invaluable because they:

- Improved overall patient health

- Enabled better deployment of resources

- Reduced patient anxiety

The pre-visit calls were also a great opportunity to confirm patient information, anticipate possible snags in the paperwork, and answer any patient questions or concerns. It had the added benefit of scoring "brownie points" with patients because the friendly phone calls confirmed that the medical center cared about them.

However, the biggest payoff came when we saw how the phone calls affected our client's overall patient scheduling and satisfaction scores:

- No-shows were reduced by 70 percent.

- Tardiness was reduced by 50 to 60 percent.

- Patient satisfaction increased by 25 to 30 percent.

We worked with another hospital, Hackensack University Medical Center, to implement calls on the other side of the service timeline. Physicians themselves would make post-visit calls to clarify the patient's discharge instructions and survey them regarding their overall perception of the hospital's service level. From these calls we gained important suggestions for improving service and garnered invaluable recognition and gratitude, which we shared with the hospital staff.

As the charts in Figures 17.2 and 17.3 show, patients who received post-visit calls indicate that they are more likely to

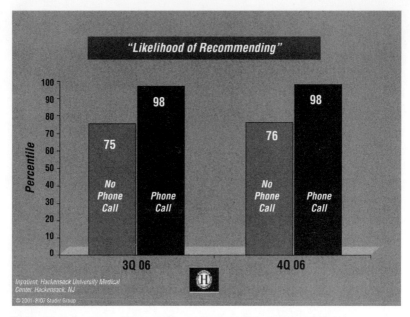

Figure 17.2 Impact of Post-Calls on Patient Perception of Care—Inpatient

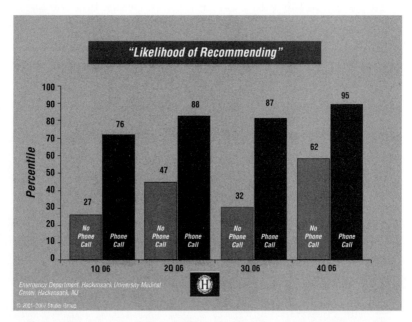

Figure 17.3 Impact of Post-Calls on Patient Perception of Care—ED

recommend Hackensack University Medical Center than patients who did *not* receive a call.

It may surprise you to hear that physicians, especially those who work in a hectic Emergency Department, have time to personally make post-visit calls. But I can assure you that Hackensack Medical Center physicians are more than willing to make time for the calls. In fact, they're excited about doing so. The reason is simple: These calls work.

They improve patient compliance and clinical outcomes. They make patients less likely to bring lawsuits. (Did you know that "poor communication" is the number-one cause of litigation?) They also remind physicians that their work really does make a profound difference in the lives of others (and because physicians are as human as the rest of us, they appreciate that affirmation).

A TECHNIQUE FOR ALL TYPES OF BUSINESS

Of course, as I mentioned earlier, you don't have to be a hospital or a health care organization to implement a pre-/post-visit call system. The principle translates seamlessly to any organization dependent on customer appointments. For instance:

- Auto service centers
- Financial planners
- Hair salons/barbershops
- Nail salons
- Weight loss centers
- Dentists
- Realtors
- Restaurants
- Interior designers
- Law firms

- Tanning salons

- Tax services

- Cleaning services

- Dog groomers

- Veterinarians

- Health spas

These courtesies, calling to confirm an appointment and calling to follow up, have a huge impact. They send the message to customers that we care, and that we've created a culture of service. This makes our customers feel valued and it makes our employees feel their work has meaning.

However, pre- and post-customer-visit calls don't just happen. They must be hardwired into an organization. *In fact, I recommend that a company attempt to call every single customer both* before *her appointment and* after *her appointment.* It's important that you determine beforehand what percentage of customers contacted constitutes success—having a goal will ensure that people really try to reach it.

Often when I make this statement to a client, he thinks the idea sounds great in theory but won't work in reality. (Again, I urge him to *relate*, not *compare*. Even if you can't follow a plan point by point, you can usually modify it to work for your unique circumstances.) Anyway, it's at this point that the client hits me with a barrage of questions. Here are a few of them, along with my answers.

COMMON QUESTIONS ABOUT PRE- AND POST-VISIT CALLS

Q: Who should make the calls?

A: Ideally, the person who performs the service should make the call. It's always more powerful when the post-visit call in particular comes from the doctor who just performed the surgery, the mechanic who fixed the car, or the aesthetician who did the facial. If the actual service provider absolutely can't make the call, it should come from the person who is "next closest" to the service. (If not the doctor, then her nurse; if not the mechanic, then his assistant.)

As for pre-visit calls, the identity of the caller is less important than the fact that the call gets made. Just make sure it's someone with a friendly voice who will represent your company well.

Q: But what if we're too busy to make the calls?

A: You're *never* too busy to make the calls. (If Hackensack Medical Center's Emergency Department physicians can make time, *anyone* can!) If leaders make it a *must-do,* then employees *will* do it. Occasionally, it may be that a particular person really can't make a pre- or post-visit call on a particular day. When that happens, the next-closest-to-the-service employee can fill in. The rule of thumb is this: Any call, even if it's not an ideal one, is better than no call at all.

Q: What if the customer doesn't answer her phone?

A: Certainly this will happen. In fact, it will happen often. (People do go out of the house from time to time and they do screen calls.) It's fine to leave a message on the answering machine, along with a number where the customer can return your call. If the answering machine doesn't pick up, try again later (at least one more time). Remember, the goal is to *attempt* to call every customer. None of us is ever likely to achieve perfection, and that's okay.

Q: But what if we do a post-visit call and the customer blasts us? What if it turns out she was really unhappy with the service?

A: Those kinds of calls certainly aren't as rewarding as the ones in which we get glowing reviews, but they're just as valuable in a different way. They give us an opportunity to salvage a customer who might otherwise be lost. We issue a standard scripted apology and go into service-recovery mode: *I am so sorry your experience with us was disappointing. What can we do to make it right for you now?*

Q: Are you saying calls should use a script (key words)? Won't that seem insincere?

A: I absolutely believe in using key words in pre- and post-visit calls. A call without these key words is a call without a reason. However, I don't mean that the caller should read the script word-for-word in a lifeless monotone voice. What I'm calling a script is really just a set of three to five questions the caller asks, with strategic key words woven in to reinforce your brand or further some goal your company has set. (See Chapter 19.) Believe me, it won't seem insincere if the caller is truly passionate about her work—which is why it's best when the actual service provider does the job.

DEVELOPING KEY WORDS FOR PRE-CUSTOMER-VISIT CALLS

The main purpose of these calls is to ensure that the customer shows up. That's it. It all comes back to the universal "time is money" adage. No-shows mean your employees are sitting idle when they should be generating profits.

And busy, overscheduled customers appreciate these reminder calls. (In today's society, who *isn't* busy and overscheduled?) In many industries appointments are made months in advance—even *years*. Think about your own experience: If you've been waiting six months for a hair appointment with an in-demand colorist, you certainly don't want to miss your one opportunity to see him. You'd appreciate a call, wouldn't you?

By the way, I recommend making these calls two or three days ahead of time for the appointment. If your customer has indeed forgotten about the appointment, you're building in enough time for her to rearrange her schedule.

The elements of a thorough pre-visit call are as follows (Figure 17.4):

- Confirm the date and time of the appointment.

- Remind the customer of the purpose for the appointment. This is a good way to ensure that you're both on the same

Confirm appointment	*"Mrs. Smith? Hello. This is <name>. I am calling to confirm your appointment for your car's quarterly oil change on <date>.*
Talk about test or appointment and why it is important	*"Mrs. Smith, this appointment is important to keep your vehicle running smoothly . . ."*
Explanation of procedure and pre-visit requirements	*"The oil change will take <time> . . . and won't require anything from you . . ."*
Directions	*"I wanted to make sure you know directions to get here . . ."*
Request customer bring any historical or tracking information necessary	*"When you bring the car in, could you please make sure the chart of past services is in the car?"*
Payment review	*"The total cost for the oil change is $25. Remember you can bring in a check or for your convenience we will take a credit card. . . ."*
Answer questions	*"Are there any other things you'd like us to look at while your vehicle is here? Are there any questions I can answer for you?"*

© 2001–2007 Studer Group

Figure 17.4 Pre-Visit Phone Call Sample

page. Let's say you're a beauty salon. If your computer system shows that Mrs. Richardson is due for a root touch-up, but she thinks she's only due for a haircut, it's better to get the discrepancy straightened out in advance.

- Go over any pre-visit instructions. If you're an attorney confirming an appointment for Mrs. Tyson's estate planning meeting, you'd remind her to bring in her will and other important legal and financial documents.

- Make sure the customer knows how to get to your office. If she seems hesitant, go over directions verbally or send her to the map on your web site.

- Give her an estimate of what the service will cost. If health or dental insurance is involved, bring up that issue as well.

- Ask if she has any further questions.

- Thank her in advance for her business.

Care and Concern	"Mrs. Smith? Hello. This is <name>. You were discharged from my unit yesterday. I just wanted to call and see how you're doing today . . ."
Clinical Outcomes	"Mrs. Smith, did you get all your medications filled? . . ."
	"Do you have your follow-up appointment? . . . "
	"Is your pain better or worse than yesterday? . . ."
	"Mrs. Smith, we want to make sure we do excellent clinincal follow-up to ensure your best possible recovery. Do you understand your discharge instructions? . . ."
Reward and Recognition	"Mrs Smith, we like to recognize our employees. Who did an excellent job for you while you were in the hospital? . . ."
	" Can you tell me why Sue was excellent? . . ."
Service	" We want to make sure you were very satisfied with your care. How were we, Mrs. Smith? . . ."
Process Improvement	"We're always looking to get better. Do you have any suggestions for what we could do to be even better? . . ."
Appreciation	"We appreciate you taking the time this afternoon to speak with us about your follow-up care. Is there anything else I can do for you? . . ."

© 2001–2007 Studer Group

Figure 17.5 Post-Visit Phone Call Sample

DEVELOPING KEY WORDS FOR POST-CUSTOMER-VISIT CALLS

Again, these calls are a good way to shore up customer relationships. All questions should be aimed at making sure the customer was satisfied, figuring out what (and who) is working well in your company, and harvesting ideas for improvement.

Generally, these calls shouldn't last any longer than two minutes. We want to connect with the customer on a sincere level, not overwhelm him with questions!

It's important to determine the best times for these calls. It is usually best to wait a day or two after the appointment to make these calls. This gives the customer time to reflect on the service you provided and/or get used to the product you sold her.

Elements of a thorough post-visit call are as follows (Figure 17.5):

- Express care and concern. Let the customer know that you're calling because his satisfaction is important to you.

- Inquire specifically about the outcome of your transaction. For instance: *Do you feel comfortable with your new haircut? . . . Is your truck running well? . . . Are you happy with the financial strategy we worked out with you?*

- If any follow-up action is needed, remind the customer about it or ask him to do it:
  - *You may get a survey in the mail in the next week or so. Will you please take a moment to fill it out and return it? Your feedback is very important to us.*
  - *Mr. Smith, as you know, regular oil changes extend the life of your engine. Would you like to go ahead and schedule your next one right now?*
  - *Have you sent in the warranty for your new office furniture yet?*

- Ask the customer if there was a particular employee who did an excellent job for him. Here, you're looking for opportunities to reward and recognize outstanding employees.

- Next, ask about overall service and process efficiency: *Was it a good experience? Could it have been better? How, specifically, could we change the process to make it better?*

- Thank the customer for his business.

That's it! Of course, you'll want to make a mental note to share positive feedback with any employees the customer raved about, and you'll want to correct any mistakes he may have identified.

For the most part, however, any significant changes based on these calls will occur over time. When you see a pattern of customers consistently complaining about the same issues—or people—you'll know it's time to act.

Both pre- and post-visit calls show customers that we care about them. They appreciate that as much as they do the products and services we provide. Perhaps even more. Much in the same way that we seek to build an emotional bank account with our employees, these calls help us build a service bank account with our customers. If we later drop the ball, they're far more likely to give us another chance.

When we implement these calls, we end up with happier customers who are more pleasant to serve, who keep coming back, and who refer us to their friends and family. We end up with happier employees who see firsthand that their work makes a difference. And we end up with a more efficient and prosperous company that consistently gets excellent results—results that last.

KEY POINTS FOR HARDWIRING RESULTS

- In a global marketplace, every company must become a customer-driven service company.

- Customers today have higher expectations than ever. And when companies go out of their way to provide great service, customers *really* notice it. What's more, they really appreciate it. Pre- and post-customer-visit calls are a critical ingredient of good service.

- Pre- and post-customer-visit calls increase profitability by:
  - Reducing the number of no-shows
  - Improving the customer's perception of service and making it more likely that she'll come back again and recommend your organization to someone else
  - Helping you identify problems in your staff or processes so that you can fix them
  - Providing positive feedback that boosts employee morale

- Pre-customer-visit calls should be made a few days before the scheduled appointment. The caller should:
  - Confirm the date and time of the appointment.
  - Remind the customer of the purpose of the appointment.
  - Go over any pre-visit instructions.
  - Make sure the customer knows how to get to your office.
  - Give her an estimate of what the service will cost.
  - Ask if she has any further questions.
  - Say, "Thank you."

- Post-customer-visit calls should be made a few days after the appointment. If at all possible, the person who actually performed the service should make the call. He or she should:
  - Express empathy and concern.
  - Inquire specifically about the outcome of the transaction.
  - Remind the customer about any follow-up activity.
  - Ask if anyone deserves reward or recognition.
  - Ask about overall service and process efficiency.
  - Say, "Thank you."

CHAPTER

18

ROUND ON YOUR CUSTOMERS
Determine Your Customers' *What* and Give It to Them!

Why This Chapter Is Important

EARLIER IN THIS BOOK, I DISCUSSED THE VITAL IMPORTANCE OF zeroing in on your employees' *what*—the one thing that most powerfully motivates them. In this chapter, the other side of the coin—determining what the *what* is for your *customers*—will be covered.

There's something your customers want and need from you more than anything else. When you can figure out what it is—via a technique I call *rounding on customers*—you can give it to them. Then, a lot of good things will happen. Your customers will be happy. They'll keep coming back. They'll tell other customers how great you are and bring you even more business.

But also, giving customers what they really want makes *employees* happy. Why? Because satisfying the customers' *what* brings focus to their work, improves their efficiency, and provides that all-important sense of purpose, worthwhile work, and making a difference.

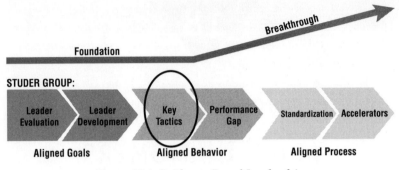

Figure 18.1 Evidence-Based Leadership

Satisfied customers lead to satisfied employees, and vice versa. Both lead to prosperous companies. And both are critical components in the quest for results that last.

• • •

All customers have a *what*. And if we know what their *what* is—and if we can meet that all-important need or desire—most customers will actually forgive us when we don't meet some of their other (less important) expectations. Finding customers' *whats* enables us to provide "individualized customer care." This boosts the loyalty factor and makes it much more likely that customers will stick with us long term.

Figuring out what the *what* is for our customers is not optional. We *must* do it. If we don't pinpoint the *what* and build our service around it, we're guaranteed to struggle. Eventually, one of two things will happen: We'll either figure out what our customers really want and give it to them, or our company will fail.

Let me tell you a story that Katherine, a client of mine, told me about a business that misjudged its customers' *what*.

> Katherine takes her vehicle to a car wash near her business office. As an entrepreneur with three young children, she has very little free time. When she first started frequenting the car wash, she found that the employees did good work, but more to the point, they did it fast. The manager worked hard to keep the cars moving through the various cleaning stations, and when the car was clean, he always walked out with Katherine to help her inspect the results.

But after a while, things inexplicably changed at the car wash. (Perhaps some consultant gave the manager bad advice!) It seemed the manager had taken his focus off moving vehicles through swiftly and seemed more interested in "pampering" his customers in his renovated waiting area. Now when Katherine brought her car in, he would meet her at the door with a drink and offer her a magazine. As irritated customers shuffled their feet and checked their watches, oblivious to the soft lighting and relaxing music, the car washing process outside was moving at a snail's pace. And when Katherine's car finally *was* ready, the manager was too busy chatting with customers to walk her out for the inspection.

The next time Katherine came in—thinking regretfully that it might be the *last* time—the manager happened to ask her how she liked the new setup. She decided to be honest with him. "I don't come to the car wash to leisurely read the paper in a cozy environment; I come for fast, efficient, reasonably priced service," she told him. "What's more, I suspect most people feel the same way. While I appreciate your attempt to provide great customer service, I think you've lost sight of what the customer really needs from you."

Fortunately, the manager took Katherine's words to heart. The next time she stopped in, having decided to give him one more chance, she found him busily moving cars through the cleaning stations. True, the ambience in the waiting room was less inviting—but she wasn't stranded there long enough to care.

Katherine's car-wash story is not unique. It's representative of the evolutionary process that most organizations go through. Frankly, many companies think they know what the *what* is for their customers, but they really don't. The reason is simple: They have never *asked*.

THE IMPORTANCE OF *ASKING*

Some years ago, I was working with an organization in Hickory, North Carolina. This company had called me in because their most recent customer satisfaction survey results were good, not great.

The leaders I was meeting with were disappointed with this luke-warm rating, to put it mildly. They had worked hard to provide what they sincerely believed was excellent service and could not understand why customers didn't agree.

So, after much hand wringing had taken place, the conversation shifted to the question, "What does excellent service look like?" We divided everyone up into groups, pulled out the flipcharts and tried to come up with an answer. People were shouting out their opinions, papers were flying around, the squeaks and scent of felt-tipped markers filled the room. Then, amid all the chaos, one employee innocently said, "Why don't we ask the customer?"

Bingo! With that one question, this person had put her finger on the truth: Excellent customer service is subjective. *Only the customer knows the answer.* If you don't ask her, you'll never know what her *what* really is. All the guessing in the world is worthless compared with the simple yet powerful act of getting the customer to tell you what she *really* wants from you.

That meeting in Hickory was a defining moment for me. It led me to consider on a deeper level than ever before how to discover what the *what* is for customers—and ultimately, deliver it.

ROUNDING ON CUSTOMERS

In Chapter 2, we discussed the importance of rounding for outcomes: regularly touching base with your employees to determine what they need (there's that *what* again!), to show them you care, and to recognize and reward their successes. Now, let's take the same principle and apply it to the men and women who buy your products and/or services.

You can gather vital information from your customers much in the same deliberate, structured way you gather it from your employees. It may not be possible to talk to your customers on a weekly or even daily basis like you can with your employees, but you can round on them in other ways. How a leader rounds depends on the nature of the company.

Back when I was a hospital administrator, my team and I had to keep two groups of customers happy: the patients and the physicians. In order to do that, we had the staff maintain *preference cards* on each. The preference card for the patient might include questions about sleep habits, food choices, and visitors. The physician cards (Figure 18.2) might include questions like, "When do you want to be called about a patient's condition?" (Some doctors

STUDER**G**ROUP

Physician Preference Card   Date:

Physician Name

What 3 items are most important to you in your practice?

1. _____
   _____
   _____
   _____

2. _____
   _____
   _____
   _____

3. _____
   _____
   _____
   _____

What is one item you would like to have improved?

Figure 18.2 Physician Preference Card

may want a call if the patient's temperature hits 100 degrees. Others aren't concerned until it hits 101 degrees.) The point is, these preference cards told us what the *whats* were for patients and physicians alike. They allowed us to individualize the service we provided not just to the two groups, but to each person in each group.

Preference cards also helped us manage handoffs effectively. We used them to make sure each employee was aware of what was important to each particular patient. Today, many of Studer Group's health care organization clients use similar preference cards in their work with physicians. (See sidebar for an example.)

Of course, preference cards work just as well for non-health care companies (we'll discuss them in greater detail later). Have you ever called a customer service representative and been transferred to three different representatives—which meant you had to explain the issue three different times? (And all this is after waiting an hour to speak to someone!) What if the first representative asked, "Tell me what I can do during this call to provide great service to you?" What if she then filled out a preference card

---

Determining Physicians' *Whats*

In health care, it's critically important to keep physicians happy. At Studer Group, we use a proactive tool to capture physician preferences and document these preferences in a format that is accessible and used by the frontline staff who work with physicians on a day-to-day basis. The Physician Preference Card (Figure 18.2) demonstrates to our physicians that:

1. We value them and respect their time.

2. Their patients are in good hands and we care about them.

3. We want them to work as efficiently as possible.

It's a simple tool that brilliantly positions health care organizations for improved patient, employee, and physician satisfaction. How might you modify this card for use with your customers, clients, or partners?

that detailed this vital information and explained why you were calling? I know I wouldn't be as nervous about being transferred to another representative if I knew that person already had the needed information.

THE THREE FACES OF ROUNDING

How you round on customers depends on who your customers are, how often you see them, and what they expect from you. If you own a hardware store, you might see the average customer twice a year. If you own an accounting firm, you might see him twice a month. If you own a health club, you might see him twice a week.

Both the man who stops into the hardware store to buy a hammer and the woman who comes into the health club to work with a personal trainer on a weekly basis can be involved in identifying service expectations—but the wise service provider (necessarily) handles the rounding in very different ways.

In other words, I'm asking you to take a *spirit-of-the-law* approach to the advice in this chapter, rather than a *letter-of-the-law* approach. Round in a way that makes sense for your company and its customers—but please *do* round.

There are three overarching principles to follow:

1. Always be clear and specific in asking questions and recording her answers.

2. Always thank the customer for her business.

3. Always do everything in your power to meet her requests.

Here are the three scenarios we've developed for our clients. Hopefully, one of them will work for you.

Scenario #1: Random Rounding

This scenario, designed for big retail stores, represents rounding in its purest form. You (or your managers) literally walk around and talk to customers as they browse the aisles of your store.

I call it *random rounding* for obvious reasons. You'll get an unpredictable cross-section of customers who are there for a whole universe of different reasons. But if you round regularly, ask the right questions, and capture their answers, you'll see a (decidedly nonrandom) pattern of customer preferences emerge. From there you can begin to operationalize the actions that meet the typical customers' *whats*.

This type of rounding has four steps:

1. Introduce yourself and state your intention: "My name is Ellen. I want to make sure you have excellent service today."

2. Ask: "Is there anything specific you're looking for or any questions I can answer?"

3. If the customer needs help and you have to leave her to find the answer, do so. Don't say, "I'll be right back." (That's too vague.) Clearly state the duration by saying something like, "I'm going to the stock room to see if we have the kind of tire you need. If not, I am going to look it up on the computer to see how long it will take us to order it. I will be back in five minutes."

    If the customer doesn't need help, say, "Remember, my name is Ellen. If you need anything else, please have me paged. I'll be glad to help you."

4. Thank the customer for coming into the store.

That's it! Walking around and talking to customers is the best way to stay in touch with their needs. Do it as often as you possibly can.

Scenario #2: Relationship Rounding

Relationship rounding is more in-depth than the first type I described because it's meant for companies that have more time with each customer. Maybe your business is a car dealership Service Department or a hair salon or an accounting firm. The point is, your goal is to build a solid relationship with each customer and keep her coming back regularly.

How does relationship rounding work? Generally, it has three steps:

1. Thank her for her business and state your intention: "Thank you for choosing us, Ms. Smith. We are excited about being your financial planner and we want to exceed your expectations."

2. Ask her to identify her needs and preferences. "What are you looking for in a financial planner? What is the most important thing we can do to make you happy?" (You're asking her what her *what* is.)

   When you ask this question, you'll get one of two outcomes: (a) She'll tell you exactly what her expectations are, or (b) she won't know what she wants. If the outcome is "a," great! You can move on to step 3. If it's "b," you have an opportunity to educate her. You'll say something like, "Well, I'm a certified financial planner and I've worked with customers like you for years. Here's what most customers are looking for."

   After you tell her, you can work together to figure out her preferences.

3. Create a customer preference card. (For example, see Physician Preference Card in Figure 18.2.) Write down everything she told you during step 2 on this card and keep it on file. Contact her once a year or so to make sure it's up to date and her needs haven't changed.

That's it! The customer preference card can help you in many ways. Obviously, it helps you provide outstanding, personalized service to each customer. If there's a handoff—you must turn the customer over to a colleague—the preference card helps you make a seamless transition.

The card also makes a good training tool. You can show several examples to new employees to help them understand the types of customers they will be dealing with and the issues these customers care about.

Finally, customer preference cards keep you from being overly dependent on employees' "institutional memory." If a key employee should leave, having this information on hand greatly reduces the likelihood of customers abandoning ship as well.

Scenario #3: Deep Impact Rounding

You may be thinking, "My business doesn't really fit into either of the first two categories. First, I'm not a store. Second, I'm not the kind of service provider that customers see on a regular basis. They may come back more than once—at least I hope they will— but it won't happen very often. So neither one of these rounding scenarios makes sense for me."

Great Teachers Find the *What* for Every Student

My daughter called me the other day to share the news that my grandson's teacher had called just to say how great he is doing— specifically, how much his focus, his reading, and his confidence had improved. While she said she was proud of Cooper's accomplishments, she quickly moved on to singing the praises of his teacher, Renee Griinke.

The teacher, revealed, focuses on what is important to Cooper—what motivates him and gives him the confidence to (as Ms. Griinke puts it) "keep his mind open for learning." She added that the teacher doesn't do this only for Cooper, but also for every child in the class. In short, Ms. Griinke finds the *what* for each child and then builds his or her learning around it.

Her personalized approach has resulted in a love for learning, a blossoming of confidence, and a hunger for achievement— certainly for my grandson and I suspect for many other students. I wish every child in America could learn this way.

Don't worry. There is a rounding solution that makes sense for businesses that don't fit the first two scenarios. I call it *deep impact rounding* because that's exactly what you're trying to do—make a strong enough impression on the customer that he comes back the next time he (or someone he knows) needs home repairs, or legal representation, or luxury spa services.

Let's use the last one as an example to illustrate how deep impact rounding can work. Let's say Mrs. Garcia comes in on her birthday for a massage, a manicure, and a facial. Train your employees to follow these four steps:

1. Thank her for her business and state your intention: "Thank you for choosing our spa, Mrs. Garcia. We want you to have a wonderful, memorable experience with us today."

2. Ask the customer to identify her expectations and preferences. You might need to gently probe to find out what is most important to her about her services, so allow enough time for this step. (Perhaps you'll find that she prefers silence during her treatments rather than a lot of chatter, for instance, or that she doesn't like when technicians hard-sell the products they're using.)

3. Write down what she says on a *customer expectations form*. See that everyone who works with Mrs. Garcia that day—the massage therapist, the manicurist, and the aesthetician—has a chance to read the form before they see her. At the end of each treatment, each one should sign his or her name.

4. Send the customer expectations form home with the customer.

Done properly, this type of rounding creates a powerful impression. Not only will the customer come back to you the next time she needs a spa day, she'll enthusiastically refer her friends to you. Best of all, she'll have hard evidence (the signed form) that you really care about her wants and needs.

And here's another benefit: Having the signatures of your employees in front of her makes it far more likely that the customer will refer her friends to a particular employee and write a nice thank-you note. Both will build employee satisfaction—a commodity for which there is no substitute!

CUSTOMER ROUNDING REALLY WORKS

Studer Group just did a study in New Mexico that revealed the power of rounding on customers. We found that the mere act of talking with customers about their expectations caused satisfaction scores to skyrocket—*even when the company didn't change its inventory, its price, or its processes in any other way.*

Finding Ford's *What* (A Consultant's Challenge!)

Many years ago, Henry Ford hired an outside consultant to help Ford Motor Company improve operations. Despite hours of research, all of the consultant's recommendations seemed to fall flat with the celebrated entrepreneur. The consultant just couldn't seem to put his finger on the *what* that drove Ford to want to change the way the company was doing things.

Finally, the outsider touched off a firestorm when he advised Ford to fire one of the company's executives. Ford obviously was angry at the recommendation, but the consultant protested, saying, "But Mr. Ford, every time I walk past his office the man is sitting back with his feet up on the desk, staring into space. He never appears to be doing anything."

Ford replied, "Not so long ago that man had an idea that saved this company millions of dollars. And, as I recall, he was sitting in that exact same position at the time!"

At that point it dawned on the consultant where he had been going wrong. In his recommendations he had been focusing on improving processes without clarifying for the venerable car builder exactly how much money would be saved. Once he understood Ford's *what,* he was able to revise his report to satisfy his client. And the "lazy" executive was retained.

It's pretty amazing what a cascade of benefits flows from this simple technique. Rounding is one of the best—and easiest—ways I can think of to show customers that you truly care about their needs. And when customers believe you care about them, the hard part is over. You're on your way to achieving results that last.

KEY POINTS FOR HARDWIRING RESULTS

- By uncovering what your customers' *what* is, you'll learn how to give them what they truly want, keep them happy, and as a result build your business. Ultimately, you'll encourage them to tell other potential customers how great you are.

- Giving your customers what they really want also makes your *employees* happy. It brings recognition to their hard work, improves their efficiency, and provides that all-important sense of purpose.

- Rounding on your customers will help you figure out how well you are serving them. It's a great way of staying on top of what improvements or changes you need to make at your organization in order to ensure that every customer is getting the service they want and need.

- The way you round on your customers depends on who they are, how often you see them, and what they expect from you. There are three different ways to round:
  1. *Random rounding:* You or your managers will walk around and talk to customers as they browse the aisles of your store. It's the best way to stay in touch with their needs.
  2. *Relationship rounding:* Companies that have more time with each customer should strive to build a solid relationship with each one based on his or her wants and needs. *Customer preference cards* are the centerpiece of this method.
  3. *Deep impact rounding:* This method is meant for organizations that won't see their customers very often, but

will probably see them again. Use a *customer expectations form*—signed by everyone who comes in contact with a given customer—to make a strong enough impression to bring her back next time she needs the type of service you provide.

KEY WORDS AT KEY TIMES

Why This Chapter Is Important

CUSTOMERS WANT TO BELIEVE THAT WE CARE ABOUT THEM. Just providing them with a good product or service isn't enough. We need to reassure them that, when they chose to do business with our organization, they made the right decision—one they won't regret.

Key Words at Key Times help us manage up our products and services and alleviate customer anxiety. They shore up customer loyalty. They help defuse customer frustration when a transaction goes wrong. They even reduce our chances of being sued. Not a bad outcome for a tool that's easy to learn and takes perhaps a minute to use!

In this chapter you will learn more about when to use Key Words at Key Times—and how to create the right ones for your company.

• • •

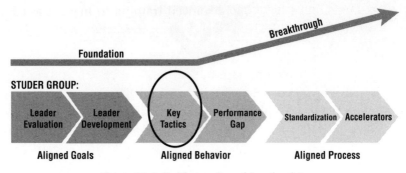

Figure 19.1 Evidence-Based Leadership

"I have a dream . . . "
"We hold these truths to be self-evident . . . "
"Friends, Romans, countrymen, lend me your ears . . . "

Words have tremendous power. The right words spoken by the right people at the right times can lift up communities, transform lives, mend relationships, break hearts—even topple empires. So it shouldn't surprise you that carefully chosen words, offered by your employees at critical points in a business transaction, can help you build a culture of service and operational excellence.

Key Words at Key Times has long been a cornerstone of my business philosophy. All my years of working in hospitals have taught me that what doctors, nurses, and other care providers say to patients makes all the difference in how their care is perceived. When you consider the frightening nature of most health care experiences, it's not hard to see why this is so. Let's pretend I'm a health care provider approaching you with a needle, getting ready to draw blood from your arm. Consider how each of these three scenarios would affect the experience:

Scenario 1: Mr. Smith, my name is Bill and I'll be doing your blood draw today. (*Reassuring smile.*) Dr. Valentine, who is one of our top physicians, by the way, will be seeing you shortly and she needs your lab results. Now, I have ten years of experience and have done this procedure thousands of times. May I see your arm? (*I gently swab your skin.*) I know you may be a little nervous, but I have had advanced training to make it as easy on you as possible. Now, just relax . . . and tell me a little about yourself.

Scenario 2: Okay, I'm here to take some of your blood. Whew! That's a big needle. Better you than me! Uh-oh . . . looks like you don't have very good veins. Sorry, but I may have to take a few stabs at it. (*I grab your arm as you cringe in terror.*) Now this may hurt, so brace yourself.

Scenario 3: (*I say nothing, just grab your arm, start swabbing, and jab the needle in.*)

Clearly, anyone who doesn't love sharp needles, pain, and anxiety would choose the first scenario over the other two! Regardless of what the person doing a lab draw says, the end result is the same: A sample of your blood is transferred from your body to a vial by way of a sharp object. But the way you feel about the procedure— as well as the person performing it and the organization he or she represents—*does* depend on the words spoken. The right words can change everything.

Key Words at Key Times is all about positioning yourself, your co-workers, your products, your services, and your organization in the best possible light. And while the best health care organizations have perfected the concept, companies in many other industries haven't yet caught on. That's too bad. Even though, say, buying an automobile may not be as momentous as having a heart transplant, customers still feel anxiety about the transaction—and your employees can alleviate that anxiety through what they say.

Any business in any industry can use this powerful technique, and many already do. Most retail stores have *key words* in place at the point of checkout. How many times has your supermarket clerk asked "Did you find everything you were looking for?" Of course, most of us have heard that particular question so many times that it's lost its impact. Most shoppers mutter an absentminded "yes" as they dig for their checkbook or debit card (even if they actually spent 20 minutes combing the store in an unsuccessful quest for some obscure Thai cooking spice).

What if instead the grocery store clerk asked, "Can you think of a product you'd like us to add to our inventory?" It's only a small shift in meaning, but it tells the customer you're looking for more than a rote yes-or-no answer. It positions you as the grocery store that really cares about meeting its customer's needs and is willing to take action to meet them. Even though most people will probably answer, "I can't think of a thing," you'll get credit for asking.

DEVELOPING *YOUR* KEY WORDS

How do you get started creating your own key words? Actually, it's a relatively simple five-step process:

Step 1. Revisit your customer satisfaction surveys.

Step 2. Based on the results, determine which issues are most important to your customers. For instance, you might find that your customers are perpetually in a hurry and care very much about timely service. You would develop key words to be spoken to customers at the beginning of the transaction, aimed at reassuring them that the business at hand will be taken care of quickly and smoothly.

Step 3. Come up with *service-recovery* key words for the inevitable occasions in which transactions don't go quickly and smoothly. If your customer satisfaction surveys reveal a different area of weakness—one in which balls frequently get dropped—develop key words for those occasions as well.

Step 4. Thoroughly train your staff on how—and when—to use key words.

Step 5. Just do it! As your Key Words at Key Times initiative gets underway, you'll find that employees naturally figure out where any shortfalls are. If you train them properly, they'll let you know what issues are being neglected, and you can develop new key words to address those concerns.

THE AIDET APPROACH TO SERVICE

When we work with health care providers, we teach them that the Five Fundamentals of Service—*AIDET*—provides a good framework for applying Key Words at Key Times. The letters stand for *A*cknowledge, *I*ntroduce, *D*uration, *E*xplanation, and *T*hank you. The approach works equally well for companies in any service industry. (See Figure 19.2.)

A—*Acknowledge the customer.* Say hello and greet the customer by name.

I—*Introduce.* Introduce yourself, your skill set, your professional certification, and your training. This builds your credibility, and the customer's confidence, right up front.

D—*Duration.* Describe what you're going to do for the customer, how long each step will take, and so forth. This alleviates uncertainty and makes the customer feel more comfortable.

E—*Explanation.* Go into detail about important aspects of what you're doing. An educated customer is a happy customer.

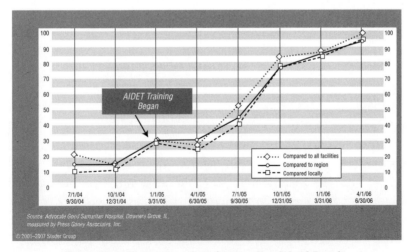

Figure 19.2 Outpatient Satisfaction Key Word Results

T—*Thank you.* Quite simply, thank the customer for choosing your spa . . . or hair salon . . . or car detailing service. "Thank you" goes a long way.

My son Quin recently had a great experience with a company that might as well have been following the AIDET script. He hired Badger Basement Systems to do some repairs and waterproofing in his home and was delighted by the level of service they provided. The company representative:

A—Greeted Quin in a friendly and professional manner.

I—Not only introduced himself and his assistants, but actually handed Quin resumes for each person who would be working on the basement.

D—Explained exactly how long the process would take. As any homeowner knows, having contract work done can be very disruptive. Knowing the duration of the process, up front, helped Quin mentally prepare himself for the chaos.

E—Explained the procedures to be done, in detail. In fact, he directed Quin to the company's highly educational web site, which has a "learning center" link that delves into reasons basements leak and outlines all the options for repair.

T—Concluded the service with a sincere *thank you.*

"The fact that the company went to so much trouble to educate me really set my mind at ease," Quin noted. "It instantly alleviated that typical consumer suspicion associated with contractors."

Do you feel intimidated now? Please don't! There is no rule that says you have to implement AIDET all at once. You can start with one or two of the letters—the letters that make the most sense for your company—and build on them as your comfort level grows.

AIDET... Even in a Taxi!

I love it when clients and associates get excited about a concept Studer Group has shared with them. It shows me that the ideas we teach truly resonate. AIDET is one concept that has generated a lot of feedback over the years. For example, I recently received the following e-mail:

Quint:

I know you love stories, and I must share with you the experience I had at California Hospital Medical Center. It shows you one can use AIDET with just about anything!

As you know, I am the internal patient satisfaction coach for Catholic Healthcare West, and I was conducting one of my coach visits. California Hospital Medical Center has implemented the strategies of AIDET and the Nursing Bundle and is well on the road to having it hardwired, even to the point of putting me into a taxi.

Anthony Benjamin, the Manager for Public Safety and Transportation, had made arrangements for a taxi to take me to the airport. When I arrived at the main entrance, Anthony was there and said:

"Hello, Sandy, your taxi is here." (A)

"This is (name of driver), who will safely take you to the Burbank Airport." (I, E)

"The ride will take about 20 to 60 minutes, depending on traffic." (D)

"He'll take such-and-such route." (E)

"And thank you once again for visiting us at California Hospital." (T)

Sandy Rush, BSN, MA, FACHE

Care Management Specialist—Patient Satisfaction

Catholic Healthcare West

The key words you use, of course, depend entirely on your company, your products, and your customers. However, I can think of several situations in which key words are especially critical:

When You Sell an Expensive Product

Don't misunderstand: I think Key Words at Key Times matters even if your business is a tiny restaurant that sells one-dollar cups of coffee. Remember, it's all about positioning. You want to make the experience of stopping every morning for that steaming Styrofoam cup as pleasurable as possible so your patrons will come in every morning. (That dollar a day adds up over time!) But let's face it: People don't have the same emotional response when parting with a dollar as they do when parting with, say, 2,000 of them at one whack.

Let's imagine that you sell high-end men's suits. During the sales process you'd manage up your product by saying, "This suit is made from the finest hand-finished cashmere, so that it's lightweight yet exquisitely textured. Note the classic profile: wide in the shoulders and slim in the waist. And this rich charcoal color is absolutely stunning. Once our tailor works his magic—and by the way, he's the best in the business—this suit will be the best wardrobe investment you've ever made."

Later, perhaps as the customer pulls out his checkbook, you'd alleviate his concern about spending so much money by saying, "Will you do me a favor? Sometime over the next few weeks, please put on this suit and take your wife out for a nice dinner. If you aren't absolutely delighted with the suit for any reason, I want you to bring it back in and we'll see what we can do to remedy the problem. Our top priority is ensuring that our customers are completely satisfied."

Key words should accompany the selling of any big-ticket item—a plasma TV, a lawnmower, a vacation timeshare. People are understandably worried that they'll get home and experience a severe case of buyer's remorse, or worse, that they're somehow getting ripped off. With a few well-crafted words of reassurance, you can put them at ease and make the experience pleasant, not nerve wracking.

By the way, the Key Words at Key Times concept isn't just a consumer thing. It works equally well in business-to-business transactions. Say a new customer is raising his pen to sign a contract specifying your company to supply 80 percent of his die-cut foam packaging insulation for the next two years. It's a pretty big moment. Who knows? His job security may hang on this decision.

Imagine how much better he would feel if, right at the moment that the customer put pen to paper, you stopped him and said, "Mr. Clarke, before you sign, I just want to reassure you that you can feel good about this decision. We want to be a valuable partner to you, and if you should ever feel that we're not meeting our end of the bargain, please speak up. We will do everything in our power to remedy the problem—and if we can't satisfy you, we'll free you from this contract with no hard feelings."

If you were that customer, wouldn't you feel much better about signing on the dotted line?

When You Provide a Personal Service

What constitutes a "personal service"? In this context, I mean that representatives of your company actually come into face-to-face contact with the customer or someone she loves or in some other way have a direct impact on her life. Perhaps you own a gym or a daycare center or a housecleaning service. Perhaps you run an upscale doggie spa and kennel. Or maybe you have an automotive detailing service that picks up employees' cars during the workday and returns them sparkling clean. (If you think this last doesn't qualify as a personal service, you've obviously never met a 50-year-old executive nervous about turning his "baby"—a restored '57 Thunderbird convertible—over to some teenage kid to wash!)

If you provide a personal service, what you're really doing is asking customers to trust you with something—or someone—they care deeply about. People are understandably skittish about letting someone cut their hair or clean their home or keep their beloved pet for a week. They would really appreciate some verbal comfort when they sit down in that salon chair or hand over their spare house key or drop off Fido on their way out of town.

I recently went to the Ritz Carlton Spa to have a facial. Now, keep in mind, I am a *man*. I am not as accustomed to being fussed over and pampered and anointed with mysterious potions as some of you female readers may be. So let's just say I was a tiny bit nervous. Maybe *nervous* is too strong; maybe I just wasn't sure what to expect. No, I take that back—nervous is *exactly* the right word!

Anyway, the aesthetician did a nice job, and I basically enjoyed the 90-minute experience. But still, I couldn't help but wonder how much *more* I would have enjoyed it if she had employed some Key Words at Key Times to put me at ease and tell me what to expect. For example: "Hello, my name is...I have a degree from...I am thoroughly trained in...Here is what you can expect during the next hour and a half...and here is what you should do when you leave here today to maximize the benefits of our session." Oh, and it wouldn't have hurt for her to reassure me that lots of men—very *masculine* men—get facials...and love them!

When Your Company Drops the Ball

Virtually everyone has suffered through a bad restaurant experience. You know what I mean: You wait an hour to get seated, then you wait another 15 minutes for the server to acknowledge you, then the kitchen gives you broccoli instead of the baked potato you ordered, and to add insult to injury, your steak is overcooked. Then, while you're waiting another 20 minutes for your replacement steak to arrive, the server spills water in your lap. In short, everything that can go wrong *does* go wrong.

If you're like most people, an experience like this causes you to become more frustrated and angry by the minute. At some point during the nightmarish meal, you probably ask to speak to the manager. What happens then will determine whether you return to the restaurant—or whether you boycott it and share the story with 15 of your closest friends. Hopefully, the manager says the right things, such as, "Mr. Smith, it seems everything has gone wrong for you tonight. I am so sorry you've had a bad experience and I want to make it right. I will be taking care of your check tonight and furthermore, because I want you to return to our restaurant, here is a coupon for ten dollars off your next meal. Please accept our sincerest apologies."

Okay, maybe the server should have deployed some key words before your resentment built to a fever pitch, but doesn't the apology make it a lot better?

Every company, not just restaurants, should have some service-recovery key words in reserve for such times. No matter how conscientious your company may be, sooner or later mistakes *will* occur. Balls *will* get dropped. Customers *will* get angry, justifiably or not. It's inevitable. And most people, when they're angry, want to hear an apology. In most cases it isn't the actual wrongdoing that makes the customer angry; it's the way that the employee handles the situation.

I have found that people usually are very forgiving when you simply say, "I am sorry our service did not meet your expectations. What can we do to make it better?"

The truth is, most irate customers *aren't* after a refund. When service has been horrifically bad, I do think it's wise to offer the customer a "financial apology." A full refund, or at the very least, a price break or a discount for future patronage is appropriate. The $50 it costs a restaurant to pick up the tab for a ruined meal is nothing compared with the thousands of dollars it loses when an angry customer refuses to darken its doors ever again.

The sad part is that many organizations could recover from a bad customer service situation fairly inexpensively—yet they choose not to. Let me illustrate with a personal story:

My family and I were making a seven-hour drive to a popular resort destination and our son got sick on the way. For the last hour and a half of our journey he was vomiting in the car. When we finally pulled into the parking lot of our hotel, we were exhausted and ready to just collapse in our room. But lo and behold, after standing in a long line to check in, we were told that the hotel didn't have our reservations and that all the rooms were full.

Needless to say, we weren't happy at all. After I applied some pressure, the customer service representative found us a room in a different hotel for one night and promised the room situation would be straightened out the next day. The next day, I stood in another long line to get an activity pass, only to be told I couldn't get one because we were checking out of the hotel. So then I had to stand in *yet another* long line at the new hotel—which, remember, was the original hotel that had lost our reservations—to get the long-awaited activity pass.

By now, I was disgusted at the string of hassles my family and I had endured, but I was even *more* disgusted at the way the resort destination company handled them. What did they do for service recovery? Absolutely nothing! I did not expect the organization to pay for my entire vacation, but refunding our money for the first botched night would have been a nice gesture. A partial refund would have been a nice gesture. Heck, even a sincere apology would have been a nice gesture! But we got none of the above.

Look, I know that an organization as huge and complex as the one in my story is guaranteed to make a mistake occasionally. I understand that. My company is far smaller, and *we* make mistakes from time to time. What's not so excusable is failing to have effective key words in place for service-recovery situations (or at least failing to properly train employees to say them).

By doing nothing to rectify its mistake and mollify an unhappy customer, this organization ensured that my family and I would seek our vacation fun elsewhere in the future. Further, it ensured that I would tell others about my less-than-magical experience. I don't care how big and successful you are, that's bad business.

Here's my point: Don't underestimate the importance of those two little key words. *I'm sorry* costs nothing to say . . . but not saying it can be costlier than you ever dreamed possible.

The bottom line is that not having key words for yourself and your employees to use on good days *and* bad can affect your bottom line. Employees need to know how to appease angry customers, make happy customers happier, and do it all while selling and protecting your products and brand. Finding the right key words for your organization is one of the best things you can do to maximize the interactions that you and your employees have with your customers. Simply put: It's great for business!

KEY POINTS FOR HARDWIRING RESULTS

- Developing your key words can be achieved by following a simple five-step process:
  1. Revisit your customer satisfaction surveys.
  2. Based on the results, determine which issues are most important to your customers.
  3. Come up with service-recovery key words for the inevitable occasions in which transactions don't go as quickly and smoothly as they should.
  4. Thoroughly train your staff in how and when to use key words.
  5. Just do it! Kick off your Key Words at Key Times initiative.

- Key Words at Key Times allows you and your employees to position your organization in the best possible light. Key words are especially critical when a customer is purchasing a particularly expensive product. They should also be used when you are providing a personal service to your customer, whether it's taking care of his pet at your kennel or detailing his beloved sports car.

- Your organization should also designate key words that will be used specifically for service recovery. Mistakes do occur, and when you are trying to appease a dissatisfied customer, what you say can make a huge difference in how she views your organization afterward. A great place to start is with this simple statement and question: "I am sorry our service did not meet your expectations. What can we do to make it better?"

ABOUT STUDER GROUP

Studer Group is an outcomes-based firm devoted to teaching evidence-based tools and processes that organizations can immediately use to gain and sustain operational excellence. Organizations see clear results in the areas of higher employee retention, greater customer satisfaction, healthy financials, growing market share, and improvements in various other quality indicators. Studer Group has worked with hundreds of organizations in health care and other industries since the firm's inception in 1998.

CEO Quint Studer and Studer Group's coaches teach, train, and speak to thousands of leaders at organizations worldwide each week, through both on-site coaching sessions and frequent speaking engagements. This ongoing in-the-trenches dialogue provides ample opportunity to spot best practices in action from first-mover innovators at many organizations. These best practices are then harvested and tested in other organizations, refined, and shared via peer-reviewed articles, Studer Group publications, and products designed to accelerate change.

Because we find that reducing leadership variance lies at the very heart of creating a consistent culture of excellence, Studer

Group helps organizations to hardwire great leadership. The firm harvests effective tools and techniques and then shares best practices for development of Leadership Development Institutes that efficiently turn training into results.

To learn more about Studer Group, please visit www.studergroup.com.

If you enjoyed *Results That* Last, you may also appreciate some earlier titles by the author and others affiliated with his company. Although they are aimed primarily at a health care audience, these books are filled with insights and principles that transcend industry—for instance, creating a culture of excellence, engaging employees, and finding meaning in and passion for one's work.

Hardwiring Excellence: Purpose, Worthwhile Work, Making a Difference, by Quint Studer (Fire Starter Publishing, 2003, perfect-bound ISBN: 0-9749986-0-5, case-bound ISBN: 0-9749986-1-3). In this best-selling book, Studer helps individuals and organizations to rekindle the flame and offers a road map to creating and sustaining a Culture of Service and Operational Excellence that drives bottom-line results. His tools, tips, and techniques help readers hardwire key behaviors to increase employee, physician, and patient satisfaction; lower employee turnover; improve quality; grow market share; and increase revenue while reducing costs.

101 Answers to Questions Leaders Ask, by Quint Studer (Fire Starter Publishing, 2005, ISBN: 0-9749986-2-1). Informed by best practices in a national learning lab of health care organizations, Studer shares his insights on how to deliver excellent patient care, engage employees, and improve physician relations for access, growth, and strong financial performance. In short, his answers accelerate the leadership learning curve. Questions are organized by topic, making the book valuable as a reference point for specific issues or on-the-spot problem solving.

What's Right in Health Care: 365 Stories of Purpose, Worthwhile Work, and Making a Difference (Fire Starter Publishing, 2007, ISBN-13: 978-0-9749986-4-0, ISBN-10: 0-9749986-4-8). This book, compiled by Studer Group, shares an inspirational story a day for an entire year. The stories, submitted primarily by health care professionals, movingly illustrate what happens when people view their work as not just a job but as a calling.

To learn more about these and other Studer Group books, please visit www.studergroup.com or www.firestarterpublishing.com. Bulk pricing is available.

Accomplishments:
  celebrating, 221–222
  of organizations, performers and, 21–23
Accountability. *See also* Accountability,
  building individual
  of leaders, 107–108
  in leadership training program, 137
  tracking method for, 208
  in violating standards of behavior, 240
Accountability, building individual:
  employee ownership benefits in, 188–190
  helping staff achieve ownership in, 61,
    195–197
  owners *vs.* renters in, 190–191
  satisfied employees in, 145
  setting expectations for employees in,
    193–195
  transforming renters into owners in,
    191–193
Agenda, common, leadership variance and,
  84
AIDET approach to service, 285–292
Alignment, instant, 71
Alliance for Health Care Research (AHCR), 79
Anxiety:
  reducing, managing up and, 45–46
  scouting report and, 47–48
Appearance, in standards of behavior, 243
Argyris, Chris, 199
Attitude, embracing "consider it done," 155
Avalex Pillar Tools, 109–111
Awards, employees and, 29

Bailey, George, 143
Baptist Hospital, Pensacola, Florida, 39
  Bright Ideas Program implementation at,
    201–202
  focus on employees' wins, 228–229
  hero recognition at, 227–228

Behavioral-based questions, in employee
  selection, 178–179
Behavior(s). *See also* Standards of Behavior
  aligning with goals and values, 62,
    105–122
  leaders and standardizing, 81–84, 86
  measurement aligns with, 90–91
  recognized, 212
Best practices, harvesting, 154–155, 158
Blame game, 35, 38
Blog of Studer Group, 172
Bosses:
  employees and, 46–47
  sending regular notes to, 48
Branding, 75–77, 87
Bright Ideas Program:
  at Baptist Hospital, 202
  at Holy Cross Hospital, 201, 205–206
  steps for implementing, 204–208
Building emotional bank account,
    employee satisfaction and, 148

Cascading exercise, 111–113
Celebrations, group, encouraging, 221, 223
Challenging leaders, 68
Change:
  of reward/recognition, 214–216
  values driving, 58
Cleveland Clinic Foundation, 204, 255
Coach, as step process with middle
  performers, 15
Collins, Jim, 96
Commitment:
  to excellence, 61
  to purpose, 58
Communication:
  of Bright Ideas Program, 204, 208
  double loop, 200
  between employees, 49

Communication (*Continued*)
  in leadership evaluation, 113
  in leadership training program,
    135–136
  poor, 154–155
  ranking staff by, 9, 10
  in Standards of Behavior, 244
Competence, ranking staff by, 9, 10
"Consider it done" attitude, embracing,
    155–156
Consistency with reward/recognition,
    221–222, 223
Conversations:
  with high performers, 11–14, 23–24
  with low performers, 17–20, 23
  with middle performers, 14–17
Co-workers, managing up, 45–46
*Creating the New American Hospital: A Time
  for Greatness* (Sherman), 63
Credibility with employees, establishing,
    153–154, 158
Criticism, leaders and, 68
Culture:
  building to challenge leaders, 68
  creating shift in, 46–50
  of excellence, creating, 66–67
Curriculum, in leadership training
  program, 135
Customer-driven service, 252
Customers. *See also* Customer satisfaction;
    Rounding on customers
  AIDET approach and, 285–292
  employees and, 146
  finding difference makers through,
    229–230
  handoff of, 43–46
  low performers and, 7–8
  pre- and post-customer-visit calls and,
    253–254
  reducing anxiety of, 445
  service to, 247
Customer satisfaction:
  employee satisfaction and, 146–147
  handoffs and payoffs of, 43–44
  providing personal service and, 289–290
  role of organizations in, 290–292
  selling expensive products and, 288–289
  services of companies and, 96–98

Decision Matrix, 177, 178
Deep impact rounding, 276–278
Deming, W. Edwards, 107
DESK (describe, evaluate, show, know)
  approach, 17–20
Development of leaders, 124–126
Diagnosing employee satisfaction, 148–149
Differentiating Staff Worksheet, 8–10
Double loop communication, 200
"Double Loop Learning in Organizations"
  (Argyris), 199

Eddy, Buz, 237
Efficiency, standard of behavior for
  improving, 238

E-mail to employees, "What's your *What?*,"
    168
Emotional bank account building,
  employee satisfaction and, 148
Employee attitude surveys, conducting,
    38–39, 46
Employee of the Month (EOM), 221–222
Employee retention:
  critical key to, 126–129
  key question for, 151–153
  Trump Organization and, 184–185
Employees. *See also* Accountability,
    building individual; Employee
    retention; Employee satisfaction;
    Employee selection; Hiring employees;
    New employees; Rounding for
    outcomes
  bosses and, 46–47
  communication between, 49
  empowering, 155–156, 159, 160–170
  financial performance and, 99–101
  helping connect the dots, 68–72
  helping develop keywords, 48
  rounding for outcomes and, 25–33
  termination and firing of, 9–10, 21
  turnover of, 25, 93, 94, 126
Employee satisfaction:
  building blocks of, 145–147
  emotional bank account building and,
    148
  power of, 145
  purpose of company and, 143–145
  solid foundation and, 61
  ways to get started, 147–157
Employee satisfaction survey, 149–151, 168
Employee selection:
  first 90 days after, 174–175
  method for hiring new staff, 85
  overview of, 171–174
  peer interviewing skill for hiring,
    175–176
  step-by-step process of peer interviewing,
    176–179
  as strategy in transforming employees,
    192
  30- and 90-day new-employee meetings,
    179–184
Employee survey rollout, step-by-step guide
  to, 149
Employees' *what*:
  application of the principle to all,
    162–163
  knowing, 163
  overview of, 161–162
  pursuing, 168–169
  story about, 164–167
Employee tracking log, 11, 23
Empowerment of employees, 155–156, 159
Environment, supportive, creating, 67–68
EOM. *See* Employee of the Month (EOM)
Evaluation:
  align process, leadership variance, 84
  of staff performance in organizations,
    8–10

Evidence-based leadership, 27, 33
Excellence:
    commitment to, 61
    perfection *vs.*, 73
    Pillars of (*see* Pillars of Excellence)

Feedback system, developing written,
    49–50
Finance:
    as pillar of excellence, 63–66, 110
    various levels and, 99–101
Finance leaders, leadership variance and,
    77–78
Financial transparency, organizations and,
    99–101, 103
Firing employees, 21
Flywheel, organizational, 57–58, 72
Ford, Henry, 278
Ford Motor Company, 278
Foundation building:
    basics of, 55–57
    Five Pillars of Excellence, 62–68
    helping employees connect the dots,
        68–72
    organizational flywheel and, 57–58, 72
    prescriptive to-do's in, 60–62
    principles for, 61–62
    results and, 62
    self-motivation and, 58–60
    steps to creating supportive
        environment, 67–68
Fry, Art, 203

Goals:
    aligning behavior with, 62, 105–121, 239
    cascading, leadership evaluation tool
        and, 111–113, 121
    leadership and, 69–70
    setting for Bright Ideas Program, 204, 208
*Good to Great: Why Some Companies Make
    the Leap . . . and Others Don't* (Collins),
    96
Greeting and interacting, in standards of
    behavior, 242
Growth, as pillar of excellence, 63–66, 110

Hackensack University Medical Center,
    255–257
Handoffs and payoffs, managing, 43–46
Hardwired system, for recognition, 220
*Hardwiring Excellence: Purpose, Worthwhile
    Work, and Making a Difference* (Studer),
    126
Hero recognition, power of, 227–229
High performers:
    conversations with, 10–14, 22
    percentages in organizations, 20–21
    performance gap with low performers,
        7–8
    problems and, 9
    questions of, 13
Hiring employees:
    impact of selection and first 90 days,
        174–175

peer interviewing and, 175–176
step-by-step process for peer
    interviewing, 176–179
as strategy in transformation, 192
30- and 90-day new-employee meetings,
    179–185
Holy Cross Hospital:
    Bright Ideas Program at, 200–201,
        205–206
    group celebration, 221
    hero recognition at, 228–229
    patient survey, 189–190
Hot Topic, 43

IBM (International Business Machines),
    63–64, 136
IEPs. *See* Individual education plans (IEPs)
Improvement, measurement and, 89–103
Individual education plans (IEPs), 116
Information, leaders and, 26
Instant alignment, 71
Insurance, 59–60
Intellectual capital, harvesting:
    basics of, 199–201
    implementing Bright Ideas Program,
        204–208
    moving beyond suggestion box, 201–208
    3M bright idea, 203
    training leaders and, 201–204
It's a Wonderful Life (movie), 143–144

Jazwick, Liz, 82
Jones, Dori, 236

Key words:
    AIDET approach to service, 285–292
    benefits of, 281–284
    helping employees develop, 48
    for patients and families in emergency
        department, 79
    power of, 246–247
    for pre- and post-customer-visit calls,
        260–264
Key Words at Key Times:
    benefits of, 281–284, 293
    developing, 284
    as successful business philosophy, 247
    when providing personal service, 289–290
    when selling an expensive product,
        288–289
    when the company drops the ball,
        290–292
Knowledge, ranking staff by, 9, 10

LDIs. *See* Leadership development
    institutes (LDIs)
Leaders. *See also* Employees' *what*; Leaders,
    creating and developing; Training
    leaders
    accountability of, 107–109
    building passion and purpose, 55–73
    low performers as, 5–6
    managing up to improve performance,
        35–51

Leaders (*Continued*)
  monthly progress report, 114, 115
  90-day plan, 114, 115–120
  objective evaluation system for, 105–107, 120
  return on investment and, 101–103, 104
  rounding for outcomes and, 25–33
  senior, financial matters and, 100
  termination of, 9–10
  the *what* in empowering employees, 160–170
Leaders, creating and developing. *See also* Leaders training
  development of, 124–126
  employee retention, 126–129
  leadership development institutes, 132–137
  principles for, 129–132
Leadership competencies, 127
Leadership development institutes (LDIs), 132–137
Leadership evaluation tool:
  key to, 109–111, 120
  rolling out, 111–113
Leadership variance:
  consistency equals sustainable results, 78–80
  finance leaders and, 77–78
  leaders and standardizing behavior, 81–84
  organizations and, 75–77
  reducing, 84–86, 87
  transformation process, 85–86
Leaders training, 201–202
  curriculum for, 129
  evaluation of, 113
  necessity of, 16–17, 123–124
  to respond to bright ideas, 205
Letter-of-the-law approach, 273
Listening, in Standards of Behavior, 244
Logistics, in leadership training program, 136
Low performers:
  conversation with, 17–20, 23
  customers neglect by, 7–8
  employees and, 29
  in organizations, 3–5
  percentages in organizations, 20–21
  shapes and sizes of, 5–6
  teams and impact of, 154
Loyalty factor, 247

Making a difference, in organizational flywheel, 58
Managers:
  employees' requirements from, 27–30
  frontline, financial matters and, 100
  role in customer satisfaction, 290–292
Managing up:
  art of, 40–43
  creating the cultural shift and, 46–50
  handoffs and payoffs, 43–45, 50
  to reduce anxiety, 45–46

tasks and benefits of, 35
the we/they phenomenon and, 35–36, 37–40
Measurement 101:
  employee turnover and ripple effect, 94
  financial transparency as new value, 99–101, 103
  frequency of measurement, 94–96, 103
  helping people understand metrics, 98–99
  measurement aligns behavior, 90–91
  measurement and improvement, 92–93
  moving 4s to 5s, 96–98, 103
  overview of, 89–90
  for process improvement, 91–92, 95
  return on investment, 101–104
Middle performers:
  conversation with, 14–15, 22
  percentages in organizations, 20–21
  performance gap with low performers, 7–8
Mistakes and punishment, 68
Money, leadership development and, 125
Monthly progress report, 114, 115

New employees:
  activity in orientation of, 71
  selection method for hiring, 85
  30- and 90-day meetings with, 179–185
90-day plan, 114, 116–120
"No-excuses" policy, 67
Notes, sending to bosses, 48

Objective evaluation system, 105–106, 120
Objective measurement, in organizations, 89
Organizational change, leadership training and, 130–132
Organizational excess, process for achieving, 86
Organizational flywheel, 57–58
Organizations. *See also* Leaders; Purpose
  aligning behavior with goals and values in, 105–122
  assessing current status of, 90–91
  financial transparency and, 99–101
  hardwiring strategic direction of, 65
  information and time in, 26
  monitoring progress in, 114–120
  moving to the next level in, 3–24
  objective measurement in, 89
  percentages of different performers in, 20–21
  providing tools for employees in, 155
  returning to sense of purpose in, 120–121
Oversight committee, establishing to rescue bright ideas, 206–208, 209
Ownership, in standards of behavior, 244–345

Passion, leaders and building, 55–73
Peer-interview certified, 175
Peer interviewing:
  as skill for hiring right people, 175–176
  step-by-step process for, 176–179

INDEX

Pensacourt Health, Racquet & Fitness Club, 241–245
People, as pillar of excellence, 63–66, 110
Peoples First Community Bank, 247
Performance. *See also* Managing up
  areas of, 9
  gap of, 7–8
  management of, 193
  performers and, 3
  reward/recognition and, 215
  of staff, ranking, 8–10
  staff and drivers of, 25–27
Performance review, of employees, 106–107
Performance standards, 176–177
Performers, high. *See* High performers
Performers, low. *See* Low performers
Performers, middle. *See* Middle performers
Personal connection, making, 30
Personal service, providing, 289–290
Phelps Group, 24
Physicians' preferences, 272
Pillars of Excellence:
  department's goals alignment with,
    109–111
  organizations and, 62–68
Positioning:
  Key Words at Key Times and, 283
  of product and employees, 42
Post-It Notes, 203
*Pour Your Heart Into It: How Starbucks Built a
  Company One Cup at a Time* (Schultz
  and Yang), 236
Power:
  of hero recognition, 227–229
  of reward and recognition, 217–218
  of satisfied employees, 145
  of words, 282
Pre- and post-customer-visit calls:
  benefits of, 251–253
  common questions about, 258–260
  customer service and the bottom line,
    254–257
  developing keywords for, 260–264
  exceeding customer expectations,
    253–254
  technique for all types of business,
    257–258
Preference cards, 271–272, 275
Prescription, successful leaders and, 62
Prescriptive to-do's, 60–62
Process for reviewing, Bright Ideas Program
  and, 204, 208
Product positioning, 42
Products, selling expensive, 288–289
Professional conduct, in standards of
  behavior, 242
Professional development:
  employees and, 29
  as requirement from managers, 29
Professionalism, ranking staff by, 8–10
Program for recognizing heroes, 230
Progress, monitoring, 114–120
Promotions/participation, in standards of
  behavior, 244

Public address announcements, standard of
  behavior for, 238
Punishment, mistakes and, 68
Purpose:
  of company and satisfied employees,
    143–145
  employee satisfaction and, 145–147
  foundation building and, 55–73
  of organizations and employees, 127

Quality, as pillar of excellence, 63–66, 110
Questions:
  about pre- and post-customer-visit calls,
    258–260
  after few days of training, 35–37
  of high performers, 13–14

Random rounding, 273–274
Recognition system, putting in writing, 221
Recognize/reward. *See also* Recognizing
    difference makers
  basics of success, 211–214
  change of, 214–216
  hardwiring thank-you notes, 217, 218–220
  of high-performer employees, 31
  impact of small prizes, 214
  for innovation, 205, 209
  leaders' resistance to, 216–217
  overview of, 211–214
  power of, 217–218
  as requirement from managers, 29
  scheduling and implementing, 221–223
  WOW award, 212–214
Recognizing difference makers:
  finding, 229–230
  overview of, 225–227
  power of hero recognition, 227–229
Recruiting high performers, 11–14
Relationship rounding, 274–275
Rembis, Mike, 28–29
Respect, in standards of behavior, 241
Restaurant industry, 42
Results:
  of employee satisfaction, 150
  flywheel and, 62
Results-oriented companies, employees in,
    70
Results-oriented leaders, 146
Retail stores:
  key words of, 283
  random rounding for, 273–274
Retention of employees, 126–129, 151–153,
    184–185
Return on investment, 80, 101–103, 104
Reward. *See* Recognize/reward
Ripple effect, employee turnover and, 94
Roosevelt, Franklin D., 156–157
Rounding for outcomes:
  of good performers, 220
  leaders and, 147–148
  method and skill of, 25–27
  reasons for, 27–30
  Rounding 101, 30–32
  successful, tips for, 33

Rounding log, 31, 220
Rounding on customers:
  benefits of, 278–279
  deep impact rounding, 276–278
  gathering information, 270–272
  importance of asking, 269–270
  random rounding, 273–274
  relationship rounding, 274–275
  technique of, 267–269
Rounding relentlessly, employee
  satisfaction and, 148

Safety awareness, ranking staff by, 9, 10
Scheduling reward/recognition, 220–222
Schultz, Howard, 236–237
Scouting reports, 30, 46–48
Self-motivation, 58–60, 86
Service, as pillar of excellence, 63–66, 110
Service culture, building. See also Standards
    of Behavior
  corporate culture and, 61
  key words and, 246–247
  loyalty factor and, 247
  overview of, 235–237
  tool for, 238
  Zappos.com, 249–250
Service recovery key words, 291
Sherman, Clay, 63
Silver, Spence, 203
Single loop communication, 200
Skills, leaders and lack of, 16–17
Social theme, in leadership training
    program, 136
Spirit-of-the-law approach, 273
Staff:
  drivers of performance of, 25–27
  evaluating performance of, 8–10
  financial performance and, 101
  leaders and selection of, 174–175
  low performers, percentage of, 15
  ranking performance of, 8–10
Staff meeting attendance/participation, in
    Standards of Behavior, 243
Standardized process, development of, 86
Standard of the Month, creating, 240
Standards of Behavior:
  creating, 239–245
  power of key words, 246–247
  reason for working, 245
  sample of, 241–245
  Studer Group and, 238
Starbucks, 236–236
Studer Group:
  blog of, 172
  Standards of Behavior, 238
  web site of, 178
Subtraction is addition, in organizations,
    20–21
Suggestion box, moving beyond, 201–208
Support, as step process with middle
    performers, 14–15
Support—coach—support process, middle
    performers and, 14–15

"Taking You and Your Organization to the
    Next Level" seminars, 37, 77
Tasks explanation, as strategy in
    transforming employees, 192–193
Teamwork:
  effects of, 39–40
  ranking staff by, 8–10
Tenacious, meaning of, 5
Terminating employees, 9–10, 21
Thank-you notes, 217, 218–220, 223
3M, 203
Time, leaders and, 26
Tools and equipment:
  companies providing, 155
  as requirement from managers, 28–29
Tracking method for accountability, 208
Training leaders:
  in basic competencies, 85
  lack of training, 16–17, 36–37
  in organizations, 129–132
  questions after few days of training,
    35–37
  to respond to bright ideas, 201–202, 205,
    209
Transparency:
  with employees, 156–157, 159
  in financial matters, 99–101
Transparency/sharing of information, as
    strategy in transforming employees,
    192
Trump Organization, retention of
    employees at, 184–185
Trust with employees, 156–157, 159
Truthfulness with employees, 156
Turnover of employees, 175, 184–185

Value domain, 123
Value(s):
  aligning behavior with, 62, 105–122
  as requirement from managers,
    27–28
Variance, 80, 81, 87
Vulnerability, leaders and, 67–68

Wall Street Journal, 22
Watson, Thomas J., 138
Watson Wyatt, 127–128
Web site, Studer Group, 178
We/they phenomenon, in managing up,
    35–36, 37–40, 50
"What you permit, you promote," 82–83
Whibbs, Vinnie, 28
Wiley, Ralph, 188
Workplace:
  cultures, managing up and, 42
  top incentives, 220
Worthwhile work, in organizational
    flywheel, 58, 59–60
WOW awards, 212–214
Written departmental feedback systems,
    49–50

Zappos.com, 249–250